MAR 0 7 2014

Experiencing Rhythm

Experiencing Rhythm:
Contemporary Malagasy Music and Identity

By

Jenny Fuhr

CAMBRIDGE
SCHOLARS
PUBLISHING

Experiencing Rhythm:
Contemporary Malagasy Music and Identity,
by Jenny Fuhr

This book first published 2013

Cambridge Scholars Publishing

12 Back Chapman Street, Newcastle upon Tyne, NE6 2XX, UK

British Library Cataloguing in Publication Data
A catalogue record for this book is available from the British Library

ISBN (10): 1-4438-5047-0, ISBN (13): 978-1-4438-5047-6

TABLE OF CONTENTS

LIST OF ILLUSTRATIONS

ACKNOWLEDGEMENTS

First of all, I would like to express my warmest thanks to Erick Manana, who continues to encourage me and invite me to learn and perform Malagasy music. Thank you so much for sharing and for making me understand the treasures of *lova-tsofina!*

Another special thanks to Bebey Rakotomanga, who has helped and supported me greatly during my research stays in Antananarivo.

I would also like to thank all the artists and musicians from Madagascar who I have had the privilege to meet during my research. Without their time and energy, this project would have not been possible.

My sincerest gratitude to Prof. Ulrike Meinhof for her infectious enthusiasm and support, to Prof. Alex Knapp, Prof. Phil Bohlman, Dr. Thomas Irvine and Dr. Heidi Armbruster for their supportive advice and encouragement.

A big thank you to Bernd Leideritz for helping in putting together the book's DVD and to Adam Dunn for his accurate reading and most helpful corrections.

More people have inspired and supported this work in numerous ways; My deepest thanks to Birger Gesthuisen, Hasina Samoelinanja, Oriane Boulay, Thea Bjaaland, Hauke Dorsch, Gabriele Budach, Marie-Pierre Gibert, Meike Reintjes, Hery Ritsoka, Ferry Fuligno, Eulalie Ramamonjisoa, Passy Rakotomalala, Felana Aliderson, Tefinjanahary Tantelinirina, Miriam Lormes, Hilke Engfer, Birgit Ellinghaus, Herbert Labenski, Akgül and Cahit Baylav, Eliška Sýkorová and Lova Razafimahazo.

I would like to express my gratitude to my big, loving, and growing family. Without your love and warmest support, this book would have not been completed.

Fisaorana mitafotafo no atolotro an' ireo mpitendry sy mpanankanto gasy izay nahafoy andro sy fotoana ary nanampy ahy be dia be, nahafahako nanantotosa ity boky sarobidy amiko ity.
NY MOZIKAN' i GASIKARA no MAMPIVAZO ny FOKO!
Sitraka ho enti-matory tompoko!

Jenny Fuhr

CHAPTER ONE

MUSIC IN CONTEMPORARY MADAGASCAR

Introduction

This book centres upon experiences of "rhythm" in "Contemporary Malagasy music" (Randrianary 2001). My study is fundamentally based on my own experiences as a practising musician regularly learning, playing and performing with musicians from Madagascar. Challenging the long-established and still-existing boundary between those who make music and those who write about it, I try to present the story of a profound intercultural (musical) dialogue that I have shared, experienced, and lived with Malagasy musicians over the past seven years in both Madagascar and Europe. I am going to tell a story about falling in love with a music whose combined familiarity and strangeness have captured me from the first moment I heard it on CD and with which I have engaged ever since– as both researcher and musician. It is a story about posing and tackling questions of sameness and difference that draw on my dual role as musician-researcher and therewith also challenge other boundaries, such as that between researcher and researched. Despite the fact that many ethnomusicologists are musicians–and many musicians are involved in research–experiences gained through "musicking"[1] (Small 1998) and the way we talk about music and express our experiences of music-making are almost always described as two separate worlds between which translation seems difficult if not impossible (e.g. Titon 1997, Rice 1997). In my analysis, however, I have made particular use of the connections I see between the ways in which we discuss and talk about music and our actual

---

[1] Small (1998) proposes the new verb "to music" (with its present participle or gerund "musicking"), as music should, in his opinion, be understood as an activity rather than as a thing. He explains that his definition of "to music" goes beyond the meanings of "to perform" or "to make music:" "To music is to take part, in any capacity, in a musical performance, whether by performing, by listening, by rehearsing or practicing, by providing material for performance (what is called composing), or by dancing" (Small 1998: 9).

experiences of playing and performing the music, arguing that both constantly inform each other.

British music journalist Ian Anderson once wrote that to him, music from Madagascar sounded "like everywhere and nowhere else at the same time" (Anderson 1994). Due to the island's shape and its particular location off the Mozambique coast, Madagascar is often referred to as the "footprint between Africa and Asia."[2] The effects of the many waves of migration over the centuries (cf. Deschamps 1972) can be seen, heard, and experienced today in the diverse musical practices of the island's artists. The sounds of Mexican street bands, songs of the Alps[3] and a "tropical version of Irish music"[4] are only a few examples of the diverse associations that appear when Malagasy music meets Western ears. With regard to the island's history, these associations are not surprising. The balancing act between new and familiar sounds, between unity and diversity, and between difference and sameness characterises Western experiences of Malagasy music. But the islands' musicians themselves also talk constantly about these seemingly contradictory associations and experiences–a fact which turns music from Madagascar into an exceptionally rich area for research into questions of identity. What makes music sound "Malagasy"? Or: What is Malagasy music? The musician Samy (alias: Samuelson Rabenirainy)[5] once explained to me that he believed Madagascar to be a "successful melting pot" where all civilisations met. And in this, he sees the reason for both the ease with which everyone can relate to (or even identify with) the music and the adaptability of Malagasy people to new situations or other musics.[6]

However, despite these intriguing contradictory issues and the entanglement of diverse cultural encounters, Madagascar's music has hardly been researched so far and very little has been written on the island's musical traditions, particularly concerning contemporary and popular musical styles.

A good overview of existing works on the music of Madagascar is the "Archives Virtuelles de la Musique Malgache (AVMM)" (the virtual archive of Malagasy music), initiated by Vienna Professor August Schmidhofer in

---

[2] An expression also used by some of the Malagasy musicians I met during my research.
[3] Ian Anderson (1994).
[4] Interview with Paddy Bush, London, 2.3.2006.
[5] Due to their extremely long family names, most Malagasy musicians have nicknames/stage names. I give complete names in the first appearance of each musician, and then use their nicknames or stage names thereafter.
[6] Interview with Samy, Antananarivo, 7.12.2007.

1998.[7] This virtual platform provides bibliographic and discographic references and gives access to a considerable number of pictures and music samples. The country's musical instruments have been described by several researchers, most importantly by Curt Sachs (1938), Gilbert Rouget (1946), Norma McLeod (1977) and in Silvestre Randafison's (1980) book on organology. With regard to musical genres, the *hira gasy*, a peasant's music and theatre tradition from the High Plateaux region has been dealt with in three relatively recent works by Ingela Edkvist (1997), Didier Mauro (2001) and Géraldine Vatan (2004). August Schmidhofer (1995) has written a study on xylophone traditions in Madagascar with a particular focus on African musical influences, whereas Marie Aimé Joël Harison (2005) has focused on European influences on Malagasy music. Other scholars have conducted research on particular regional music styles. For example, Ron Emoff (2002) has analysed the possession music of Madagascar's East coast (*tromba*) and French ethnomusicologist Julien Mallet has published a number of articles and a book on *tsapiky* music (Mallet 2000, 2004, 2007, 2008, 2009). More general works are Nora McLeod's article on the status of musical specialists in Madagascar (Mc Leod 1964) and a bibliography concerning ethnomusicological works on Malagasy music that has been published by Mireille Mialy Rakotomalala (1986) for the Musée d'Art et d'Archéologie in Antananarivo. The same author in 2003 published the *Madagascar. La musique dans l'histoire*, a book that aims to describe the island's music within its historical and socio-cultural contexts, emphasising for example the close relationship between music and everyday life. Another Malagasy scholar, Victor Randrianary, in 2001 published *Madagascar. Les chants d'une île*, a book that gives an overview of the musical traditions of the different regions, focusing on the origins of each and aiming to understand the music as embedded in its cultural contexts.

Ulrike H. Meinhof (2005a), and Meinhof in collaboration with Zafimahaleo Rasolofondraosolo (2003, 2005b) have published articles that deal with the experience of Malagasy popular artists in the diaspora. Following on from this, Meinhof continued to research Malagasy musicians' transnational networks and in collaboration with Nadia Kiwan published a book on *Cultural Globalization and Music*, looking at artists from both Madagascar and North Africa (Kiwan and Meinhof 2011).

At present, more and more Malagasy musicians are transnationally connected (Kiwan and Meinhof 2011) and more and more intercultural music projects take place. This not only sheds new light on the role the

---

[7] AVMM (2013).

metropolitan centres of the South, such as Madagascar's capital Antananarivo, play as hubs for the musicians and their musical careers (Kiwan and Meinhof 2011: chapter 2) but is also a wake-up call for researchers to think outside fixed cultural boundaries and conduct self-reflexive research that focuses on both the individual experiences of those we work with and our own (e.g. Rice 2003). Music from far-away countries directly affects our lives in numerous ways (e.g. Aubert 2007) and so-called "world music" has become part of our everyday experience. This also means that ethnomusicological research is not only happening in far-away places, but needs to follow the trajectories and experiences of the individuals involved. These thoughts gain particular importance with regard to a place like Madagascar whose name already epitomises for many people remoteness and distance, a fact that the musicians themselves reflect on. We only need think about Hitler's absurd "Madagascar plan" of relocating all Jews to Madagascar; or about the German saying "Geh dahin wo der Pfeffer wächst" ("Go to the place where the pepper grows!"), a phrase expressing the wish to send someone away as far as possible; or about the three Dreamworks *Madagascar* films about a group of funny and likable animals–that do not exist in real on the island. The latter appears particularly ironic as hardly a month passes in the international media without the announcement of the discovery of a new animal or plant species on the Big Island in the Indian Ocean, known for its microclimates and its fauna and flora, of which 90 % is said to be endemic.[8]

In 2011, the BBC produced a three-part series called *Madagascar. The Land Where Evolution Ran Wild*, narrated by David Attenborough. Its advertising text summarises well the immense fascination that Madagascar's wildlife creates and the extraordinary attention that it receives:

> Lying just off the coast of Africa, Madagascar is a land of misty mountains, tropical rainforests and weird spiny desert scrub. Here the wildlife has evolved in splendid isolation to become strange and totally unique. (…) one of the few places left on Earth where there are still wildlife mysteries, waiting to be discovered.[9]

Far fewer people know that the country is currently suffering from a severe political crisis, as news coverage by Western media has been lacking. The political tensions and power struggle at the present time mirror former crises in the country since its independence from France in

---

[8] WWF (2013).
[9] Gray and Summerill (2011).

1960 (such as in 1972, 1992, and 2002).[10] Since the beginning of 2009 when opposition leader Andry Rajoelina started protests against President Marc Ravalomanana, the country has been in turmoil, causing severe social and economic hardship. At the point of writing, the political situation has not been resolved and remains subject to unexpected change. Despite the fragmentary news coverage, the crisis has destroyed the island's image as a "safe tropical paradise." Private tourism operators reported an almost-100% cancellation rate at the beginning of 2009 and the crisis has hit foreign investment and battered the tourism sector.[11]

Obviously, this situation has also affected the musicians and thus, indirectly, the island's music. The island's capital Antananarivo is described as a "place of fear and desire, jealousy and triumph–and the passage obligé for all but a few musicians en route for transnational migration" (Kiwan and Meinhof 2011: 23). The reason for the important position that the capital holds appears to be the steadily growing facilities of the music industry. Further, international cultural institutions and embassies are often domiciled in capitals and, especially in Antananarivo, it is these institutions that remain the main supporters for local artists (Kiwan and Meinhof 2011: chapter 3; Fuhr 2006). However, without denying that most artists have experienced Antananarivo as a possible gateway and have somehow profited from the capital's infrastructure, the on-going political crisis is shaping and changing this picture in a dramatic way; Malagasy musicians based abroad have been and to some extent are still restricted in their ability to return home to give concerts, a crucial impact as many express their need to return "home" from time to time to gain inspiration and to "re-source."[12] Further, rising criminality brings not only mistrust and fear as a result of increasing attacks and robberies–also recently more and more experienced by musicians with whom I work–but also turns the organisation of cultural events, especially at evening times, into a challenging, if not impossible, business. Finally, the enduring crisis has lead to international sanctions, with development money frozen and political relations becoming tense, which knocks support for local artists and the promotion of cultural events quickly off the institutions' agenda.

The immense attention that Madagascar's natural wealth receives in comparison to political, social or cultural developments in the country is also something that musicians there recognise. Although they value this

---

[10] For a detailed account of the former political crises, see for example Randrianja and Ellis (2009).

[11] For further information on the present crisis, see Randrianja (2012).

[12] Various discussions with Bordeaux-based singer and guitarist Erick Manana. See also Meinhof and Triandafyllidou (2006).

attention, they are also critical. Many bring up the topic of the island's environment in their music and songs. They praise the natural wealth, but very often they also point at the dangers of human beings destroying the environment they live in and often live off. Ricky (alias Ricky Randimbiarison) is a singer and percussionist based in Antananarivo, where he founded the "Rarihasina Cultural centre," a base for workshops for students as well as other cultural activities (see Fuhr 2006). He regularly performs in Madagascar (but also in Europe) as a solo artist and in different small groupings. He often joins the group "Madagascar AllStars," who have as one of their permanent members the singer and guitarist   (alias Zafimahaleo Rasolofondraosolo). Dama Mahaleo also performs solo and with other groups, and as a duo with singer and guitarist Erick Manana (alias Erick Rafilipomanana) in Madagascar, Europe, and Canada. However, Dama Mahaleo is especially known as a member of Madagascar's legendary group "Mahaleo", that was born out of the island's 1972 rebellion against the neo-colonial regime and that still performs regularly, in Madagascar and also for Malagasy communities abroad.[13] Dama Mahaleo and Ricky, for example, have created a project called "Voajanahary" ("natural"), which features both artists in musical performances and also aims to create environmental awareness in Madagascar. Both artists have also participated in a campaign supporting the environmental policy of former President Ravalomanana of enlarging protected areas of Madagascar, a policy he presented at the "World Park' Congress" in Durban in 2003.[14] I have also realised that it is not only through songs but also through announcements and discussions during concerts that musicians try to create more awareness for the Malagasy people and their culture, explaining (to foreign and Malagasy audience alike) that Madagascar is not only about flora and fauna; the people living of the island, their culture, language, customs etc., and their problems and needs also need attention.[15] This observation made by the musicians also applies to the priorities of academic literature. Compared to research

---

[13] For more information on the group "Mahaleo," please see Meinhof (2005a); Rasolofondraosolo and Meinhof (2003). There is also a film about the group "Mahaleo" that was produced in 2005 by Marie-Clèmence Paes, Cesar Paes, and Raymond Rajaonarivelo, see Rajaonarivelo and Paes (2005).

[14] Following this congress a film was produced by USAID called "Madagascar: a New Vision/Madagasikara: *fijery vaovao*." Subsequently two big concerts were performed on the same theme staring Ricky and Dama Mahaleo. Both, the film and the concerts finally were put together on the DVD "*Ny dian'I Mananilatany.*"

[15] For a detailed discussion on this topic, see Meinhof (2005a).

undertaken on the island's natural environs, there is far less literature on Madagascar's people, culture, and society.

There is a vast body of French-language colonial literature as well as literature in English, Norwegian, and Malagasy from the same period. The School of Oriental and African Studies (SOAS, University of London), for example, holds the "Hardyman Madagascar Collection," the largest personal collection on books about Madagascar in existence, donated by Mr. J.T. Hardyman whose parents worked for the London Missionary Society (now called the Council for World Mission), who himself lived in Madagascar from 1946-1973.[16] Within colonial and missionary literature, Malagasy music only appears as a side topic, if at all.

The island's history has been discussed and analysed by different authors, the most important being Hubert Deschamps (1972), Mervyn Brown (1979), and with their most recent publication, *Madagascar: a Short History,* Randrianja and Ellis (2009). Some political events and periods have received academic attention; during colonial times, the influence of Protestant Missionaries (e.g. Bonar A. Gow 1980) and the Malagasy revolt against French colonial power in the 1890s (e.g. Stephen D.K. Ellis 1985); the country's socialist period under president Didier Ratsiraka from 1975-1993 (e.g. Ferdinand Deleris 1986; Roger Rabetafika 1990); but also political developments since 2001 (e.g. Jean-Loup Vivier 2007). The most recent publication analyses the current political crisis that started in February 2009 (Randrianja 2012). In general, there is far more relevant literature, anthropological studies included, in French than in English.

With regard to Anglophone anthropological studies on Madagascar, a very prominent scholar is Maurice Bloch who has, since the late 1960s, published a considerable number of books and articles. Whereas his earlier works mainly concern the High Plateaux region and the Merina culture (Bloch 1968, 1971, 1986), more recent works by him focus on the *Zafimaniry*, a population living in the Eastern forest area of Madagascar (Bloch 1999, 2006).

Scholars have focused on topics such as gender and social structure (e.g. Richard Huntington 1987); identity in connection with spirit possession (Lesley A. Sharp 1993); authority and fertility (Oliver Woolley 2002); the remembrance of colonialism (Jennifer Cole 2001), or power and "development disconnect" (Ritu Verma 2009). A significant publication is *Ancestors, Power and History in Madagascar*, edited by Karen Middleton

---

[16] Turfan (2013).

(1999). It is a collection of articles by scholars expert in different geographic regions, each of whom reassesses the importance of ancestors for changing relations of power, emerging identities and local historical consciousness. In the introduction, Middleton writes that almost all ethnographic works published between 1970 and the early 1990s state that the relationship between the living and the dead is a key to power, fertility, and blessing in Malagasy culture (Middleton 1999:1). Looking at publications since then, the importance of the ancestors continues to be emphasised (e.g. Sophie Blanchy et al. 2001, Raymond-William Rabemananjara 2001, Robert Dubois 2002). This includes connections with both the *famadihana*, the reburial of the ancestors (e.g. Pierre-Loïc Pacaud 2003) where music plays an important role, and with *tsapiky* music, a genre from the South-West of Madagascar (Julien Mallet 2008 and 2009).

In my experience, tourist guidebooks about Madagascar and tourism discourses sometimes treat the island almost as though unpopulated, praising the unique natural environments and advising everyone to quickly leave the capital to discover the rural countryside and "the real Madagascar." While the island's nature and wildlife is declared amongst the richest in the world, the current political crisis has reinforced Madagascar's ranking as one of the world's poorest countries and worst economies.[17] While different waves of migrations have brought a broad palette of diverse influences, the same language–Malagasy–is spoken everywhere on the island, albeit with various dialects.[18] While geographically Madagascar forms part of the African continent, a large part of the people living on the island, especially in the region of the High Plateaux do not think of themselves as African.[19] The list would be easy to continue. It is this unique environment of an island entangled in somehow contradictory stories and developments that we also encounter in its music. Within my study on Contemporary Malagasy music, it is the existence of seemingly contradictory and competing discourses on the music and music making that has become the crux of my research:

---

[17] The World Bank (2013).

[18] The spread of Malagasy throughout the island can be described as a "continuum of dialects (…) with mutual comprehensibility (…) estimated at no less than 60% of the lexicon even at the extreme ends of the continuum" (Rasolofondraosolo and Meinhof 2003: 130)

[19] Various discussions with musicians from the High Plateau region. See also chapter 4-6.

"Contemporary Malagasy Music" (Randrianary 2001): "6/8 rhythm" meets *Lova-tsofina*

In 2005, I conducted research on the strategies and personal experiences of a number of musicians working in and around the "Rarihasina cultural centre" in Madagascar's capital Antananarivo. The centre was founded in the mid-1990s by a group of Malagasy artists, most prominently singer and percussionist Ricky, to create a Malagasy forum for artistic exchange and the preservation of the country's heritage. The artists' main aim was and still is to become more independent from the dominant foreign institutions in a situation marked by almost complete absence of a state cultural policy (Fuhr 2006). What surprised me at the time was the enormous variety of musical styles I encountered; it was impossible to define this group of individual artists solely by the musical styles they perform. Even the musicians themselves–and this is true for almost all musicians that I met throughout the last seven years–have difficulties explaining their music, or do not consider terms or categories such as "traditional" or "popular" appropriate for their own music. However, through my ethnographic research, in which I focused on the music itself and especially engaged in musical practices myself, I came to understand the significance of the Malagasy concept of *lova-tsofina* that the musicians very often describe as the base of Malagasy music-making. It consists of the two words *lova*, meaning "heritage" and *sofina*, meaning "ear." With one or two exceptions, none of the musicians I worked with could read or write music. The idea of *lova-tsofina* (see chapter 5 for a more detailed account) is oral transmission; it is not only described as a method to learn, play, and compose Malagasy music by many of the musicians. It is more: a frame of mind (*"état d'esprit"*); a way of living, seeing and experiencing the world; a way of using one's own ears as a means for self-assurance and yet at the same time, a gateway and instrument for intercultural exchange and encounters. With regard to the significance the *lova-tsofina* holds for the musicians I work with, I argue that the music they play and create could best be understood and defined by the notion of "contemporary music" (*"la musique contemporaine"*) used by Malagasy ethnomusicologist Victor Randrianary (2001). He describes "contemporary music" in the Malagasy context not as a style, but as an attitude of the musicians who embrace new musical forms and create musical syntheses while keeping and using their own tradition. He emphasises that "tradition" here needs to be understood as inseparable from the notions of "creation" and "openness" (Randrianary 2001: 128).

Following Rice's principle aims of a "subject-centred ethnography" (Rice 2003; see also chapter 3) I have worked with a group of individual musicians who share some elements and experiences in spite of their significant differences across musical styles, genres, and practices. The music they play and perform is made for consumption, performed on stages and often produced on recordings. It is produced with the aim of selling it to the international music market (where it is often labelled as "world music"). In other words, it is not the kind of music that is played in functional or ceremonial contexts, such as music played at funerals, in churches or specific music such as trance music (cf. Emoff 2002, Schmidhofer 2013). Closely related to the musicians' strategies to reach the "world music market" is another aspect that unites them all: their relation and bond to the capital Antananarivo, whose significant role I have already mentioned above. Most musicians I work with are based in Antananarivo or are frequent visitors. Of the Malagasy musicians based in Europe, many come from Antananarivo and for all of them the capital has definitely been a place of great importance, a sort of "trampoline" for their musical career (Kiwan and Meinhof 2011).

One of my first observations when I started to focus more on the music itself was that the musicians constantly talk about a rhythmic structure they all share despite an enormous variety of regional musical particularities. Within their discussions about this rhythmical structure, the specific term and concept of "6/8 rhythm" is constantly used and contested. "Rhythm" seems to be the starting point for the musicians' search for a collective musical identity and this is where the challenge of competing discourses becomes obvious: the concept of "6/8 rhythm" in Western music theory has grown out of and is based on the idea of musical notation (Arom 1991, Dudley 1996). The fact that the "6/8 rhythm" is so deeply rooted in the idea of musical notation seems at first glance to contradict the indigenous concept of oral transmission, the *lova-tsofina* that the musicians also emphasise in discourse about their own music and their experiences of music making.

However, in this study I argue that we need to go beyond the study of competing discourses in search of other relevant criteria, for which shared music-making and the analysis of the constant interrelation of musical experiences and discourses holds the key.

With regard to African music studies, much research since the 1950s has been dedicated to the topic of "rhythm" (e.g. Brandel 1959, Chernoff 1979, Kauffmann 1980, Arom 1991, Temperly 2000)–a fact that has caused much debate and criticism, most prominently from Kofi Agawu (2003). He argues that research on African music so far has been marked by a constant search for difference, ignoring indigenous theories and understandings of music (Agawu 2003). My own study challenges these dominating Western analytical perspectives on music, and in particular the prevailing use of Western music notation as the main analytical tool. It substantiates topical methodological needs and aims expressed within the so-called "new fieldwork" and the "new ethnomusicology" (e.g. Hellier-Tinoco 2003). Self-reflexivity and the focus on relationships are highly debated issues and have been essential to scholarly debates on ethnographic fieldwork across disciplines even as researchers have realised that their implementation and practical application remain difficult. In short: there is still a gap between theory and practice (e.g. Cooley 2003, Hellier-Tinoco 2003).

I suggest that we often underestimate the significance of the mutual integration of musical experiences and ethnomusicological research. Despite the long-standing claim of the importance of a performance-based approach in ethnomusicological research (e.g. Hood 1960), not many scholars have actually pursued this aim on a practical level (Baily 2008). Following the principle ideas of Rice's "subject-centred ethnography" (Rice 2003), I propose that it is only through shared experiences and shared music-making that we can fully integrate the voices of the people we work with and hence, conduct research "with" rather than just "on" people and "their music." Throughout the last seven years, I have worked with Malagasy musicians both in Antananarivo, Madagascar and in Europe and further afield. Outside of Madagascar itself, this has mainly meant France, which has the biggest Malagasy diaspora community, but also Germany, Switzerland, the UK and Canada. As I am currently still involved in musical projects and performing with Malagasy musicians in Europe and Madagascar, this study should be understood as a "snapshot" of on-going research.

Fieldwork Experiences

My very first experience of "musicking" Malagasy music was listening to a CD that I had found by chance, part of my father's CD collection in the family home, a recording from the 1990s of various Malagasy artists in Germany that formed part of the "World Music Network series" produced by German radio station WDR.[20] Listening to this CD sparked the greatest emotional response to music I had ever felt, combined with an insatiable curiosity to understand this music and why it had this strong effect on me.

---

[20] World Network 18 (1993).

It was a kind of "initial experience" (cf. Rice 1994), which was followed by the immediate urge: to find more recordings of Malagasy music; to get to know musicians from Madagascar; to attend concerts and rehearsals; to many attempts to learn from and play along with recordings at home. This led, perhaps inevitably, to my very first research trip to Madagascar in spring 2005, followed by several more extended stays in Antananarivo and very many shorter trips within Europe over the last years.

Many ethnomusicologists talk about field research situations which have raised questions of "reciprocity" (e.g. Hellier-Tinoco 2003, Titon 1997). French scholar Mallet, who has worked in South-western Madagascar on *tsapiky* music for a long time, writes that a foreigner who is interested in the music is directly regarded by musicians there as a producer (Mallet 2009: 25). Mallet therefore describes how he tried to create a relationship with the musicians that was different to the musicians' a priori expectations and hopes:

> Il fallait que je leur fasse comprendre et accepter une relation à l'autre, par le biais de leur musique, différente de celle qu'ils connaissent et pour laquelle ils ont des outils, des repères construits sur la base d'argent, repères qui constituent aussi des formes de défenses, de protections. Il fallait que j'atténue progressivement cette double extériorité du producteur vazaha, cet a priori qui m'était naturellement assigné. J'ai tenté d'effacer les « Monsieur Julien » et de dépasser les discours tout faits, liés aux opportunités que je pouvais représenter, l'ambiguïté d'un rapport fondé à la fois sur la méfiance des musiciens et sur leur espoir de voir leurs parcours se prolonger jusqu'andafy (à l'extérieur, à l'étranger) (Mallet 2009 : 25).[21]

Field research is part of real life; we are often taken by surprise or even pulled into some sort of "field politics" by our fieldwork participants (Hellier-Tinoco 2003: 24, 32). I have definitely been taken by surprise many times, especially during my first stays in Antananarivo. Here is an example: A musician, who invited me to come to a rehearsal at his house, picked me up with a taxi. While driving in the taxi, I realised that we were

---

[21] "I had to make them understand and accept a new form of relationship based on their music. This relationship was different to what they knew and to the rules they were used to, e.g. rules based on money which also worked as a form of protection. I had to gradually weaken the double exteriority of a vazaha producer that had been naturally assigned to me. I tried to stop them calling me "Mister Julien" and to go beyond both the already fixed discourses that were linked to what I could offer them and the ambiguity of our relationship based on their combined mistrust and hope that I would help them find their way to andafy (abroad)" (my translation).

going a completely different way (which I could only tell as I had been to his house before). I therefore asked where we were going and he said that he needed to pick up something from a friend. We parked just in front of the Ministry of Culture. When I proposed to wait in the car, he persuaded me to come with him as it would not take long and we could have a chat while waiting. I suddenly found myself in a big black leather chair, facing this "friend"–an official from the Ministry. Although I did not say a word, my Malagasy was good enough to understand that the musician was begging money for himself–though in my name–as my research definitely would prove his music to be worth supporting. It worked. Although I cannot know for sure, I had the feeling the official understood exactly what was going on.

However, in contrast to Mallet, who argues that being a musician himself also created some kind of mistrust among the *tsapiky* musicians, in particular with regard to the "stealing of songs" (Mallet 2009: 29), I found that my being a musician added a merely positive dimension to my research.

One of the very first things I did in Antananarivo during my first research trip in 2005 was to find myself a teacher to start learning the most famous Malagasy instrument, the bamboo zither called *valiha*. Since the age of five, I had been trained in Western classical music (violin, recorder and piano) and had a particular interest in baroque music and historical performance practice. Doné Andriambaliha, my teacher at the Rarihasina Cultural Centre, insisted I learn by ear –we generally recorded every lesson–as well as teaching me a little of the *koritsana*, a Malagasy percussion instrument, in order to better understand the accentuation and underlying rhythmical patterns. I very much enjoyed starting a completely new instrument and building a small repertory of Malagasy songs from the High Plateaux region. However, learning the basic technical skills on a new instrument takes some time; sometimes I thought that I would like to feel more comfortable with the instrument's technical side in order to concentrate on the actual moments of musicking. All the happier was I when in 2006 I got to know singer and guitarist Erick Manana who immediately encouraged me to try to use my violin, an instrument not foreign to Malagasy music.[22] Erick Manana started to teach me many songs from his home region, the High Plateaux, and his own compositions. Again, I relied on learning by ear, using only recordings and no note-taking to memorise new tunes.

---

[22] See Randrianary (2001) for information about the Malagasy traditional violin *lokanga* and Harison (2005) for information about the arrival and use of European instruments in Madagascar.

I had not played Malagasy music as part of a public concert until Erick Manana invited me to perform one song with him at his concert at the "Olympia" music hall in Paris in November 2009. He persuaded me because he was convinced the Malagasy audience[23] would be delighted to see a *vazaha*[24] musician performing on her violin in "proper Malagasy style." During the last days of intensive rehearsals with all musicians somewhere in the outskirts of Paris, we took a spontaneous decision: I had brought one of my recorders, thinking that there might be an opportunity with so many musicians to experiment and play together. It was my Renaissance soprano recorder, favoured by me because its sound is strong but soft and easy to vary. I had never played any Malagasy music with my recorder before. However, the legendary Malagasy flutist Rakoto Frah (who died in 2001) was a long-time musical companion to Erick Manana; both were members of the group "Feo Gasy." To my regret, I had not met Rakoto Frah in person. I know the few recordings of his work by heart, have seen a few rare video recordings of him and have listened to hundreds of stories about him by Malagasy people, especially musicians, who had played with him. I spontaneously tried to play the song "Bitika" that we had prepared with my violin on this Renaissance recorder the evening before the concert. It worked astonishingly well, so we decided I would change instruments during the song, taking the recorder out as a surprise in the second half of the song. Although I never properly learned Malagasy flute-playing before this particular event, I could say that I had done so indirectly and unconsciously by listening to recordings, watching videos, transferring already-learned knowledge and experiences from my violin and *valiha* playing onto the recorder and above all, remembering every little detail and re-listening again and again to stories and memories of Rakoto Frah to the extent that it almost felt like I actually knew him.

It's no exaggeration to say the concert at the "Olympia" has become a turning point in my musical life. Since then, I have performed regularly with Erick Manana and a great variety of the musicians he continually works with, in France, the UK, Switzerland, Germany, Belgium, Canada and more recently also in Madagascar; the biggest highlights have been the concerts in the CCESCA in Antananarivo in June 2011 (the recording of which is now available on DVD[25]) and the concert in May 2012 in the Palais du Sport, Madagascar's biggest indoor venue, hosting more than

---

[23] As Erick Manana had expected, although there were *vazahas* in the audience (even from other European countries, such as Sweden, Germany, or Norway), the majority was Malagasy.

[24] Malagasy term for foreigner, literally meaning "well observed."

[25] Erick Manana and Jenny (2011).

7000 people. I have also started to sing–a fact that had a very strong effect on Malagasy audiences (see chapter 6).

Erick Manana was born in Antananarivo but moved to France at the age of nineteen. As a child, he was particularly fascinated by the typical musical genre of the High Plateaux region, the *hira gasy*,[26] an influence that can be heard in many of his compositions. I have come across numerous descriptions of *hira gasy*–"peasant's theatre," "Malagasy street opera," a "mixture of polyphonic singing, orchestra, and acrobatic" or "Malagasy theatre à la Brecht" to name but a few.[27] The variety of elements and influences that can be found in *hira gasy* performances has attracted researchers from different disciplines (see for example Edkvist 1997, Didier 2001 or Vatan 2004). Erick Manana argues that as an artist, his office was his heart and his main tool the *lova-tsofina*, which means that his experiences of living in a foreign country, meeting musicians from different backgrounds, or travelling to other countries can be heard and experienced in his own music. One of his projects in which I also participated, was the "malagasising" of standard jazz tunes and manouche tunes[28] that we performed at the Festival "Nuits Atypiques" in Langon[29] in July 2010.

Yet another experience–and with regard to Erick Manana's musical background a complementary experience of musicking–was my encounter with the *hira gasy* group "Tarika Ra-jean Marie," from Feonarivo, who came to Germany in March 2010.[30] In collaboration with the Theater an

---

[26] See Edkvist 1997, Didier 2001 or Vatan 2004 for more information on the *hira gasy*.
[27] See for example WDR3 Musikkulturen (2010).
[28] For a detailed account on manouche music and the legendary manouche guitar player Django Reinhardt, see Gelly and Fogg (2005) and Dregni (2006).
[29] The concert at the Festival Nuits Atypiques in Langon in July 2010 was in a way symbolic to me as it was exactly on that stage that legendary flute player Rakoto Frah performed with the group "Feo Gasy" shortly before he died and where the CD "Ramano", one of my main sources of Malagasy flute music, was produced, see Feo Gasy (2000).
[30] The initial idea of bringing a *hira gasy* group to Germany was born during one of many meetings with a Malagasy friend of mine, Hasina Samoelinanja, who works as Malagasy teacher, tourist guide, translator and is also a professional *kabary* (speaker) in Madagascar (*kabary* forms also part of a *hira gasy* performance). This idea made me contact Rolf Hemke who is working at the Theater an der Ruhr, which organises many Africa-related music and theatre projects. The project with the *hira gasy* group "Rajean-Marie" from Feonarivo was then organised by the Theater an der Ruhr (Mülheim an der Ruhr) within their series *Klanglandschaften Afrika* ("Soundscapes Africa") in collaboration with the

der Ruhr (Theatre in Mülheim, Germany), the German radio station WDR and the cultural secretariat of the federal state of North Rhine-Westphalia we invited for the first time ever a *hira gasy* group to perform on a German stage. This project allowed me to spend a very intensive time with these artists. Despite a strict and dense timetable, we found moments to play together and I profited from attending all rehearsals, recording sessions and live performances. A reunion with these musicians took place when I invited them to watch our concert in the CCESCA in Antananarivo in June 2011, which for many of them had been the first experience in their home country of going to and listening to a concert in an indoor venue with a fixed starting time, a seated audience and entry tickets.

As will become clear, my research over the past years has been geographically scattered across different places. But it has also been shaped by the increasing intensity of my own learning, playing and performing of Malagasy music, from the first few *valiha* lessons to a semi-professional position as a regularly performing violinist, flutist and singer. External factors, such as the enduring political crisis, have also had an effect on my research, such as preventing me from going to Antananarivo for a relatively long period of time: between autumn of 2008 and the summer of 2011.

A steady element throughout these years has been and still is my effort to concentrate on the interrelation of discourses and musical practices: I have never regarded or experienced different field research activities, such as interviews, rehearsals, informal meetings or musical performances, as separated from one another. Rather, regardless of the timespan that sometimes lies between these different activities, I have always searched for and made use of the connections between them. I often refer back to my interviews, and have realised that my musical experiences often help me to better understand and analyse discourses. In turn, reading, listening to, re-discussing or reflecting upon discourses also helps me to further develop my musical skills.

All ethnographic interviews I conducted have been open and explorative; they did not follow any prefixed questions or questionnaires. Further, numerous informal conversations before and after concerts and

German radio WDR3 (Cologne) and the Kultursekretariat NRW (Cultural Secretariat of the Federal State of North-Rhine Westphalia). It included two days of studio recording and three live performances, with the performances particularly adapted to a German-speaking audience. For more information, please see WDR3 Musikkulturen (2010). I was in charge of supporting the artists throughout their stay in Germany (the very first trip ever outside Madagascar for all members of the ensemble), so I was involved in the project from beginning to end.

rehearsals, when visiting people at their homes, when meeting someone by chance in a café, in the streets, in a CD shop or at market stalls, or during taxi drives[31] have added significantly to my research ideas and results.

I conducted almost all interviews in French, a second language for me as well as most interviewees. Informal conversations, meetings, or discussions during rehearsal have more often been held in Malagasy. My knowledge of the Malagasy language is still basic, but it helped me gain valuable knowledge, as for example through my asking for specific definitions, terms, and concepts, or for meanings and interpretations of Malagasy proverbs and sayings; and most importantly, through my learning of Malagasy song lyrics.

During this process, I did not feel any sort of language barrier during my research. Rather to the contrary, the fact that I am not a French native speaker is often perceived with a kind of benevolence, if not relief, and therefore much facilitated conversation and exchange. The attitude of many Malagasy people towards France and French people is in general still very much shaped by the colonial history of the island. The political crisis of 2009 only boosted this tension, showing once more that the ex-colonial power is still highly influential.

The topic of "rhythm" was not planned at all from my side; I hit on it only during my field research. There are a few important circumstances that I would like to consider: the main conversation language has been French, which might have increased the emphasis on the "6/8 rhythm," considering that this is a concept that has grown out of Western music theory. Having said this, there is discord among the musicians whether a term for "rhythm" actually exists in the Malagasy language. When I asked for a translation of "6/8 rhythm" I was told either that there was not a word for it or that it was mainly foreigners who called it "6/8 rhythm" (see chapter 4). A much bigger effect on my research and our discourses in my eyes has been my double role as musician and researcher. The musicians' knowledge about my own Western musicological training, for example, certainly had an impact on their choice of words. My musical background

---

[31] Antananarivo taxi drivers have turned out to be a particularly illuminating source of information. I have had the chance to express my gratitude to all the Antananarivo taxi drivers: In 2011 Erick Manana composed "2CV an-dRandria," a song dedicated to the taxi drivers of Antananarivo, praising their knowledge and expertise of the old but still working 2CVs. We recorded the song in April 2011 and the video clip was broadcast as publicity for our concert tour in Madagascar in June 2011. Ever since, people keep relating me to that song; taxi drivers in particular, show their gratitude for our appreciation of their job. See video example 1 ("*Ny 2CV an-dRandria*") on DVD.

also occasionally led to a situation in which someone asked me to explain the rhythmical structure of Malagasy music with the help of Western notation ("Jenny, you should be able to explain the 6/8 correctly"). I usually said that I would be happy to explain how the "6/8 rhythm" was understood and used in Western music theory, but that I personally felt that it was difficult to use it for describing Malagasy music. In fact, I realised that when I mentioned the *lova-tsofina* in any kind of conversation and explained that it was through this concept and approach (i.e. not using any kind of notation) that I have been learning and performing Malagasy music, Malagasy people seemed to immediately agree and often showed their sympathy that I recognise and appreciate this indigenous concept. However, some also seemed to be surprised, if not slightly disappointed, often arguing that someone was needed who was capable of explaining Malagasy music to Western listeners and musicians in "their" language, i.e. using Western notation.

Ethnomusicologists with research experience in different music cultures and countries have emphasised the positive effect that shared music making have had on their fieldwork situations and relationships (e.g. Rice 1994, Baily 2008, Mallet 2009; see chapter 3 for a detailed discussion). My own research experience lines up with this; although it is true that with regard to the missing cultural infrastructure and support for artists, music-making in Madagascar is an environment often dominated by jealousy and rivalry, the fact that I presented myself not only as an academic researcher but also as a musician facilitated and opened conversations.

My double role as musician and researcher especially helped to loosen or even cross the boundary between the "researcher" and the "researched." I can recall quite a few situations in which I felt like the one being "observed," "researched" and the one raising attention and causing curiosity. When in summer 2008 I did not take my own violin with me, as I was afraid at the time that tropical weather could damage the instrument, I had the idea of borrowing an instrument in Antananarivo. This idea turned into a three days' search with numerous phone calls and endless taxi and bus journeys, through which I got to know new parts of Antananarivo, including many new people, musicians, music shops and instrument-makers. Even more importantly, people got to know me as well. I received phone calls from people I did not know who had heard I was looking for a violin. The whole process of searching for a violin propelled interest in me to a new level. When I finally found a violin, the bridge broke after a few days (probably because of the sultry tropical weather!), which took me on another two days' journey through Antananarivo trying to find a replacement. Again with the help of many people, I finally found one in a small music shop. When I sat down in the corner of this shop to try to affix the bridge to the violin, I was soon surrounded by a group of people observing me and taking pictures of me "at work," and I became the one telling my story and answering questions.

Ever since, I always bring my own violin with me. The more concerts I play, especially in Madagascar, but also within Malagasy communities in Europe, Canada and the US, the more I ask myself to what extent the boundary between the "researcher" and the "researched" still exists, if at all. Already after the concert at the Olympia in Paris in November 2009, but even more so with the concerts in Madagascar in June 2011 and May 2012, there has been significant media interest in me as a German-born musician performing Malagasy music. Numerous newspaper articles, TV broadcasts, concert critiques, discussions in Internet forums, comments on videos available online, reactions of concert audiences, or personal information I receive testify to this attention, curiosity, and amazement that my engagement in Malagasy music making has created so far.[32] In my home country, Germany, my engagement in Malgasy music-making also attracts attention,[33] raises questions and creates curiosity; during a concert with our "Compagnie Erick Manana–Jenny" that we played at the Philharmonic of Berlin in May 2013, for example, well-known German journalist Roger Willemsen interviewed me on stage and asked me to reveal and explain "my story," the story of a German-born musician with classical music training singing and playing Malagasy music to German audiences.[34]

Within this development, a few aspects are of particular interest as they directly relate to questions of identity, a key topic of this book. Malagasy audiences often compare my own flute playing to Rakoto Frah, sometimes to such an extent that they see a kind of incarnation of him in me. Comments on my violin-playing usually emphasise amazement that a foreigner plays like *mpihira gasy* (Malagasy term for musician playing in the *hira gasy*), much as to my singing style is often compared to the particular usage of the voice in the olden High Plateaux songs called "*Kalon'ny fahiny*."[35] All these responses, surprisingly, draw on a

---

[32] For examples of newspaper articles see: Ratsara (2011a, 2011b), Rado (2011) or Heimer (2012). For examples of comments on internet videos, see Youtube Madatsara (2013).

[33] See for example Heimer (2013).

[34] The philharmonic of Berlin in 2011 initiated the concert serie "Unterwegs" ("on the way") featuring word music ensembles from around the globe. See Berliner Philharmoniker (2013).

[35] See for example Ratsara (2011b).

connection to the past, projecting something onto me that might carry the risk of being lost and forgotten (see chapter 6 for a detailed discussion on these and more examples).

Finding myself in the position where people start to know and recognise me, becoming extremely curious about everything in my life and myself as a personality, has become another challenge to my continuing research. Especially in Madagascar itself, a negative effect is that it becomes ever more difficult to observe situations quietly or take part in any kind of event without attracting attention. However, a very positive effect, I feel, is that this level of recognition has helped to create a deep exchange of musical experiences that questions Western-dominated discourses on music and music-making and goes beyond cultural boundaries, a profound intercultural dialogue that I hope to present and explain with this book.

Outline

I understand the video and audio samples on the book's DVD not as accompanying material but as an integral part of the book, so would encourage every reader to make use of them where mentioned in footnotes. As much as I have tried to make the musicians' own voices heard by providing original interview material (sometimes at great length), these samples also form part of my argument about the importance of analysing experiences of "musicking" and discourses about music interdependently.

Chapter 2 focuses on the concept of "rhythm," giving a state-of-the-art account of theoretical discussions of the topic. What is "rhythm" and how is it understood, explained, and explored in academic research? By analysing the different themes that have caused controversy and critique across different academic disciplines, this chapter sheds new light on "rhythm" and challenges long-established and Western-dominated theories, in particular regarding the historiography of scholarship on African rhythm.

Chapter 3 argues for participatory research and the need for the intersection and mutual integration of musical practices and ethnomusicological research. It thereby depicts and challenges different boundaries that are often created and experienced, such as the boundary between the "researcher" and the "researched," or differently said, between those who make the music and those who write about it. This chapter outlines my bottom-up approach and use of the main principles of a "subject-centred ethnography" (Rice 2003), arguing that it is only through this approach that it is possible to follow Agawu's demand for a "presumption of sameness" (Agawu 2003), a research attitude that prevents researchers ignoring the voices of the people with whom they work, making them aware of the risk of imposing a Western analytical perspective and approach.

Chapters 4-6 explore in great detail my field research material, analysing and interconnecting interview materials and musical experiences. Through in-depth examples, this set of chapters gives a clear and concrete understanding as to how it is both necessary and possible to integrate musical practices into ethnomusicological research and analyse discourses about music (and music-making) and musical experiences in a constant interrelation. Whereas chapters 4 and 5 focus closely on the musicians' discourses about the two issues that have come to the fore–the "6/8 rhythm" "versus" the *lova-tsofina*–chapter 6 emphasises shared musical experiences. For the purpose of clear arrangement and easier understanding these materials are presented in this order though they need to be read and understood as being closely interrelated.

Chapter 4 studies the terminological confusion around the concept of "6/8 rhythm" in the Malagasy context, linking theoretical discussions and debates to concrete fieldwork material. Analysing how different identity questions are negotiated through this particular term and concept, the chapter starts with the question of how this term is used and understood from a Western perspective. It then concentrates on where, when and how exactly it appears in the Malagasy context, investigating how it relates to the controversial and strongly debated "theories on rhythm." As there is no shared or agreed terminology among the musicians, the focus here is on the individual musicians' usages and understandings of this particular concept.

Chapter 5 focuses on a seemingly contradictory aspect, namely the musicians' experiences that relate to the indigenous concept of oral transmission, the *lova-tsofina*. Following from the previous chapter, this one investigates how identity is constructed through the musicians' discourses about the meaning and origin of "rhythm" in Madagascar. Arguing for the importance of listening to the musicians' own concepts and ideas about music and musicking, the chapter's analysis takes a sensitive, self-reflexive approach, taking into account my own double role as researcher and (Western classically-trained) musician.

Chapter 6 concentrates on musical experiences, both my own and those of the musicians. Hence, it links the two previous chapters to the experiences I have gained through learning, playing, and performing with Malagasy musicians, using concrete examples and interview material as well as music and video footage to show how discourses about music, music-making and musical experiences are analysed interdependently. Coming back to the crux of my research, the chapter focuses on the understanding of and relation between the "6/8 rhythm" and the *lova-tsofina*.

CHAPTER TWO

THEORISING "RHYTHM"

Introduction

The previous chapter introduced the crux of my research, namely the existence of supposedly contradictory discourses on Malagasy music. There is, on the one hand, the consistent appearance and use of the Western concept of "6/8 rhythm" which is in its original context based on the idea of musical notation. On the other hand, Malagasy musicians consistently emphasise the importance of the Malagasy indigenous concept of oral transmission–the *lova-tsofina*–as the base for Malagasy music-making.

This seeming contradiction is crucially important because "rhythm" appears to be the starting point for the musicians' search for a collective musical identity; despite the many different influences that can be heard, seen and experienced in the music of Madagascar and the diversity of existing music dance and instrument styles in the different regions of the island (cf. Randrianary 2001), all musicians I worked with claim there is a rhythmical base in Malagasy music common to all (see chapter 4, 5, and 6). Throughout my research over the past years with Malagasy musicians I have continuously tackled this issue of a shared rhythmic base, bringing together individual understandings, explanations and experiences, including my own. This process of exploring the existence and meaning of such a structure will be explained in detail in chapters 4-6. For now, it is necessary to take a close look at the concept of "rhythm" in general.

What is "rhythm"? How is it understood, used and explained in academic research? How has "rhythm" been explored and analysed in studies on African music cultures? This chapter sheds new light on "rhythm" and intervenes in the historiography of scholarship on African rhythm. By analysing long-established theories on "rhythm," I aim to challenge the use of prevailing Western analytical discourses and perspectives on music, particularly on rhythm. With this study, I would like to encourage scholars to reflect upon the ways we represent knowledge in academic work, especially with regard to links between music and oral culture as in the case of Malagasy music. The following discussion of "rhythm" shows that the boundary between those who make music and those who write about music, i.e. between the researchers and those "being researched," very often leads to ignorance about indigenous ideas and theories. In other words: the ignorance of the voices and experience of the people we work with.

The next chapter (chapter 3) therefore tackles methodological issues relevant to current debates concerning fieldwork and ethnomusicological research methods; it explains how I integrated musical experiences in order to go beyond a study of seemingly contradictory discourses and how I analysed shared musical experiences and discourses in a constant interrelation in order to fully integrate theories, ideas and experiences of researcher and "researched" alike.

What is "Rhythm"?

The ethnomusicologist Mieczyslaw Kolinski claims to have discovered some "fifty different meanings of the word 'rhythm'" (Kolinski 1973: 494). Numerous scholars throughout different disciplines point out the "terminological confusion" (Arom 1991: 182) and the number of terms describing somehow-related or even similar concepts and meanings seems endless. The author Apel argues that

> [i]t would be a hopeless task to search for a definition of rhythm which would prove acceptable even to a small minority of musicians and writers on music (Apel 1946: 639, cited in Arom 1991: 186).

Of particular interest to scholars of various disciplines have been the notions of "metre" and "measure," notions that seem at the same time to have caused the most discord. This, in turn, has resulted in a high number of competing interpretations of these terms, especially among those who have looked at non-Western, particularly African, music. Because of this discord and the many different interpretations, scholars have also invented a large number of new concepts related to "metre" and "measure." However, the usefulness of these new terms has been questioned and even strongly criticised by authors specialising in African or Cuban musics. Acosta (2005) and Agawu (2003), for example, argue that these newly-invented terms emphasise stereotypes—such as that African or Cuban rhythms are "complex"—and that they also contribute to ideologies of difference by searching for and focusing on the notion of "otherness."

Many scholars from different disciplines also emphasise the close relation that rhythm has with language or other cultural aspects.

Interestingly, the concepts of "measure" and "metre" seem to appear in all discussions of various aspects concerning the general topic of rhythm, a fact that needs to be considered when looking at the "6/8 rhythm" in the Malagasy context. It is therefore important to examine this emphasis and search by scholars across disciplines for something tangible and measureable in music, i.e. a way to put "rhythm" into writing.

The Concepts of "Metre" and "Measure"– Different Interpretations and Understandings

Even a glance at the articles on "metre" and "measure" in the *The Oxford Companion to Music* (2007-2012) reveals a confusing aspect, which is the different usage in American and British English. The definition of "metre" seems clear as the:

> pattern of regular pulses (and the arrangement of their constituent parts) by which a piece of music is organized. One complete pattern is called a bar. The prevailing metre is identified at the beginning of a piece (and during it whenever it changes) by a time signature, which is usually in the form of a fraction; the denominator indicates the note- value of each beat and the numerator gives the number of beats in each bar.[1]

The confusion starts with "bar" and "bar-line." In British English the latter is used for the vertical line that is drawn through a staff or staves of musical notation, indicating division into metrical units, i.e. "bars." American English refers to this metrical unit as "measure" and reserves the term "bar" for what British English refers to as the actual "bar-line."[2] The notion of "measure" in British English, again, has a very particular meaning as a term referring to a specific moderately slow and stately dance in duple time of the sixteenth and seventeenth century.[3] As we will see in what follows, many authors have very particular and individual definitions of these concepts. This is also the case in the Malagasy context; whereas almost all musicians constantly use the concept of "6/8 rhythm," many different meanings and individual understandings are attached to it (see chapter 4).

The ethnomusicologist Simha Arom has paid a lot of attention to the notion of "measure." He writes that originally "measure" was just a way of assembling a given number of beats that derived from what was known as

---

[1] Latham (2007-2012)
[2] Hiley (2007-2012).
[3] Oxford Music Online (2007-2012).

"tactus" in the Middle Ages (Arom 1991: 189). Since about 1600, however, the sense of the notion of measure as entities grouped as for example 3/4, 4/4, or 6/8 with the underlying alternation of strong and weak beats has "sharply constrained all cultured Western music" (Arom 1991: 179-180). Van Leeuwen (1999) confirms Arom's explanations. He writes that while during the Middle Ages "eternal" time and plainchant dominated, in the Renaissance period music began to be divided and measured and composers introduced the bar line (Van Leeuwen 1999: 37). Hiley[4] also confirms that the earliest usage of bar lines can be found in music written in tablature in the early fifteenth century. He further writes that even until the sixteenth and seventeenth centuries, bar lines did not always immediately precede the main accented beat. The first beat of the bar and the strong beat therefore did not always coincide. It was only after the mid-seventeenth century that it became the rule to precede main beats with bar lines.

Arom remarks that all definitions in dictionaries as well as education at music schools and conservatories are still based on a contrast between strong and weak beats in music (Arom 1991: 180). He analyses several definitions of "measure" by various authors, as for instance Kolinski (1973), Chailley (1951), Cooper and Meyer (1960) and Herzfeld (1974) and comes to the conclusion that all of them "provide for accentual ranking within the measure" (Arom 1991: 187). Dudley also agrees that Western musicians and its listeners assume that metric pulses were consistently accented, for instance the first note in a 3/4 metre or the first and fourth note in a 6/8 metre (Dudley 1996: 272). Arom's critique goes even further. He argues that for most authors accentuation is actually the foundation of rhythm and only the presence of accents in itself implies the existence of rhythm (Arom 1991: 187). "Rhythm" and "metrics" are thus inconceivable without each other (Arom 1991: 184). Most authors see difficulties in adopting this interpretation of rhythm and in particular that of measure to non-Western musics, especially when it comes to music transcription; some also see its limits regarding Western music.

Dudley (1996), for example, argues that European music has more variety of rhythmic feel than can be explained by concepts such as 3/4 or 4/4. His example is "a waltz feel," a description which already says much more about the character of a piece than saying it is in a 3/4 metre (Dudley 1996: 274). These remarks about the interpretation and use of "metre" founded in Western music culture seem to be the starting point for many

---

[4] Hiley (2007-2012).

critiques. In addition, there are some relevant new concepts and terms, which I will now analyse in more detail.

Martin R.L. Clayton (1996) has undertaken research on "free rhythm." Although his study refers to music without metre, he makes some important remarks about the use of the concept. He criticises two presumptions: first, that of a given particular accentual ranking and, second, that all pulses are temporally equal:

> The terms 'strong' and 'weak' beats will almost certainly prove inappropriate to many musics; we cannot assume the temporal equality of pulses; neither can we assume that a periodic pattern necessarily begins or ends at any particular point (that there is a 'beat one') (Clayton 1996: 328).

He offers a large variety of examples of "free rhythm" from around the world and criticises other scholars' neglect of studying "free rhythm" (Clayton 1996: 323). He has found several reasons for this, the main ones being the absence of concepts and methods in (Western) musicology that account for the existence of metre, and the fact that our musical perception and analytical thinking therefore developed largely through the study of metric musics. In addition, ethnomusicologists have not yet reported any indigenous theories about "free rhythm" (Clayton 1996: 326-327). Clayton's argument is that all "metrical systems" have in common a dependence on pulsation. "Metres" repeat and therefore create periodicity, through which they become a framework for rhythmic design. Terms such as "strong" or "weak" beats are, however, misleading since patterns are not necessarily marked by dynamic accenting or de-accenting. He therefore suggests thinking of metre as a "cognitive representation" rather than an objective quality of the music itself (Clayton 1996: 328).

Several authors who work on African music go one step further, saying that these terms are worse than misleading, that time signature and the contrast of strong and weak beats actually lack a way to differentiate between the many patterns of accents that are possible in a musical period. And in much African music, for example, main beats are conceived but not audibly accented (Dudley 1996: 272). Arom refers to this phenomenon as "abstraction of the notion of metre and strong beats" ("abstraction de la notion de mesure et du temps fort") (Arom 1984: 6). Dudley concludes that metre is therefore something entirely separate from rhythmic accent and that African musicians have many different kind of metres that can be described as, for example, a 4/4 measure (Dudley 1996: 273). Arom also comes to the conclusion that rhythmic systems in African music make no use of the notion of "measure" and the associated feature of "strong" and "weak" beats. In order to have an accurate description of these systems, he asks to develop "a precise and univocal vocabulary, i.e. one in which the meanings of two terms never overlap" (Arom 1991: 201). He therefore promotes the notion of "pulsation" rather than using the term "measure" that has grown out of a long established Western musicology:

> Pulsations are an uninterrupted sequence of reference points with respect to which rhythmic flow is organised. All the durations in a piece, whether they appear as sounds or silences, are defined in a relationship to the pulsation (Arom 1991: 202).

From his point of view, pulsation is not equivalent to rhythm. Rather, for there to be rhythm, "sequences of auditive events must be characterised by contrasting features." He recognises three different features through which this can happen: by accents; by tone colours; by durations. Considering all possible combinations of these three features, Arom concludes that there are nine different ways to create rhythm. And this is when his concept of "metre" comes into play: One of the combinations, namely that of identical durations with regular accentuation, he identifies as "metre" and suggests that "what is called metre in music is thus the simplest form of rhythmic expression" (Arom 1991: 202-203).

Gerhard Kubik (1969, 1974, and 2010) also takes up the notion of "pulsation." In contrast to Arom, he writes that especially in several forms of instrumental African music, musicians refer to two, three, or even four on-going pulsations (Kubik 1969: 57). This implies the absence of a common guide-pulse as a reference points by all players and means that each player relates his or her part to individual reference pulses which can stand in various relations to each other. Scholars usually refer to this as "interlocking" (Kubik 1974: 247).

Rhythm in African Music and the Invention of New Terms

The question whether Malagasy music can or should be categorised as African music is a difficult one. According to my own experience, in Western music shops, in music magazines, or on music-related Internet sites, it is usually classified under the header of "Africa," mainly due to its geographical position. Looking at the musicians' own discourses, the categorisation is far less clear. Identities and questions of belonging constantly shift, as we will see in chapters 4-6. Generally, I have had the experience that people from the High Plateaux region tend to establish a border between Africa and themselves, emphasising that people from this region were descendants of Indonesian people, whereas Malagasy people from the coast ("*Côtiers*") are more likely to be descendants of former African slaves.[5]

As already seen above, many scholars, especially those studying African musics, have invented new terms and concepts they find more appropriate for their subject.[6] Whereas some of these concepts and terms, like the idea of "interlocking," have been taken up in wider scholarly discussions, others have never made their way beyond the work in which they were originally invented. The most significant critique of using these newly invented concepts specifically for African music has come from musicologist Kofi Agawu. He has conducted much research on African music, especially on music from his home region in Ghana, but is also a classically trained scholar of Western musicology. In his *Representing African Music* (2003), he criticises in no uncertain terms numerous scholars who have worked on music in different regions of Africa. His main point of critique concerning the topic of rhythm is already well summarised by the title of one of his chapters, "The Invention of 'African Rhythm.'" He explains that rhythm and the particular complexity of rhythm has been brought up so consistently as a central theme throughout the discourse on African music that it is now taken as a commonplace:

> That the distinctive quality of African music lies in its rhythmic structure is a notion so persistently thematized that it has by now assumed the status of a commonplace, a topos. And so it is with related ideas that African rhythms are complex, that Africans possess a unique rhythmic sensibility, and that this rhythmic disposition marks them as ultimately different from us (Agawu 2003: 55).

Based on the argument that rhythm was the most sensationalised parameter in African music, Agawu describes several problems. The first problem is that African music supposedly constitutes a homogenous body. Agawu explains his critique by using different perspectives. Whereas in the quotation above he speaks from a Western researcher's point of view (by

---

[5] For a detailed discussion of the old conflict between the High Plateaux and the "*Côtiers*" and especially how it acquired a particular political salience in the twentieth century since the French colonisers had made use of the established power structures of the Merina to rule the island, see Deschamps (1972).

[6] Stephen Blum (1991) in his article on "European Musical Terminology and the Music of Africa" examines problems that arose as European terminology was applied to African music by early comparative musicologists towards the end of the 19th and the beginning of the 20th century, particularly looking at the works of E.M. Hornbostel and concepts, such as "musical system," "musical thinking," "motive," or "melodic motion".

stating "different from us"), a few pages ahead of this he speaks from the perspective of someone from the African continent, using exactly the same argument: "*Our* complex and diverse continent is virtually unrecognizable in the unanimist constructions employed by *some researchers*" [Emphasis mine] (Agawu 2003: 59). "Africa" as such cannot be grasped as a unified cultural phenomenon or a fruitful epistemological referent, he argues. This false idea of a singular Africa creates another severe problem: the retreat from comparison (Agawu 2003: 60).

> The choice of an appropriate comparative frame is already ideological. Indeed, a determined researcher could easily show that the sum of isolated experiments in rhythmic organization found in so-called Western music produces a picture of far greater complexity than anything that Africans have produced so far either singly or collectively. One could, in short, quite easily invent 'European rhythm' (Agawu 2003: 61).

"African rhythm," Agawu argues, should therefore be called an "invention, a construction, a fiction, a myth, ultimately a lie" (Agawu 2003: 61). Agawu agrees with other scholars that the semantic field of rhythm is not a single, unified, or coherent one, but one permanently entangled with other discourses, such as the Western music being "balkanized into separate domains" (Agawu 2003: 61, 63). Agawu demands an ideology of difference to be replaced by an ideology of sameness "so that–and this is somewhat paradoxical–we can gain a better view of difference" (Agawu 2003: 67).

Philip Bohlman critically remarks that it was the use of musical notation that often gave scholars the idea of effacing difference and "Otherness" within their research. In his article on "Musicology as a political act" he argued that musicology[7] was going through a "political crisis" and "profound moral panic," criticising in particular the constant attempt in musicology of "essentializing music" (Bohlman 1993: 419). To Bohlman each sub-discipline privileges different forms of essentialization, with the most wide-spread form being the persistent use of musical notation:

> By making and essentializing its object, musicology situates itself in a particularly Western position of wielding power. Notation, for example, becomes a convenient way of collapsing time and space, thereby removing all sorts of Others–Western and non-Western–to the plane of the universal. By rendering all musics in Western notation, one creates a universe of music and then succeeds in controlling it (Bohlman 1993: 424).

---

[7] Bohlman emphasises that "musicology" as understood here also includes ethnomusicology, music theory and music criticism (Bohlman 1993: 418).

Bohlman here raises the issue of power which he emphasises even more with regard to notation and music from oral tradition:

> By transcribing and notating music from oral tradition, we demonstrate our power and knowledge, but ipso facto keep the transmitters of oral tradition from acquiring the same measure of power (Bohlman 1993: 424).

Methodological and theoretical debates throughout the last twenty years have raised the issue of power and challenged the critique of music being essentialised by scholars. But still the demand for written reference of music in academic works remains prevalent and the use of musical notation a matter of course. With regard to African musics and rhythm, scholars have receded more and more from notating the music merely in Western notation style. However, only very rarely do we encounter the indigenous theories or concepts used by the musicians themselves. Instead, the question of how to notate African music has led scholars to the creation and invention of a large number of new concepts and terms.

Right at the beginning of his chapter entitled "Polymeter, Additive Rhythm, and Other Enduring Myths" Agawu presents a list of no less than 38 new terms that have appeared in the literature on African music so far (Agawu 2003: 72-73). The notions of "polyrhythm" and "polymetre" are widely used and very well known among scholars. Arom's major publication (with more than 600 pages on African music) is even entitled *African Polyphony and Polyrhythm*. "Polyrhythm" is understood as the simultaneous use of two or more contrasting rhythms in a musical texture (Agawu 2003: 79). It has to be distinguished from "polymetre," which is the

> simultaneous use of more than one meter in an ensemble composition. Each functional component of the texture, be it an instrument or a group, is said to expose a distinct rhythmic pattern within its own metrical frame, apparently without any obvious regard for a larger coordinating mechanism. (Agawu 2003: 79).

Although Agawu still questions the term "polyrhythm," he argues that the phenomenon it describes is easily grasped and also exists in European music. The degree of repetition inherent in African polyrhythm might, however, make a difference:

> What perhaps distinguishes the African usages is the degree of repetition of the constituent patterns, the foregrounding of repetition as a modus operandi. If this counts as a difference, it is one of degree, not of kind (Agawu 2003: 81).

Agawu does see, though, reasons to reject the notion of "polymetre," the most important being that there are no indications that polymetre is relevant in the discourses among those African musicians who are the actual "carriers of the tradition." Although some ideas of metre are recognised in some indigenous discourses (e.g. where dancers put their feet), there is no evidence of the simultaneous use of different metres, which shows that polymetre has been imposed on African music (Agawu 2003: 84-85).

Scholars working on African music have given their attention to another term: "additive rhythm" as opposed to "divisive rhythm." "Additive rhythm" describes a pattern in which non-identical or irregular durational groups follow one another. A single 12/8 bar, for example, may be divided additively into 5+7 or 3+2+2+5, but not into 3+3+3+3. "Additive rhythms" can appear within one bar or between bars or even groups of bars. The distinction between "additive" and "divisive" rhythms was first made by Curt Sachs, who understood the earliest examples as "rhythms of the body" specifically designed for dance. These became dominant in European music from the seventeenth century onward. The later additive rhythms he thinks of as "rhythms of speech;" he sees their origin in language and the asymmetrical periodicities in speech. Sach's term became prominent within the ethnomusicological discourse on African music through his student Rose Brandel (Agawu 2003: 86-87).

Brandel (1959) has developed the concept of the "African *Hemiola* Style." She argues that African music is always based on duple and triple rhythms. However, there is one distinction to be made, namely between "vertical *hemiola*" and "horizontal *hemiola*." The first one describes what in Western music is often referred to as *hemiola*, namely triple rhythms sounding against duple rhythms. The latter means that the "conductor's beat" frequently changes from triple to duple rhythm. In this horizontal *hemiola*

> the change in the conductor's beat occurs in a short time span, as in a regular change from 6/8 to 3/4 or on frequent changes in meter: 5/8, 7/8, 8/8; at other times the hemiola will be wide-spread and sectional with several measures being in 3/4 and another section being in 6/8 or other configurations (Kauffman 1980: 397-398).

Kauffman (1980), who has reassessed various theories of African rhythm, sees some potential (as well as some weakness) in Brandel's approach. On the one hand, her distinction between horizontal and vertical *hemiola* opens up the possibility of dealing with both polyrhythmic relationships and individual patterning. He also favours Brandel's focus on the duple and triple changes, something central to all African music and usable for many other musical areas in the world, such as the additive rhythms of Eastern Europe or the Middle East or the divisive rhythms in Western music. One of the weaknesses Kauffman remarks is that Brandel reduces African music to Western notation, which he regards as a result of her lack of experiences in African music. He therefore concludes that "even though Brandel's theory has potentialities for a total explanation of the gestalt of African rhythm, its realization seems to be inadequate" (Kauffmann 1980: 398). A much stronger critique of her approach comes from Agawu, who has analysed many of her transcriptions of African music. She mainly transcribed from recordings and never had "the benefit of seeing the music and hearing the dance" (Agawu 2003: 90); one of her main mistakes when transcribing the music is that she placed a bar line before any perceived accent, which then produced "some unfortunate results" (Agawu 2003: 90). Agawu's main critique, however, is that she ignores the African musicians' own perceptions of their music.

> Brandel's Stravinsky-style scores confer an enviable complexity on ordinary African dance music, but they do not reflect the way African musicians conceive of their music. A Mangbetu woman dancing (…) is unlikely to think in terms of 3/8 followed by 5/16 followed by 6/16, then 7/16 then 3/8 (Agawu 2003: 90).

In my own research, my main aim has been to focus on the musicians' own perceptions and understandings of their music. I have not in any way tried to explain Malagasy music from a Western musicological perspective but have instead analysed the musicians' own discourses and musical experiences, including my own musical practices. This, for example, has made me aware of and made me use the *lova-tsofina*. At the same time, it has also made me aware of the musicians' constant use of the Western term "6/8 rhythm." However, instead of thinking of this as an already-defined Western term that has "migrated" to Madagascar, I have searched for and analysed its meaning and the musicians' individual usages and understandings of it in my particular research context (see chapter 4).

Brandel is not the only one who claims African music to be additive. The Ghanaian musicologist Nketia (1974), for example, says "the use of additive rhythms in duple, triple, and *hemiola* patterns is the hallmark of rhythmic organization in African music" (Nketia 1974: 131). Interestingly, Nketia is also quoted by Arom in order to underline his argument against the usage "additive rhythm" as he writes that "[t]he African learns to play rhythms in pattern" (Nketia 1963:10, cited in Arom 1991: 207). The fact that rhythmic formulae are learnt as a whole without being broken down into single constituents seems for Arom to be the proof that terms such as "additive" or "divisive" rhythms actually do not make sense for African music (Arom 1991: 207).

Yet another term seems to have gained importance within the discourse on African music: "cross rhythm." The idea here is that two different rhythmic patterns unfold in the same time span. An example would be a musician who beats two equal beats with the one hand, and three equal beats with the other hand within the same time span, i.e. one hand in 6/8 the other in 3/4 (Agawu 2003: 92). Agawu remarks that this was so much a part of the lore on African rhythm that "it would seem almost perverse to question it" (Agawu 2003: 92). He argues that it seems very unlikely that the musician think of this time span as being divided in this way and that therefore the resultant pattern, namely the 6/8, holds the key for understanding. If someone says he or she is performing in "cross rhythm" it actually means that it is a performance in a 6/8 metre. Yet, he admits that it is nevertheless worth looking at different hand movements in order to think about the possibility of independent articulation:

> It is true that the resultant is articulated with timbral distinction between left and right hands, and that looking at what the hands play separately may encourage thinking in terms of independent articulations. But there is no independence here, because 2 and 3 belong to the same Gestalt (Agawu 2003: 92).

Agawu draws some conclusions from his harsh critique on all these invented terms and concepts for African music. He argues that the persistency of these terms in the literature on African music can be interpreted in two different ways: either as a discourse on "Africanism," mirroring that of "Orientalism," indicating "those nuggets of African cultural identity that survive in the New World" (Agawu 2003: 95); or, these terms need to be regarded as inventions and myths, as "power-based constructions of knowledge motivated in part by a search for self through imagined differences" (Agawu 2003: 95). He further argues that it is "fashionable" to invoke such constructs as "Orientalism" or "invention." The cause for "these sorts of errors" lay in inadequate research, as for example if ethnographic data is insufficient, indigenous conceptions are disregarded or hasty conclusions are made. Agawu then goes one step further to suggest that these errors are also made in other musicological research and are not unique to research on African music. Within this thought, however, he depicts a bigger problem, namely that there always has to be a notion of "otherness" with regard to Africa:

> But therein lies the root of the problem: the denial of nonuniqueness to Africa. To imply that no portrayal of Africa is legitimate, complete, or of interest if it does not establish an ultimate African difference is to saddle Africa with an enormous critical burden (Agawu 2003: 95).

Looking at literature on other non-Western music, as for example Latin American music, quite similar schemes appear which might challenge Agawu's critique that it was Africa alone that was carrying this "enormous critical burden" (Agawu 2003: 95). Within discourses on other musical regions, there also seems to be a strong focus on "rhythm," criticised and questioned along similar lines. One example is the discourse on rhythm in Cuban music (e.g. Acosta 2005). Leonardo Acosta equally argues that too often the voices of the musicians are ignored when the musicians themselves and their own musical experiences should be regarded as the ultimate "authority" (Acosta 2005).

Rhythm in Culture and Language

Confusion and discord caused by the concept of "rhythm" is not limited to scholars conducting musical analyses. Many different theories and ideas have been developed, for example, about rhythm embedded in culture or language. This becomes relevant to my own research as many Malagasy musicians draw similar connections (see chapter 5). Interesting in this respect is, again, the scholars' focus on the concepts of "metre" and "measure."

Justin London (2004) has developed a definition of metre which runs against most of the other understandings of it that I have discussed so far. Instead of only asking "What is metre?" he finds it useful to instead think of what metre is for. He argues that metre is perceived as being "for something" as well as "part of" something. It is "for something," because metric counting can help musicians hear how the music should go. But metre is also perceived as part of the music's feel or "groove." When a musician plays according to a particular metre, it means they are giving a series of tones a certain rhythmical shape and nuance. If the same series was played under a different metre, the expression of timing and dynamics would be different as well.

London therefore thinks it necessary to make a very clear distinction between "rhythm" and "metre." "Rhythm" is about patterns of duration, often called "rhythmic groups." These patterns are not based on the actual duration of each musical event; rhythmic patterns can be played, for example, *legato* or *staccato*. In London's view, "rhythm" is about the structure of temporal stimuli, whereas "metre" involves our perception and of these stimuli. "Metre," in contrast to "rhythm," involves "our initial perception as well as subsequent anticipation of a series of beats that we abstract from the rhythmic surface of the music" (London 2004: 4) With reference to Gjerdingen (1989) he puts it the following way: "if 'meter [is] a mode of attending,' then rhythm is that to which we attend" (London 2004: 4). In order to emphasise this point, he gives a very detailed definition and a "guiding hypothesis" of his understanding of "metre:"

> meter is a particular kind of a more general behaviour. The same processes by which we attend to the ticking of a clock, the footfalls of a colleague passing in the hallway, the gallop of a horse, or the drip of a faucet also are used when we listen to a Bach adagio, tap our toes to a Mozart overture, or dance to Duke Ellington. As such, meter is not fundamentally musical in its origin. Rather, meter is a musically particular form of entrainment or attunement, a synchronization of some aspect of our biological activity with regularly recurring events in the environment (London 2004: 4).

This understanding of metre mirrors the theories of some of the musicians that the Malagasy rhythm is inherent in everyday life (see chapter 5). They say the rhythm can be heard in everyday activities, such as the pounding of rice, the bus drivers' shouts to gather passengers, or the *zebu* cows pulling the cart.

London speaks of "metric behaviours" and argues that these are learned, rehearsed and practiced. He emphasises this idea by saying that musical rhythms are often stereotypical, stylistically regular and (hence) familiar. What happens therefore is that "we fit, so to speak, patterns of events in the world to patterns of time we have in our minds" (London 2004: 4). "Metre" is therefore more than a part of the "representation of reality" and should be understood as "entrained behaviour." By this, he refers to "moving with the music;" the fact that music engages and encourages our bodily movements, as in tapping toes, dancing, etc. These "behaviours," he argues, are practiced from earliest childhood and although there are differences between every person concerning rhythmic sensitivities and abilities, almost everyone can to some extent run, walk, perform or at least listen. Further, the capacity for entrainment is universal. Metre is always, in all cultures and contexts, subject to the same basic formal and cognitive constraints. Rhythmically regular patterns will tend to give rise to similar metrical structures and similar musical effects (London 2004: 4-6). "Metrical entrainment" for London is also about a "complex matching of listener expectations to hierarchical structured patterns of temporal invariance that are characteristically present in the music" (London 2004: 143). This means that performers and most listeners are very familiar with at least some specific styles and performers and through this context of concrete knowledge and experience their "metric skills" are formed and honed (London 2004: 143).

About fifty years before London's work, Richard Alan Waterman (1952) introduced the term "metronomic sense," suggesting quite a similar approach to metre as something deeply embedded and learnt in culture. Applying the term to African music, he aims to describe the sense that is "at the basis of African rhythm" [...] "This sense is part of the 'perceptual equipment' which musician and listener share, having acquired it in the process of assimilation to their own culture." Therefore he also refers to it as a "cultural pattern" (Waterman 1952, cited in Arom 1991: 181). Waterman proposes one particular method in order to find out about this "cultural pattern," namely to let the musicians do hand-clapping to a recorded piece (Arom 1991: 111). London reflects on a similar method but argues that it is still an open question in many studies as to what extent participants are counting "metrically" when they clap or tap their feet. It is also not evident if participants form or employ mental images related to the performance (such as imagined melodies or speech rhythms). London (2004) writes that there are definitely questions that are highly relevant in these studies; for instance, if subjects were counting in twos or threes or if they were imagining a melody or rhythmic cadence while clapping or tapping (London 2004: 13).

This brings us back full circle to questions of accentuation with regard to metre. London writes about a tendency we have to impose a sense of accent or groupings on a series of identical tones or clicks. This has long been identified as "subjective rhythmicization" (Bolton 1894; Meuman 1894). London regards this as a misnomer as it is the listener's sense of differentiation of the stimuli into twos, threes, or fours that is really subjective. Considering his own definition of "metre," London therefore prefers the term "subject metricization" (London 2004: 14-15).

Robert Kauffmann (1980) addresses the importance of the individual perception of music (rhythm in particular) and also acknowledges the impact of the relation that every society has with time. The aim of his study, "African Rhythm: A reassessment," in which he discusses various studies on African rhythm, is to provide a theoretical basis that allows for assessing African rhythm in terms that also make comparisons between African and non-African societies possible. He argues that for an all-encompassing view of rhythm, there is a need to look at "the influences of a culture's time sense upon all aspects of its musical time" (Kauffmann 1980: 400). He mentions several factors that determine time, such as the nature of the physical movements accompanying music, such as dance or instrumental technique, the rhythm of a language and the social structures of a society. He distinguishes two different levels that should be taken into regard when studying rhythm. To study the "macrorhythm" means to study a culture's time-sense and its formal structure, whereas the study of the "microrhythm" looks at the perceptual present, i.e. what we actually feel in one specific moment, including for example metric rhythmic configurations or the relationships of different parts (Kauffmann 1980: 400-401). London also emphasises the importance of people's individual perceptions of the music. He wants to find a way which allows mediating between the abstract and theoretical categories of a tempo-metrical type and the timing behaviours that we actually encounter as listeners and performers (London 2004: 159-160). He has therefore developed his "Many Meters Hypothesis" which focuses exactly on the point that each experience of music is different and personal. London explains that many studies on rhythmic perception and performance distinguish musicians (usually instrumentalists) from "unskilled or naïve subjects;"[8] the differences, however, are not as great as one might initially expect. He provides two explanations for this claim. Firstly, experimental tasks such as tapping to a metronome or judging the duration of an empty interval are very unlike real-world musical behaviours. Secondly, most people are highly experienced listeners as music has an almost ubiquitous presence in our lives. He admits that

> some of us may have a special interest in one or more particular musical styles, and thus have a sensitivity to the rhythmic nuances of that style, whether it is the cadences of different hip-hop poets, the differing senses of swing among jazz drummers, or the phrasing habits of particular classical pianists. Such nuances are almost always produced and judged in a metrical context (London 2004: 144).

Generally, however, our metrical skills concerning musical contexts are related to other skilled rhythmical behaviours, such as speech production and comprehension, listening to and visually tracking moving objects, as well as motor control behaviours such as walking, running, dancing and doing sports. These behaviours are practiced from earliest childhood and the more familiar we get with a particular rhythm, the more skilled our attentional behaviours tend to become (London 2004: 144). A musical experience is always an experience of a particular piece or a particular performance; we do not, for example, encounter a "generic 4/4"

---

[8] Like London, other authors have very sharply criticised this assumption; see for instance Blacking (1973).

but rather a pattern of timing and dynamics that is particular to a piece, a musical style or a particular performer. London's "Many Meters Hypothesis (MMH)" suggests:

A listener's metric competence resides in her or his knowledge of a very large number of context-specific metrical timing patterns. The number and degree of individuation among these patterns increases with age, training, and degree of musical enculturation (London 2004: 153).

Yet another approach is that of the linguist Theo van Leeuwen (1999). In his book *Speech, Music, Sound* published in 1999 he aims to explore the common grounds of these three fields by integrating them; something which he says "many contemporary musicians, poets, filmmakers, multimedia designers and so on already do in practice (and what children have always done)" (Van Leeuwen 1999: 4). Many authors point out the relation of language and music, specifically regarding rhythm. Herzfeld (1974), for instance, regards language as the origin of all rhythm:

The model for musical rhythm is the lilt of language with its ups and downs, its contrasts of stress and absence of stress. (…) Rhythm is also not an independent feature. It cannot be considered separately, but is rather a temporal ordering to which the notes are submitted (Herzfeld 1974: 445), cited in Arom 1991: 293).

Van Leeuwen also highlights the rhythmical aspect. One of his main arguments is that sound is either measured or unmeasured; he insists that there is no in-between. If measured, it then needs to be distinguished in metronomic and non-metronomic time. In the first instance sound is governed by an implacable regularity given perhaps by a metronome; in the second, sound, though measured, subverts regularity and stretches, anticipates or delays as in, for instance, human speech or movement (Van Leeuwen 1999: 7).

Van Leeuwen sees a direct link between the way in which a society handles musical time and the same society's handling of social activities in general, the society's "order of time" (Van Leeuwen 1999: 39). In his view, time is not to be regarded as a phenomenon of nature, but as a human activity; one should therefore speak instead of "timing." In order to exemplify this, he speaks of the change that the clock, pioneered in Benedictine monasteries, has brought to society, quoting Lewis Mumford:

Benedictine rule gave human enterprise the regular collective beat and rhythm of the machine; for the clock is not merely a means of keeping track of the hours, but of synchronizing the actions of men (Mumford 1934: 13, cited in Van Leeuwen 1999: 37).

With the Industrial Revolution, the clock became a major tool for control of labour and later of other human activities. This was also the reason why punctuality became a key virtue among members of bourgeois society. This goes in hand with what happened to music during this period. At this point, music began to be measured and the system of bar lines was introduced (Van Leeuwen 1999: 37). He calls the Western approach to music a "divisive approach" as people often experience a contradiction between the objective (clock) time and the subjective ("felt") time. The dominant form of musical time, however, is one in which everyone synchronises to the same beat (Van Leeuwen 1999: 55). Van Leeuwen speaks of "monorhythmic music" (as opposed to "polyrhythmic music") in which there is always a main beat. He recognises, however, that there is a possibility for notes in the melody to either anticipate or delay the beat in order to create a tension between the "objective" and "subjective" time (Van Leeuwen 1999: 58).

According to Van Leeuwen, two kind of "counting" or "time signatures" have dominated in "high" Western music, "duple time" and "triple time," both including an implicit accentual ranking. Duple time is "ONE two ONE two" or "ONE two THREE four ONE two THREE four;" triple time "ONE two three ONE two three." He argues that "most of the things we do (walking, running, shivering and so on) have a binary rhythm" (Van Leeuwen 1999: 47). Triple time is hence the more "artificial" metre. As an explanation for this, Van Leeuwen looks to dance and says that duple time has always been associated with collective dances, such as procession dances. During the Baroque period collective dances went into decline and collectivity became a matter of public parades and military marches, more devoted to expressing national ideas than actual community values. Triple time, on the other hand, had been associated with "closed couple dance" (Van Leeuwen 1999: 48).

> So there was on the one hand the procession dance, with its forwards movements, symbolizing progress, exploration, expansion, and nationalistic values, and on the other hand the closed couple dance, expressing the ethos of individualization, self-expression and privacy (Van Leeuwen 1999: 49).

Van Leeuwen then uses these explanations to draw some conclusions about non-Western music. He joins the many authors (as shown above) who point out the significant meaning and peculiarity of rhythm in African music, focusing on "polyrhythmic music" in African societies. He explains that "polyrhythm" means that each member of the group follows his or her own "internal clock," which musicians from various African cultures have referred to as "weaving in and out" (Van Leeuwen 1999: 55). Societies in which this approach to rhythm is common have been called "polychromic" societies (Hall 1983), societies, "where the regime of the clock has never gained as much of a foothold as it has, for instance, in Europe or North America" (Van Leeuwen 1999: 55).

Malagasy Rhythm(s)

Malagasy musicians also often reflect upon "internal" or personal rhythms or how the "rhythm of everyday life" in Madagascar and the rhythm of music reflect each other. Chapters 4-6 will focus in detail upon the musicians' individual understandings and experiences of "rhythm." Here, I will have a brief look at the extent to which "rhythm" has appeared in literature on music from Madagascar. So far, there has not been any work on Malagasy music specifically dedicated to the topic of rhythm. In a few works, however, some authors touch upon aspects of rhythm in Malagasy music. The specific concept of "6/8 rhythm" also appears in some works and, related to this, a reoccurring theme–also in the musicians' own discourses (see chapter 4-6)–is the rhythmical structure of overlapping binaries and ternaries.

The Malagasy musicologist Rakotomalala (2003), for example, in her book *Madagascar: La musique dans l'histoire*, analyses the effort that many researchers have made to find a method of transcription that would work for Malagasy music, especially for its "famous complex rhythm" ("rythme réputé complex"). Rakotomalala describes this rhythmic structure as a combination of binaries and ternaries, though she emphasises that it is better to say that the rhythm was *thought* in binaries and ternaries. She therefore claims the existence of a "mental structure" ("structure mentale") with regard to rhythm. Musicians, however, tend to improvise a lot, which makes it harder to identify the "initial rhythmical principle." The issue of overlapping binaries and ternaries and what musicians feel, think, or hear while musicking is a topic that I will come back to in chapters 4-6; it has become of great importance in my analyses, especially of my own musical practices.

This rhythmic structure that Rakotomalala identifies as one of the "most typical Malagasy" elements of the music also mirrors a common Malagasy expression: *"Maromarotra iraisana"*–which she translates as "the disagreements that we share" (*"les différends que l'on partage"*).

This, she concludes, is why the Malagasy rhythm is either in two but thought in three, or is in three and thought in two. Sometimes these two rhythms are played simultaneously. A very interesting point she mentions is that everything from poetry to instrumental music in Madagascar is grounded and based on this rhythm. And she adds that sometimes the "rhythm of speech" ("*rythme de la parole*") determines the "musical rhythm" ("*rythme musical*") (Rakotomalala 2003: 43-44). The idea that the Malagasy language is closely interrelated with the music is an idea that many of the musicians share and that I have also come to understand through my own musical participation (chapters 4-6).

The idea of a structure of overlapping binaries and ternaries also shines through in Julien Mallet's (2008) studies of a particular musical style, *tsapiky* music in South-Western Madagascar. In this article, he offers a dense description of a *tsapiky* live performance, explaining that there is a particular moment in the music where one guitarist leads the other players into a certain part of the musical piece, called *kilatsake*. In order to announce this changeover, he either makes a very fast plucking movement with his right index finger or plays a ternary rhythm "against" the consistent binary rhythm of the other musicians of the group (Mallet 2008: 169).

The most detailed explanations of rhythmical aspects in Malagasy music can be found in Randrianary's book *Madagascar. Les chants d'une île* (Randrianary 2001). The Malagasy ethnomusicologist invites the reader to a musical journey throughout the island, stressing that although he is himself an academic, he is not aiming particularly at an academic audience. In contrast to Rakotomalala's work, Randrianary devotes different chapters of his book to the musical phenomena of the different regions of the island: the North, the East, the High Plateaux, and the South-West. Therefore, the topic of rhythm does not appear as a generic Malagasy phenomenon, but rather appears at different sites within the dense and detailed descriptions of musical performances and is explained in the particular regional musical context. This is interesting insofar as many of the musicians often point to regional differences despite the shared rhythmic base as we will see in chapters 4-6. Whereas the title of the first chapter on the North even includes the term "rhythm" ("*Au rythme des ouvertures: Le Nord*"), it is in the chapter on the music of the High Plateaux region that the topic appears most prominently. However, there is one occasion in this first chapter, where Randrianary also emphasises the existence of overlapping binary and ternary rhythms. He writes about the musical genre of *salegy*,[9] which originates from the still-practised genre called *antsa*. Despite one being the roots of the other, there is one big difference between these two styles: the timbre created through the percussion. In *antsa* people clap their hands in a particular way, whereas in *salegy* music the percussion is usually created with musical instruments (Randrianary 2001: 26). Randrianary writes that his collaboration with the musicians often raises the question of whether the rhythm of these styles is in binaries or ternaries:

> *Ces expériences concernant le rythme en collaboration avec les artistes posent le problème de leur nature : binaire ou ternaire. Quand on a l'occasion de regarder les gestes musicaux, il devient évident qu'il s'agit du rythme binaire. On voit quelqu'un au moins qui bat en permanence : un ! deux ! un ! deux ! un ! deux ! Cependant, d'autres personnes battront des valeurs divisibles par trois* (Randrianary 2001: 26-27).[10]

This idea of binaries and ternaries recurs later in Randrianary's book where he writes about Rakotozafy, a famous player of the Malagasy zither *marovany*,[11] who died more than thirty years ago.[12] He explains that for Rakotozafy, the tierce and likewise the number three played a very important role. Someone who transcribed his music decided to write it in a 3/8 metre. And yet, the persistent ambiguity of binaries and ternaries in this music is so blatant that other metres, such as 2/8, 6/16, or 7/16, could be considered instead. With regard to Rakotozafy, Randrianary even speaks of an "obsession" to put the accent on the third beat, creating something of a personal musical leitmotif (Randrianary 2001: 120-121).

In Randrianary's chapter on the music of the High Plateaux region, the topic of rhythm is put under a sub-section entitled "*l'énigme du rythme*" ("the mystery of rhythm"), which contains two main statements. First,

---

[9] For more information on *salegy* music, see Eyre (2002); Terramorsi and Rajaonarison (2004).

[10] "These experiences of rhythm in collaboration with the artists have raised questions concerning the problem of their nature: binary or ternary. When we have the chance to observe musical gestures, it becomes evident that it is a binary rhythm. We see at least someone who permanently beats; one! two! one! two! one! two! Meanwhile, others beat measures that are divisible by three" (my translation).

[11] Malagasy term for box-shaped *valiha* (a Malagasy type of zither). Marovanys are typically built out of wood or metal and exist in the Southern parts of the island, in the region of Tuléar (Randrianary 2001: 156).

[12] The film "Like a God When He Plays", produced by Cécilia Lowenstein and featuring Paddy Bush (first broadcast on 30th August 1998 by Channel 4) tells the life of this legendary musician. See Lowenstein (1998).

Randrianary explains that the frequent usage of 12/8 is one of the typical phenomena of this region. He calls it an "asymmetrical metre" and reflects upon its roots; many scholars have already described this metre as a pan-African phenomenon. And despite the European and Asian influences in the region of the High Plateaux, Randrianary himself also agrees that "*il s'avère plus légitime d'admettre que le rythme 12/8 asymétrique provient de l'Afrique continentale plutôt que de l'Asie ou de l'Europe*"[13] (Randrianary 2001: 77). The second argument is about the characteristics of rhythm in that region. He argues that the Malagasy term that is most used for rhythm in the High Plateaux region was *ngadona,* a term also used when, for example, people talk about pounding the rice or about a footstep during a march. Further, a particular rhythm called *manonjanonja*, apparently one of the most frequent rhythms, designates the movements of the coming and going of waves (Randrianary 2001: 74-75).

Again, this mirrors aspects that come up in the musicians' discourses; many argue that rhythm is closely related, if not inherent, to Malagasy everyday life. Images of nature also appear in these descriptions (see chapter 5). Randrianary also uses Western notation to transcribe some of the typical rhythms of the High Plateaux region, but without putting these into bar lines or a particular metre (Randrianary 2001: 75). He also often uses the term "polyrhythm" (as discussed above). He does not, however, explain exactly what he means by this in the Malagasy context. For instance, he does not say whether he would call the structure of overlapping binaries and ternaries a polyrhythmic figure. He uses the term in an aesthetic way that leaves out technical description. For example, in the chapter on the South-Western region he writes about a particular instrument called *kiloloky* and how it is used in communal musical events. The term "polyrhythm" forms part of this dense description:

> *Les voix de femme entrent en jeu responsorial avec l'ensemble kiloloky. Il y a souvent là la plus belle exécution de polyphonie et de polyrythmie. Les cris de joie et les jeux vocaux fusent à tue-tête* (Randrianary 2001: 87).[14]

Apart from the rhythm called *manonjamonja* in the High Plateaux region, Randrianary generally emphasises a strong relation between nature and music in Madagascar. In the chapter on music in the East, he talks

---

[13] "it prooves legitimate to assume that the asymmetrical 12/8 rhythm comes from the African continent rather than from Asia or Europe" (my translation).

[14] "The women's voices enter into a responsorial play with the *kiloloky* ensemble. That is where the most beautiful execution of polyphony and polyrhythm is. The crows and the vocal games burst out loud with this singing" (my translation).

about a little island called "Nosy Mangabe" that is very famous for its natural environment. In the "musical description" of the nature of this place, Randrianary uses a couple of terms, such as "polyrhythm" or "polyphony" that also come from a Western academic discourse. His rather philosophical questions at the end–whether it is the human beings who copy nature or vice versa–further emphasise the notion of the connectedness of music and natural environment in Madagascar:

Nosy Mangabe est l'une des plus connues. De véritable polymusiques, polyrythmies, polyphonies dans des timbres différents se succèdent continuellement : cascades, vagues, oiseaux, grenouilles, lémuriens. Ce grand concert de la nature fait de cet endroit inhabité une vraie source. Dans tout l'est, hommes et animaux utilisent les différentes espèces de bambou comme instruments de musique ou espace musical. Les petites grenouilles se mettent au creux de ces plantes pour émettre leurs voix. Les notes défilent formant des lignes mélodiques et des rythmes complexes selon le procédé dit du 'hoquet'. (...) Est- ce que l'homme imite– inconsciemment peut-être–la nature ou est-ce la nature qui imite son maître, l'homme ? Perpétuelle question (Randrianary 2001: 57).[15]

In line with many other scholars–and probably to the biggest regret by Agawu–Randrianary towards the end of his book returns to the topic of rhythm with the statement that rhythm is the "identity card" of the African continent (*"la carte d'identité d'Afrique continentale"*). Even if Madagascar is definitely part of the African continent, he writes, it still has its particularity with regard to rhythm and vocal techniques:

Le rythme est considéré comme la carte d'identité de l'Afrique continentale ; sans renoncer à cette appartenance, la Grande Ile est quant à elle un sanctuaire des techniques vocales (Randrianary 2001: 114).[16]

---

[15] "Nosy Mangabe is one of the best known. Real polymusic and polyrhythm in different timbres continually succeed each other: cascades, waves, birds, frogs, lemurs. This big concert of nature turns this uninhabited place into a real source. Everywhere in the East, human beings and animals use the different sorts of bamboo as musical instruments or musical space. Little frogs sit in the hollow of these plants to emit their voice. The notes pass by, forming melody lines and complex rhythms like a 'hiccup'. (...) Is it mankind who–maybe unconsciously– imitates nature or is it nature that imitates its Master, mankind? Perpetual question" (my translation).

[16] "Rhythm is considered the identity card of the African continent; without denying its belonging, the Big Island is a sanctuary for vocal techniques" (my translation).

These techniques include musical styles, such as *antsa, rija,* or *jijy,*[17] partly being forms of semi-singing or semi-speaking (Randrianary 2001: 114). The important position of the voice and singing in Madagascar is often mentioned by Randrianary, giving his book its title: *"Les chants d'une île"* ("The songs of an island").

As the previous discussion has shown, the topic of "rhythm" is not only always present in scholarship on African music but it is the most contested issue. I certainly agree with Agawu's and Acosta's main critique that the voices of the musicians are often left unheard within a predominantly Western analytical perspective on musics. Without making any regional restrictions, I argue that we need to understand these critiques as a wake-up call to reflect upon the framing and nature of our research.

To what extent should we include indigenous theories, perspectives and ideas about music by those playing and actively engaged in the process of music-making? Whose discourses, languages, or terms should we use? Should the essence of our ethnographic research not be to sharpen our ability to search for, take on, and compare different perspectives and thereby scrutinise our own ways of understanding and seeing the world? Whereas methodological and theoretical needs related to these aims have already been discussed and are topical issues within recent scholarly debates on ethnographic fieldwork, there still seems to be a gap between theory and practice. In other words, links are lacking between the aims of contemporary ethnographic research and the reality and requirements of the academic contexts we work in, as I will discuss in the next chapter. I argue that it is necessary to go one step further than Agawu (2003) and move towards finding concrete methodological approaches that take seriously his critique of the dominant Western analytical perspectives and discourses to allow for the integration of indigenous theories, ideas and understandings of music into our academic works.

---

[17] When I interviewed the *sodina* player Rageorge (see also chapter 6), Sammy helped me with translating. At some point during the interview, both musicians gave me a vivid example of the *jijy* tradition: Sammy doing percussion with his mouth and Rageorge improvising about everyday life in Antananarivo. See sound example 1 on DVD. Another example of improvised singing/semi-speaking accompanied by hand clapping can be seen in video example 2 (01:03-01:20): During a rehearsal in Berlin in May 2013 we prepared a hand clapping exercise for a workshop that we gave for the education programme of the "Stiftung Berliner Philharmoniker" (see also chapter 6).

CHAPTER THREE

MUSICKING RESEARCHERS
AND RESEARCHING MUSICIANS

Introduction

The previous chapter analysed already existing theories of "rhythm," particularly challenging the historiography of scholarship on African musics. Although "rhythm" appears as a contested issue that has caused much confusion and debate, one consistent research angle comes to the fore: a persistently Western analytical perspective and the use of particular discourses derived from it. This has one important consequence: it emphasises the boundary between those who make music and those who write about it, i.e. between the "researcher" and the "researched." The result is a lack of recognition of indigenous theories, concepts, and ideas (Agawu 2003). This chapter tackles this methodological challenge and deals with the question of how to cross these boundaries.

Ethnomusicologists are often musicians who get involved in the music cultures they research. Or should we say that musicians often are or become ethnomusicologists? Either way, many scholars agree that significant knowledge can be gained through "musicking" (Small 1998) and through integrating these experiences into our research. However, researchers describe the immense difficulty they experience in trying to express verbally what they experience musically (e.g. Seeger 1977, Rice 1997)–a difficulty shared and expressed by many Malagasy musicians in a similar way. Hence, despite a continuing debate within the discipline of ethnomusicology, in which the need for more performance-based approaches to research and the integration of musical practices into analyses are suggested, not many scholars have actually put this into practice (Baily 2008).

Closely related to the topic of researchers as musicians (and vice versa) is the need for both a sensitive approach towards fieldwork relations and a greater degree of self-reflexivity. These remain topical issues in theoretical and methodological discussions within the so-called "new ethnomusicology" and "new fieldwork" (e.g. Hellier-Tinoco 2003). And yet, their proper implementation remains difficult. I argue that the mutual integration of musical experience and ethnomusicological research can actually respond to these methodological and theoretical needs. I suggest an interdisciplinary approach that guards against the assumption that musical experiences and the discussion of these experiences are exclusive and separate worlds which resist translation from one to the other. I propose to study discourses and musical experiences in a constant interrelation, interdependently, combining ethnomusicological methods, such as ethnographic fieldwork, participant observation and shared musical experiences, with discourse-analytical methods. With this approach, it becomes possible to grasp experiences gained through musicking and our talking about music and music-making as one. It is only through a bottom-up approach and by following the main principles of a "subject-centred ethnography" (Rice 2003) that we can apply Agawu's demand for a "presumption of sameness" (Agawu 2003)–a research attitude that will prevent researchers from ignoring the voices of the people with whom they work and make them aware of the risk of imposing a Western analytical perspective.

Key Terms

It is a common and well-known phenomenon within anthropology that research questions are specified and refined during the process of collecting data. Ethnographic research is not about going into "the field" in order to prove a hypothesis that has been worked out before.

I only hit upon my particular research topic during fieldwork; my research questions developed during this process. I did not think a lot about rhythm in Malagasy music to begin with, though I had always been captivated, perhaps irritated, by its structure and by the frequent mis-match between my foot-tapping and that of the musicians both when listening and when trying to play. I concentrated on rhythm and found myself observing the tapping of feet during concerts, comparing Malagasy and *vazaha* feet. I had discussions, even arguments, with friends about whether a particular Malagasy piece was in two or in three, i.e. whether accents were following a binary or ternary rhythmical pattern. In retrospect, however, I would consider these kinds of experiences and trains of thought to already be part of my fieldwork. Many anthropologists agree that there is "no clear break in the temporal flux," of our research as Watson (1999) describes it, and "the period in the field is simply part of the ongoing temporal experience of coming to an understanding of other people" (Watson 1999: 2).

One might think now that I have fallen right into Agawu's trap (see previous chapter) in that my reflections could be read as if I had been deliberately searching for difference and that "rhythm" (once again!) had been key to finding it. However, I hardly ever brought up the topic of rhythm myself, especially not at the beginning of my research or when I met people for the first time. Sometimes, it happened that a musician with whom I had been talking for a long time introduced me to another musician friend with words such as "This is Jenny. She is eager to understand our rhythm. Can you talk to her?," making it impossible for me to start a new conversation and see whether the topic of rhythm would be brought up by my dialogue partner. Most of the time, the musicians themselves instantly directed the conversation towards the topic of rhythm. Whereas this obtrusive directing towards rhythm can be seen as a unifying and general phenomenon among the musicians, the way they brought up the topic and what kind of theories, ideas and opinions they expressed about it was immensely diverse as it will become obvious in chapters 4-6. Something, however, which shines through all the musicians' diverse discourses, is that the topic of "rhythm" appears to be the starting point for their search for a collective musical identity.

Many researchers have shown that music is a powerful tool in the construction of identities (e.g. Waterman 1990, Stokes 1994, Frith 1996, Connell and Gibson 2003, Biddle and Knights 2007) and different elements, such as melody, harmony, stylistic variations, instrumentations and lyrics are used to negotiate and respond to questions of self-understanding and belonging. Rhythm has also been recognised as an important source for people to reflect upon questions of who they are and where they belong–or where or to whom they do not belong to (e.g. Monson 1999, Neustadt 2002).

Identity is a highly complex but widely used term that has been given much attention–and many definitions. However, instead of asking what identity is, here I consider it much more useful to search for key notions that relate to and constantly appear within identity debates–both in scholarly discussions and in the musicians' discourses on their own music and their experiences of musicking. The notions that come to the fore are "experience" and the dichotomy of "Self" and "Other." Simon Frith (1996) for example argues that "identity is mobile, a process not a thing, a becoming not a being" (Frith 1996: 109). Identity should be seen as an "experiential process which is most vividly grasped as music." He argues that music seems to be the key to identity because "it offers, so intensely, a sense of both, self and others, of the subjective in the collective" (Frith 1996: 110). In the same spirit, ethnomusicologist Rice (2003) argues that experience is not an inner phenomenon, but is inseparable from interaction with the outside world and other people (Rice 2003: 157, 160). Considering that scholars emphasise the need to focus and carefully reflect upon relationships when we conduct field research, it is not surprising to find that the notion of "experience" and the dichotomy of "Self" and "Other" play crucial roles in methodological and theoretical debates on the nature of ethnographic fieldwork. Ethnographic research should be seen, as Rice (2003: 160) puts it, as a constant process of understanding the shared space of experiences and individual positions.

The Idea of "Self" and "Other" within Ethnographic Fieldwork

In order to understand recent scholarly debates and theories on fieldwork, it is necessary to take a brief historical survey. In the first decades of the twentieth century, anthropological paradigms underwent immense changes. With the emerging new schools of British social anthropology, represented mainly by Bronislaw Malinowski in England, and American cultural anthropology, represented mainly by Franz Boas, new conditions were set that can be seen as reactions to the evolutionary anthropology of the nineteenth century. One of the most important changes appeared as a reaction against the persistent Eurocentric point of reference (Stocking 2001: 42-42): the demand for intensive long-term fieldwork[1] (Cooley 2003: 5). Cooley argues that before Boas and Malinowski's "radical proposal" of long-term fieldwork for scientific research purposes, fieldwork presupposed the influence of the researchers on the people studied as it was mainly undertaken within the frequent interrelated contexts of missionary work, colonial administrations and national movements (Fabian 1991: 132, 135). Although Cooley admits that this might be a broad generalisation, as there are many examples of fieldworkers that did not aim to colonise, nationalise or convert their informants, literature on the history of anthropology criticises early anthropology for being closely intertwined with colonialism and missionary work (Cooley 2003: 5). These reflections on anthropological history are very important to bear in mind; as Kisliuk (1997: 27) reminds us, we still encounter these legacies in the ethnographic past. Despite the anthropologists and ethnomusicologists' intentional examination of this "ethnographic past" and the effects that earlier anthropological works have had, hardly anyone denies that fieldwork always has an impact on the

---

[1] See for example: Malinowski (1962) [1922]; and Boas (1936).

people we work with. This also becomes evident in book titles such as *Time and the Other: how Anthropology Makes its Object* (Fabian 1983), *When They Read what We Write* (Brettell 1993), or *Shadows in the Field* (Barz and Cooley 1997). Hellier-Tinoco (2003) speaks of a crisis in representation that in the late 1970s and 1980s brought a surge of attention towards reflexivity, which we find evidence of in the works of Marcus and Fischer (1986) and Clifford and Marcus (1986). Ethnographic writing became more reflexive in the way that both, those researched as well as the researcher were included in the picture.[2] Self-reflexivity among the researchers also directed attention towards relationships. Hellier-Tinoco (2003) sees a reason for the emphasis on relationships in the unexpected experiences that many researchers have during their fieldwork:

> they have been taken by surprise in terms of their field relations, to the extent of being unwittingly and unexpectedly pulled into the politics of their fieldwork context (Hellier-Tinoco 2003: 24).

However, although most researchers are conscious of the impact of fieldwork, many scholars still see problems, especially concerning the gap between theory and practice. Cooley (2003), for instance, criticises the lack of attention given to the nature of the impact of research and Hellier-Tinoco (2003) argues that although scholars more often reflect upon field relations in theory, there is still a lack of proper planning and thorough debate (Hellier-Tinoco 2003: 24). These critiques are grounded on more general reflections concerning the very nature of fieldwork and how it defines the role of the fieldworker.

Cooley (2003) coined the term "peasant-love"-fieldwork for Malinowski's fieldwork method. This term has its roots in Central European Slavic history. According to Ernest Gellner, Central European Slavic ethnographers had been influenced by a kind of nationalism and populism that encouraged them to explore "a peasant culture in the hope of preserving and protecting it, above all from encroachment by rival nationalisms" (Gellner 1998: 115). Characteristic of this ideology was the emphasis on the ethnographic present rather than the past (Cooley 2003: 8). Cooley argues that even if we do not take peasant-love literally, we still hope and even expect as a researcher to find and make friends in the field. This suggests a new model, the "friendship model," also mentioned by

---

[2] Recent research shows that ethnographers more often also focus primarily on their own person and hence become their own main research object. Prominent works in the so-called field of "auto-ethnography" are for example Reed-Danahay (1997, 2001), Ellis (2004), Chang (2008), or Khosravi (2010).

Titon (1997) and Hellier-Tinoco (2003). Cooley describes friendship as the "most benign form of interpersonal relationship" and explains that it still takes the risk of containing not completely-formed or -realised motivations and ideologies. He suggests that what could be seen as a latent nationalism that inspired Malinowski's peasant-love fieldwork is nowadays replaced by an emerging "globalism" that we find within the fieldwork model of the late twentieth and early twenty-first century (Cooley 2003: 10).

Many scholars have raised the issue of power within ethnographic fieldwork. Anthropologist Heidi Armbruster (2008) for example writes about the uneasiness that we often feel, wanting to be friends with the people whom we want also to study. Asking how our "friendship" relationships in the field relate to our making of our own academic identities (Armbruster 2008: 136), she argues that much "ethnographic tension" is created when we try

> to reconcile our politically and our academically biased selves. While the former is about the alignment with the powerless, the latter still is, in many ways, about the alignment with the powerful (Armbruster 2008: 138).

Cooley similarly argues that fieldwork is always about the politics of power and access to experience and information. This is why he sees a need for a deliberate step back from "friendship" as a model for fieldwork, an argument that he underlines with provocative questions:

> Is friendship a liberal humanist means for global re-colonization–for re-appropriating the other? Is friendship a gesture from those with power and wealth to those without in a new colonization of the other in order to mine ethnographic data? (Cooley 2003: 12).

Hellier-Tinoco stresses that friendship and human relationships in fieldwork form a central theme in scholarly discussions. The main point, she argues, is that relationships, classified either as "friendship" or other forms, should be seen as interactive encounters that therefore depend on forms of reciprocity (Hellier-Tinoco 2003: 25). An example of this comes from Titon (1997), who writes about an experience during fieldwork where his role as "only being a researcher" was questioned; the musicians he worked with also saw some potential in their encounter with him:

> my relationship with them added a dimension: I became someone who might be able to promote them, to help them in their careers, instead of just a young man hanging around older ones and trying to learn music from

them. Besides friendship I now had a tacit contract with them (Titon 1997: 88).[3]

The focus on relationships and the urge to define these relationships in the field has led many researchers to reflect upon the idea of "Self" and "Other" within their work and in-field encounters. Cooley (2003) explains, for example, that the "friendship model" is characterised by a belief in cultural relativity, human equality, and interpersonal relationships. It is therefore based on the idea that we are all basically "one" and that ethnography may be a tool to help us realise this one-world ideology. We aim to better understand the "Self" by researching the "Other," for there is no real distinction between "Self" and "Other," he writes (Cooley 2003: 10-11). The ideas of "Self" and "Other" have been much theorised in literature on anthropological methods and fieldwork in particular. Researchers have asked themselves to what extent they can see themselves as researcher and those "being researched" as potentially interchangeable, and if there was something like "dialogues that typify the fieldwork experience" (Hellier-Tinoco 2003: 27). For Titon (1997), fieldwork requires and imposes a certain sense of separation from to the Self-Other dichotomy. Kisliuk (1997) argues that "the deeper our commitment in the field, the more our life stories intersect with our "subject's," "until Self-Other boundaries are blurred" (Kisliuk 1997: 23). Hellier-Tinoco writes that in any case, if the experience in the field is dialogical and interpenetrating between researcher and researched, this will affect the relations in many unforeseen ways (Hellier-Tinoco 2003: 27). Titon (1997) proposes to place an emphasis on "connectedness," on regarding ourselves as emergent rather than autonomous selves. We are connected selves "enmeshed in reciprocity" (Titon 1007: 99). For Hellier-Tinoco, the connection that Titon describes can be seen as a shift away from the treating scholarship, the field and life as fundamentally separated towards regarding the field as an intrinsic part of our lives. This also means that we maintain our relationships in the field with the same responsibility, reciprocity and commitment that we give to relationships in "normal" life (Hellier-Tinoco 2003: 32).

These debates show that a shift has occurred which now places field relations at the centre of the fieldwork project. Interactive encounters between the researcher and the researched have become increasingly essential to the discipline of ethnomusicology. Many ethnomusicologists speak of a "new fieldwork" that reconfigures "the field" as experience

---

[3] The same problem is discussed in Kiwan and Meinhof (2011: Introduction) who refer to these interconnections as "accidental hubs."

rather than place (Hellier-Tinoco 2003: 25-26). Barz (1997) describes the major paradigm shift in ethnomusicology in such a way; the focus lies now on "doing" and "knowing" fieldwork, rather than on representing fieldwork (Barz 1997: 205). However, scholars have discussed the question of how we can finally represent, make sense of, or "translate" our experiences into academic works across disciplines.

The Notion of "Experience:" "Narrativisation of Experiences" and "Musical being-in-the-world" (Titon 1997)

Sociolinguists argue that narratives are essential for people to make sense of their experiences in life. It is through narratives that we negotiate questions of who we are and who we are not, as well as where we feel we belong or do not belong (Meinhof and Galasinski 2005; Thornborrow and Coates 2005). Scholarly discussions and theories across disciplines have for several decades directed their attention to narratives as the "narrativization of lived experience is one of the most fundamental processes of making sense of our lives" (Meinhof and Galasinski 2005: 101). Narrating our lives is therefore an important source for making sense of our experiences. It is through narratives that we also structure and interpret our experiences (Cheshire and Ziebland 2005: 17). What is often referred to as the "narrative turn" in sciences–not only in the humanities and social sciences, but also in natural sciences–goes back a long way, to Nietzsche's observation that "there are no facts but only interpretations" (Nietzsche (1956/1844-1900): 903; cited in Meinhof and Galasinski 2005: 72). Some theories have therefore emphasised that there is no such thing as an "outside fixed reality," but that reality is instead constructed through social interaction and narrativisation of our experiences. Meinhof and Galasinski (2005) argue that it is through narratives that we also order our experiences in a "tellable" form which is interpretative and evaluative at the same time (Meinhof and Galasinski 2005: 72, 102). Thornborrow and Coates (2005) write about the pervasive role that narratives play in our lives; it is through narratives that we tell ourselves–and each other–who we are and are not. Narratives are therefore central to our social and cultural identity (Thornborrow and Coates 2005: 1, 7). Many scholars agree that identity is created through narratives, which again is related to the enforcement of a sense and perception of "Self" and "Other." Narratives "construct, display and reinforce our sense of self (Schiffrin 1996), and relate this sense of self to others in our social worlds (Bruner 1986)" (Cheshire and Ziebland 2005: 17). The way we speak is implicated in how we position ourselves in the different contexts of our lives. By telling our lives we constantly position ourselves against spaces and people, taking an at-least-implicit stance on the degree to which we belong to each (Meinhof and Galasinski 2005: 71). This constant identity shift between in-groups and out-groups through narratives will be of importance throughout chapters 4-6.

The discipline of ethnomusicology adds yet another dimension of experience (or of making sense of our experiences), which becomes especially relevant to debates on identity and the dichotomy of "Self" and "Other," namely the possibility of what Titon (1997) calls "musical being-in-the-world." He describes this as an ontology that centres on knowing people through collective music-making as shared musical experiences might also lead to shared understanding (Titon 1997: 94). Many ethnomusicologists have argued that their experience of "musical being-in-the-world" has offered them insights and paths towards understanding that other methods, such as linguistic methods, could not achieve. Even more important for some was that the musical experience allowed them to go beyond the insider-outsider or "Self" and "Other" distinction that is often so crucial to much ethnomusicological thinking. The ethnomusicologist Rice (1997), who has worked in Bulgaria for a long time, writes that he has "moved to a place untheorized by the insider-outsider distinction." Talking to the people had already directed him towards an emic understanding, he writes. When he tried to understand the Bulgarian insider perspectives through words about music, he thought that he could be satisfied with the results. However, he then realised that he

> ran into the limits of this language-based method and its associated theory of culture. I encountered precisely the 'linguocentric predicament' that Charles Seeger (1977: 47) would have predicted for me (Rice 1997: 109).

Considering this predicament, Seeger suggests that the aim should be:

> (a) to integrate music knowledge and feeling in music and the speech knowledge and feeling about them to the extent this is possible in speech presentation, and (b) to indicate as clearly as possible the extent to which this is not possible (Seeger 1977: 48).

Rice describes how participating musically and being capable of playing in the musical tradition he studied finally completely transformed him:

Although the linguistic methods of cognitive anthropology had helped me narrow the gap between emic and etic perspectives, I could not in the end close that gap completely. When, on the other hand, I abandoned those methods and acted musically, it seemed as if I fell right into the gap between insider and outsider, into a theoretical 'no place' that felt very exciting, if not exactly a utopia. I was neither insider nor an outsider (Rice 1997: 110).

Similarly excited, Titon (1997) describes his own musical experience during research and how this influenced his sense of "Self:"

Making music I experience the disappearance of my separate self; I feel as if music fills me and I have become music in the world. But I also experience the return of the knowing self. The experience of music making is, in some circumstances in various cultures throughout the world, an experience of becoming a knowing self in the presence of other becoming, knowing selves. This is a profoundly communal experience, and I am willing to trust it (Titon 1997: 99).

As these examples by Rice and Titon show, ethnomusicologists emphasise the experience of participatory musical contexts. One of the main aims for the researched as well as for the researcher is therefore to ask and find out what it is like to make and to know music as lived experience (Titon 1997: 87). This aim actually implies that the experience of "musical being-in-the-world" should be seen as in permanent interplay with the narrativisation of experiences. Even if the shared music-making adds another dimension of understanding experiences, the process of telling each other about these experiences and (even more so) the writing of an ethnography later will always challenge the researcher as well as the researched by demanding that one puts into words what one has experienced musically. Many ethnomusicologists have reflected upon narratives as a path towards the understanding of making and knowing music as lived experiences. Barz (1997), for example, describes ethnography as an integral part of the translation of experience and in this way also as a kind of extension of the "field performance." He even speaks of "performative writing," arguing that

[f]or most field researchers the period of 'translation' is frustrating, where nothing, including the self, is at it seems, and many are now beginning to realize that field research itself is just a period of translation (Barz 1997: 208).

Titon (1997) explains that it is through narratives that we tell others about our experiences and show how we come to understand:

> Narrative, of course, is the way we habitually tell ourselves and others about our experiences, and so it emerges as a conventional form in phenomenologically weighted representations of people making music (…) ethnography becomes an experience weighted genre in which narrative includes background information, interpretation and analysis, and above all one in which insights emerge from experience: one shows how one comes to understand (Titon 1997: 96).

The Importance of Integrating the Analysis of Discourses and Musical Practices

As the discussion above has shown, musical practices and discourses about music are often described or experienced as two separate worlds; many scholars have expressed their difficulties in describing their musical experiences in words. This is also an issue raised by many of the musicians I have worked with. They often say that it is very difficult to find the "right words" to talk about their own musical experiences. Even if I agree and have made similar experiences myself, I think that we tend to give too much attention to this "problem" and thereby forget that it is not a one-way phenomenon; I argue it is not only that our narratives show how we come to understand our experiences of musicking, but also that our musical experiences show how we come to understand what we have experienced through the discourses that we create and listen to. Our discourses are informed by our musical experiences as much as our musical experiences are informed by our discourses. Before explaining my argument in further detail, there are some questions we must address. First, how has the performance approach been discussed and applied so far within the discipline of ethnomusicology?[4] Second, what are the researchers' personal experiences and how have they made use–if they have at all–of these experiences for their academic purposes?

---

[4] There is a considerable amount of literature on the ethnography of "performance," with research in this field also relating to musical performance. "Performance studies" are often intertwined or integrated with other academic disciplines, such as ethnomusicology and anthropology. However, it has also become an independent discipline and is taught as such at many universities. Prominent scholars are, for example, Conquergood (1985), Turner (1986), and more recently Denzin (2003) and Schechner (2006).

"Towards a (more) Performative Ethnomusicology" (Baily 2008)

According to John Baily (2001), learning to perform has "quite a long history in ethnomusicology" (Baily 2001: 86). He claims, however, that in 2008 only very few ethnomusicological works have actually applied a performative approach. The reason for this seems to be a problem of academic "outcome," referring to the regulations and curricula of academic work in general. He argues that, in addition to scholarly writings, multimedia or documented recordings, we would need live performances. Recent debates within the discipline support Baily's argument that there is a need within ethnomusicology to move towards "a (more) performative approach" (Baily 2008: 131).

Mantle Hood is regarded as the ethnomusicologist who institutionalised the performance approach by introducing the term "bi-musicality" in 1960 (Hood 1960). Some researchers have definitely intended to learn to play certain musics during field research prior to the 1960s but were often prevented by various reasons, including colonial situations. Jaap Kunst's experience in Bali with *gamelan* music in the 1920s and 1930s is a good example of this problem (Baily 2008:118).[5] Hood's (1960) argument that ethnomusicologists should be "bi-musical" is based on his more general idea that training in basic musicianship is fundamental to any kind of musical scholarship. The term "bi-musicality" suggests that someone is equally at ease in two different music cultures, in command of the knowledge needed to participate in each (Hood 1960: 55). Although the term is widely used and appreciated within ethnomusicology, some scholars see problems with it, or at least see the need to redefine it. Baily (2008) argues that the prefix "bi" implies an emphasis on two music cultures only, in the same way as someone is called bilingual when they have fluency in two languages. He suggests that there might be people who are involved in more than two music cultures or musicians combining different musics (Baily 2001: 86). He proposes the term "intermusability" as an alternative, fusing the words "musical" and "ability" and thus emphasising the possibility of having the ability to play several different musics (Baily 2008: 118).

Many scholars have emphasised that the performance approach brings another layer to anthropological fieldwork and that it offers advantages on

---

[5] Jaap Kunst was a colonial officer in the Dutch East Indies during the 1920s and 1930s and was unable to participate in *gamelan* performances. For further information, see Heims (1976).

many different levels. I already gave a short insight into this discussion above. Baily (2008) gives a few examples, or "points of considerations" as he calls them, of advantages of the performance approach. In his opinion, participation in musical events leads to improved opportunities for observation whilst at the same time giving you direct entry into the performance event (Baily 2008: 126). He writes that:

> [b]eing able to perform to a reasonable standard provides privileged access to the actualité (...) It was not so much that I understood the music as a performer but that being able to play it gave me an immediate and large area of common experience with people to whom I was a complete stranger. We were all heirs to a common musical tradition. Again, it was a matter of musical relationships forming the basis for social relationships (Baily 2001: 96).

The French ethnomusicologist Julien Mallet, who has been working on *tsapiky* music in the South-Western region of Tuléar in Madagascar, is also a performing guitarist. In his (2009) book he mentions advantages of being a musician, such as building relationships that go beyond the idea of "researcher"–"researched" (Mallet 2009: 28). He also reflects upon what he calls his "juggling" between his dual status as a student and as a guitarist, arguing that this has given him the ability to gain a certain balance between "inwardness" and "outwardness." In contrast to my own experiences in Madagascar, Mallet mentions that being a musician has created some mistrust among the *tsapiky* musicians, as fear of the "stealing of songs" is an important topic within the *tsapiky* music scene:

> *Jongler entre mon statut d'étudiant et celui de guitariste m'a permis de garder un certain équilibre entre intériorité et extériorité. Me limiter à l'un m'a souvent semblé trop distant, me borner à l'autre ou trop l'accentuer comportait le risque d'une méfiance de la part des musiciens, d'autant plus justifiable que le vol de chanson est un leitmotiv dans l'univers du tsapiky* (Mallet 2009 : 29).[6]

---

[6] "Juggling between my double status as a student and a guitar-player allowed me to keep a balance between inwardness and outwardness. To restrict myself to [the first] one has often seemed too distant, but to focus merely on the other one carried the risk of creating mistrust among the musicians, all the more as stealing songs is a leitmotiv in the world of *tsapiky*" (my translation). The topic of "stealing songs" also appears in Kiwan and Meinhof (2011). They describe how Malagasy musicians are aware of both the opportunities and the threats of translocal and transnational connections. Musicians in rural areas express their fear that songs are unwittingly or even purposefully taken, for example by visiting musicians, and

Mallet does not describe his own musical experiences in more detail. However, his musical education and knowledge can be found in detailed transcriptions–in Western notation–of the music he studied and learned to play.[7] My observation here mirrors Bohlman's remark that the discipline of ethnomusicology often demonstrates a primary interest in the music object. He argues that ethnomusicologists insist on

> presenting and commodifying music in Western notation, recordings, or world-music courses that fulfil the same curricular requirements as Western music courses (Bohlman 1993: 418-419).

Baily (2001) further suggests that performing the music you are researching allows you to understand the music from the "inside." He writes that when playing, you must have some knowledge about what you are doing:

> the structure of the music comes to be apprehended operationally, in terms of what you do, and, by implication, of what you have to know (Baily 2001: 94).

Another argument he gives is that learning to perform also provides insights into methods of learning and the contributions of institutions to musical training (Baily 2001: 94). Mirroring Mallet's experience, Baily writes that learning to perform can give you an understandable role in the community that you are working in, as well as helping with orientating oneself, especially in the early stages of research (Baily 2001: 95). He also reflects upon the post-fieldwork period and writes that once you have started to learn to perform, you are very likely to continue to do so after the field research as "you tend to take on the music as your own" (Baily 2001:96). This continuity can lead to situations in which the researcher suddenly becomes the "researched." It is possible that the researcher becomes an extra "source" or "archive," such as for field recordings, but also through their own direct musical experiences (Baily 2001: 96). This mirrors my own experiences, as described in chapter 1.

---

later on marked as "traditional," ignoring the author's ownership (Kiwan and Meinhof 2011: chapter 1).

[7] See transcriptions in Mallet (2009).

Understanding Musically

It has become obvious that many scholars see reasons for a need to integrate performance into ethnomusicological research. But what actually happens in practice? How can we explain what it means for a researcher to understand musically or through musicking? In other words, how can we finally integrate what we have understood into our academic "outcome"?

Rice (1994), in a book about his musical experience in Bulgaria, speaks of a new "world of music" that ethnomusicologists encounter during their research. He argues that researchers do not seek to understand the inner experience of people from another culture; it is neither the "Self" nor the "Other," he writes, that becomes the object of understanding. The researcher's interpretation seeks instead to expose a world referred to by certain symbols and symbolic behaviour. This world is a complex one of multiple meanings opened up by these symbols and available for interpretation by everyone who can experience it (Rice 1994: 7). It is therefore about learning and understanding a world suggested by music sounds, performance, and contexts (Rice 1994: 5). Rice defines musical experience as "the history of the individual's encounter with the world of musical symbols in which he finds himself" (Rice 1994: 6). This history of encounters, he further explains, consists of a dialectical movement between distantiation, inviting explanation, and appropriation that then suggests a new understanding (Rice 1994: 6). What he means by this dialectical movement becomes clear in the example he gives of his initial experience of Bulgarian music, an experience of participating in Bulgarian folk dances. Eventually, he retired from the dance and by observing to what was going on, worked out the underlying rhythmical metres, such as for example 7/8 or 11/8. He writes:

> In semiotic terms, I was beginning to understand the code used to construct musical messages in Bulgarian style, to form a structural syntactical explanation that, for all of its lack of reference to worlds beyond the music, influenced my experience of it. In hermeneutic terms, the world referenced by these music and dance symbols expanded from the narrow one of folk dancing to one that included my previous musical experiences. My expanded understanding of both the structural sense and potential reference of the music and dance altered and reconstituted my experience of them. As a result of this process of distanciation and appropriation, I was moved for the first time to wonder about the world that produced and exported these symbols to us (Rice 1994: 7).

Rice calls this example the "first hermeneutical arc" of his experiences, arguing that this process of experiencing Bulgarian music "from understanding to explanation to understanding, and from appropriation to distanciation to reappropriation" can be seen as representative of many similar moves he made during his research (Rice 1994: 7).

Baily (2008) also reflects on his previous musical experience to give a few practical examples of how his own research has informed his performances of Afghan music (playing the two instruments *rubāb* and *dutār*). He used video and film to analyse right-hand performance techniques that helped him in the "formation of a motor grammar" he can use in improvised rhythmic performance. The research also allowed him to collect a traditional repertoire in notated form. Analysing this repertoire then helped him to compose new musical pieces in a traditional style. Further, he can use his written notation to remember the repertoire. Being a researcher also allows him access to many recordings, not only of Afghan music, but also to neighbouring countries' musics in similar styles. Finally, the knowledge and musical experiences of other musics, combined with his knowledge and discussions of music with musicians coming from different musical backgrounds has helped him, for example, to explain perceived stylistic differences and gain a certain freedom in playing melodic improvisation (Baily 2008: 129-130). Baily's last example here indirectly points to the usefulness of seeing the connection between discourses about music and musical experiences. However, the emphasis in academic discourses has been on the difficulty, if not impossibility, of describing in words what we experience musically. This leads us to think mainly in one direction, namely that we need to "translate" our musical experiences into words. As this creates so many challenges, we tend to give less attention to the other direction, i.e. how discourses, in turn inform our performances. By this, I do not mean discourses as technical or methodological instructions of how to play or learn certain musics, although instructions of this kind are certainly relevant. Rather, I mean any kind of discourse created by those playing the music, even if at first glance the direct link to the music is not obvious.

My approach here guards against critiques by (for example) Agawu (2003) and Acosta (2005) that the musicians' own voices and perception of their own music were often unheard, dominated and effaced by Western (academic) discourses. Listening and engaging in discourses can also create certain awareness or inspire us about different ways of musical experience and musicking that before or otherwise we would have never thought about, never experienced, or never felt.

If, for example, the Malagasy musicians had not talked so much about the importance of the indigenous concept of oral transmission, the *lova-tsofina*, to their own music making, I would never have followed this approach myself, doing without any kind of written notation throughout my learning process. And then, in turn, if I had not applied and followed the *lova-tsofina* in my musical practices, my attention would have not been drawn to other highly important elements of Malagasy music, such as the relation between the language and the music. And in turn, if the topic of the Malagasy language had not appeared so persistently in the discourses of the Malagasy musicians, I probably would never have thought about making use of learning and knowing the lyrics for my playing or thinking about the importance of language for accentuation in even instrumental music. This then made it possible for me to make practical use of my knowledge of the Malagasy language for my musical experiences, making me able to more fully understand examples, ideas and arguments expressed by the musicians when talking about language-related issues in their music. If the Malagasy musicians had not used terms such as "*rythme mélodique*" ("melodic rhythm") or "*placement de voix*" ("placement of the voice") so often, it is unlikely I would have questioned my own understanding of "rhythm." I would have never focussed my attention so much on the interrelation of rhythm and melody while playing, so would hardly have understood (or musically felt) what musicians so often described as regional musical differences. I had heard so many stories about the relationships between different musicians, about the role of musicians in Madagascar, about certain musical legends; if the musicians had not talked so much about "*l'âme Malgache*" ("Malagasy soul") and about Malagasy cultural and ethical values, I would never have understood that Malagasy music-making is always about a certain "esprit" and attitude, about creating music with which Malagasy people can identify ("*se retrouvent*") but also about expressing your own personality through musicking at the same time. These are only a few examples of many and I will return to them in greater detail in chapters 4-6.

I have given these examples here to stress my argument that discourses and musical experiences are closely related; they inform each other. They should therefore be used and understood in both directions. In fact, this is true not only of discourses alone. As I have analysed earlier in this chapter, discourses are often the means through which we make sense of our own experiences (including our sentiments and emotions, as the last of my examples shows). Seeing our musical experiences and discourses as interrelated and interdependent is the most fruitful basis for analyses of both. Instead of only seeing difficulties in "translating" the performance approach into academic writing and difficulties in applying certain discourses to our musical experiences, we should instead make use of the connections between the two.

As explained above, Rice (1994) has integrated and analysed his own learning and playing of Bulgarian music into his academic research. He explains, for example, how he discovered a new layer of musical understanding. He realised that physical behaviour, such as hand motion, is of immense importance. When first learning to play Bulgarian music, he was very much influenced by Western discourses about music. He then discovered the importance of physical behaviour, which for him became what he calls a "conceptual source:"

> whereas my original ideas were determined by Western concepts represented in musical notation, my new understanding added the hand motions necessary to produce the sounds: physical behaviour became part of the conceptual source generating musical ideas (Rice 1994: 83).

The ways we talk about music, music-making and our experiences of musicking as well as the experiences we gain through practical engagement in shared music-making are sources of understanding. Instead of thinking of two different sources or activities, we should understand these two as inseparable and interlinked. The approach of analysing both interdependently and in a constant interrelation is fruitful because it offers new paths of understanding musical phenomena not based merely on Western analytical perspectives. But it is also necessary, as it allows us to practically apply current issues discussed and argued for in theoretical and methodological debates on ethnographic fieldwork, such as a sensitive and self-reflexive approach towards our field relations, a focus on experiences, (including the researcher's own) and therefore a balanced stance that respects the researcher's own perspective while listening to and fully integrating the voices of the people we work with. In short, it allows us to research "with" rather than just "on" people and "their music."

This research and the ideas and attitude that lies behind it is of great significance considering that our world today is "marked by socio-political upheavals and transnational mobilities" (Meinhof und Galasinski 2005: 1) which place a constant process of negotiating questions of belonging and self-understanding as part of everyone's everyday lives–a situation that also affects the academic context and hence the very nature of academic disciplines. Considering its origin and history, the discipline of ethnomusicology has undergone immense changes and has been subject to heated debates about disciplinary boundaries (e.g. Stobart 2008).

With regard to on-going ethnomusicological research projects and the discipline's recent developments, it might be surprising that people still often associate ethnomusicology with research in far-away countries, with travelling scholars speaking exotic languages or researching rare and half-forgotten music cultures or instruments. A brief look at ethnomusicologists' profiles and their expertise actually often confirms a major interest in countries far from their places of origin (and I am definitely included in this set). However, this picture is deceptive and quickly becomes blurred; while the "old ethnomusicological paradigm" (Rice 2003: 151), represented by, for example, Merriam (1964), saw the world as made up of clearly-bounded cultures with relatively static social structures, today's picture is a completely different one–with important consequences regarding our research approaches, our fieldwork methods and not at least our self-understanding and self-conception as ethnomusicological researchers.

As argued above, important changes have already been discussed and proposed on a theoretical level. However, the critical question remains of how to apply these insights in practice. I argue that the mutual integration of musical experience and ethnomusicological research and the possibility that lies therein to analyse musical experiences and discourses in a constant interrelation offers a unique chance; it allows researchers to follow the principle aims of a "subject-centred ethnography" (Rice 2003) and combine them with what Agawu refers to as a "presumption of sameness" (Agawu 2003). In the following, I will present these two methodological propositions in more detail, explaining how the combination of the two responds to and takes seriously current methodological and theoretical issues and needs as outlined above.

"Presumption of Sameness" (Agawu 2003) and "Subject-centred Ethnography" (Rice 2003)

Agawu (2003) argues that Western academic work on African music has always been a constant search for difference and has produced a persistent emphasis on "the Other." But he does not propose any concrete methodological instructions in his book to undermine those same tendencies in Western discourses or to minimise their "othering" of African music. He does, however, suggest what I consider a theoretical proposition about one's attitude as a researcher, arguing for a "presumption of sameness" (Agawu 2003: 171). He writes:

> There is no method for attending to sameness, only a presence of mind, an attitude, a way of seeing the world. For fieldworkers who presume sameness rather than difference, the challenge of constructing an ethnographic report would be construed as developing a theory of translation that aims to show how the materiality of culture constrains musical practice in specific ways. The idea would be to unearth the impulses that motivate acts of performance and to seek to interpret them in

terms of broader, perhaps even generic cultural impulses (Agawu 2003: 169).

In order to bring this important theoretical impulse onto a more concrete level, I have combined it with central aspects of Timothy Rice's approach, a "subject-centred ethnography" (Rice 2003). One of Rice's main arguments is that we need to move away from studying cultures "as traditionally understood" (Rice 2003: 152). Instead of looking at the "big picture," he claims it is much more useful to take a "bottom-up" perspective and search for individual trajectories. This involves questions about the kinds of individual experiences people have, or whom they share these experiences with, as well as their beliefs, their social status, their behaviours and their tastes. At present, we need to focus on the ways individual people and small groups of people are linked, and how they relate to each other. "Subject-centred ethnography" incorporates the main theoretical aspects of what many scholars refer to as the "new fieldwork" in ethnomusicology (see the discussion above), in that it reconfigures "the field" as an experience rather than a place (Hellier-Tinoco 2003: 25-26).

If "subject-centred ethnography" is a move towards studying subjects and the experiences of these subjects, the question comes up of what exactly constitutes a "subject." Rice proposes alternative terms, such as person, individual, self, agent or actor and explains that he uses them "somewhat interchangeably;" his main point is that the subject is "a thoroughly social and self-reflexive being." Subject-centred ethnography is not, he writes, about biography or documenting individuality (though it can also be that) but an "account of the social 'authoring'… of the self" (Rice 2003: 157). This goes back to the idea of Mikhail Bakhtin, who said that "we get ourselves from others" and that identity is construed in a process of dialogue (Bakhtin 1990 [1919]). The self-perception of the individual under conditions of modernity, Rice argues, is very different from that under pre-modern conditions; he refers to Anthony Giddens, who in *Modernity and Self-Identity* raised this issue; "What to do? How to act? Who to be? These are focal questions for everyone living in circumstances of late modernity" (Giddens 1991:70). As I explained at the beginning of this chapter, Rice stresses that experience is not an inner phenomenon but instead begins with the interactions between self and world and with others. One also has to bear in mind the expanding contexts of experiences; they are no longer contained within local isolated cultures or nation-states but are shaped by "regional, areal, colonial, and global economics, politics, social relations, and images" (Rice 2003:

160).[8] Recent studies of networks of artists from Madagascar have implemented this idea by arguing that artists make use of both transnational and translocal networks. But the analysis goes far beyond the traditional "bi-focal" of communities that link originating countries and sending countries, as so often studied in diaspora research (Kiwan and Meinhof 2011).

In terms of musical and ethnomusicological research, many have recognised and studied the mix of cultural and musical styles. That these are easily available around the globe, Rice argues, is only possible because of colonialism and the ubiquity of electronic media. Erlmann (1993) has studied the commercial genre of "world music," as have many other authors, such as Guilbault (1997) and Monson (1999). And a variety of studies on other, less-commercialised forms of transnational music-making between homelands and diaspora have been made (Rice 2003: 152-155). The ethnomusicologist Mark Slobin (1993) has provided a model for these studies and with his *Subcultural Sounds: Micromusics of the West* developed ideas that serve as a starting point for Rice's idea of subject-centred ethnography. Slobin's "suggestive epigram" that "we are all individual music cultures" (Slobin 1993: ix) is of crucial importance to Rice, who argues that by taking this idea of "individual music cultures seriously" he attempts to bring some order to the experience of a chaotic and puzzling contemporary world. Global music-making, according to Slobin, should be conceptualised in three different levels: 1. the "subculture," which embraces everything on the local level, ranging from families, neighbourhoods, through organisational committees to ethnic groups; 2. the "interculture," which includes the music industry, diaspora, and affinity groups; and finally 3. the "superculture," which includes regions, nations, and states.[9]

---

[8] The argument that today the world needs to be understood as more complex, mobile and dynamic (Rice 2003: 151) is also shared by other researchers working in a similar direction: Appadurai (1996) for example describes a new "deterritorialised" world of increasingly mobile groups and individuals. This leads to a "new condition of neighboreness" that we can enter because of new technologies of travel and documentation (Appadurai 1996: 29). James Clifford (1997) disagrees with Appadurai, stressing instead the continuity between globalisation and earlier forms of travel and rootlessness. He says that "[i]ntercultural connection is, and has long been, the norm" (Clifford 1997: 5) and proposes to focus on "routes rather than roots", on "travel rather than dwelling."
[9] For a detailed account of Slobin's concepts, see Slobin (1993).

To the third level, Rice adds Appadurai's notions of "ethnoscapes," "technoscapes," "financescapes," "mediascapes" and "ideoscapes."[10] Though he builds on these ideas, Rice argues that they are not only cultures but also "social and geographical (or sociographical) locales in which individuals experience music, along with other things" (Rice 2003: 156). The goals of "subject-centred ethnography" as Rice puts them, are

> to bring some narrative coherence to the complex and seemingly fragmented world that many social theorists, cultural critics, and ethnomusicologists are writing about (Rice 2003: 157).

One of the most important aspects for my work is the argument that we need to include our own trajectories as part of the picture; "subject-centred ethnography" proposes a shared space of musical experience and ethnography that encompasses researcher and researched alike. Although musical experience and ethnography co-occur for both, contestation occurs as the two kinds of individuals are situated very differently in the space of musical experience. Power, for example, can become an issue and can be negotiated and acted out–as for example in questions of who controls the discourse (Rice 2003: 174).

Agawu has given the issue of power also much attention. He criticises the constant search for difference within Western academic works for producing ideologically one-sided and politically disadvantageous representation of African musics. A "presumption of sameness" however, would allow for a cross-cultural vision through which we would be able to focus on the specificity of local practices (Agawu 2003: 168-169). In this criticism, he mirrors aspects of Rice's model. First of these is Rice's desire to move away from the study of cultures towards a study of the experiences of individuals; it therefore also has the aim of studying a shared space of musical experience. Rice does not in any way deny the issue of power inherent in, for example, the fact that discourses are controlled and dominated. However, he argues that his model helps to study issues of contestation by looking at the positions of individuals within this space of musical experiences. Rice describes his "preconditions" for "subject-centred ethnography" as understanding the individual as a "thoroughly social and self-reflexive being" and experience as something that "begins with interaction with a world and with others." These guard against Agawu's main critique of the consistent emphasis placed on difference: Rice's model not only embraces informants or subjects but also encompasses the field-worker or ethnomusicologist in

---

[10] For a more detailed discussion of Appadurai's notions, see Appadurai (1996).

the same way. The "presumption of sameness" is therefore inherent in the shared space of musical experiences and the individual positions involved are analysed in an equal measure.

CHAPTER FOUR

CONTESTING THE "6/8 RHYTHM"

Introduction

In the previous chapter, I outlined the possibility of the intersection and integration of musical practices and ethnomusicological research and argued for its necessity for research. The following three chapters use interviews, discussions, informal meetings, shared musical activities, concerts and rehearsals as their basic materials. The order of the chapters themselves is not meant to imply any strict chronological ordering; rather, continuous work and meetings with the same musicians allowed me to properly research discourses and experiences of musicking in a constant interrelation, studying and experiencing the flow of information in both directions. The arguments, however, must appear in some order; I have chosen this order with the intention of demonstrating how the vital element of interrelation works in practice. I have divided the work as follows: I will show with concrete examples how I have analysed discourses about music and music-making (chapters 4 and 5) interdependently with musical experience (chapter 6). Chapters 4-6, therefore need, really, to be thought of as a unit.

This chapter focuses closely on the concept of "6/8 rhythm" in the Malagasy context. Why exactly is a whole chapter dedicated specifically to a Western musical concept in a book on music from Madagascar? At first glance, the Malagasy musicians' persistent usage of this Western term might not be too surprising considering that more and more of the musicians are transnationally mobile and connected, with experience as participants in international and intercultural musical projects and collaborations that have involved them travelling to promote, explain and sell their music to foreign audiences. However, seen from a different angle, it seems not only surprising but even contradictory of another prominent theme within the musicians' discourses: the concept of "6/8 rhythm" is rooted in Western musicology and even more importantly, it is rooted in musical notation. Apart from one or two exceptions, none of the musicians I have met and worked with can read or write music. Instead, musicians emphasise the importance of learning by ear for Malagasy music making, talking about the indigenous concept of oral transmission, the *lova-tsofina* (*lova* = heritage, *sofina* = ear), as the basis of their music.

Does the "6/8 rhythm" contradict the *lova-tsofina*? If we look at it this way, the picture is definitely one of contradictory discourses existing side-by-side. If, however, we take on another perspective, the picture changes: whilst it is true that the concept of "6/8 rhythm" is consistently present and seems to be of significant relevance to the musicians, their individual usage, understanding and feeling towards it vary a great deal. Instead of thinking of a foreign concept that has travelled or "migrated" to Madagascar, it is therefore much more useful to take a bottom-up approach, investigating how, when, where and in what kind of circumstances individual musicians make use of this particular concept. The chapter's aim is not to judge in any way whether the concept of "6/8 rhythm" is suitable to describe Malagasy music. Rather, the chapter analyses and listens to the musicians' individual voices to learn how they understand and make use of this particular concept. Therefore, it is extremely important to reflect upon and sensitively integrate the particular research context into the analysis.

The Importance of the Research Context

All musicians I worked with are based in Madagascar's capital Antananarivo or at least frequently work and pass through there. They all produce music aimed at the international world music market; all of them have had intercultural musical encounters with musicians from outside Madagascar. Antananarivo can be described as the country's "cultural hub" (Kiwan and Meinhof 2011) not only because its infrastructure makes international musical encounters possible (everyone entering or leaving Madagascar passes through the city), but also because it is very different from other places on the island; languages other than Malagasy, especially French, are very important to the city because of tourism, civic administration and media. There is a cultural infrastructure (even if limited, as argued in chapter 1; see also Fuhr 2006) with concert-places and recording facilities. It is within this unique environment of Madagascar's capital and within this unique circle of musicians that the Western concept of "6/8 rhythm" appears and is important.

It happened very often that I mentioned my research topic or was asked about it (whether with other researchers, friends or taxi drivers), I would be warned that I should be careful not to generalise from Antananarivo to the countryside, since musicians from outside the city would have completely different stories to tell. Some of the musicians themselves also pointed this out to me during the interviews. This discourse mirrors discourses that I often encountered in tourism-related contexts. Reading tourist guide-books, speaking to tourists and also listening to people advising tourists, the Malagasy countryside is often glorified as the "real Madagascar," something that also shines through in some of the musicians' ideas that I will discuss in the next chapter. That musicians pointed this, as well as other examples in which they mention questions they ask themselves or projects they are involved in, shows that some of the musicians are also interested in research and that they reflect upon the research and interview situations themselves. I have already discussed in great detail my role as a researcher and to what extent my role has impacted on fieldwork situations and therefore on the research itself. This also becomes relevant when thinking about the presence of the concept of "6/8 rhythm" in the musicians' discourses. All musicians I worked with are aware of me being a Western classically-trained musician and I conducted almost all interviews in French. These two circumstances have certainly influenced the musicians in their choice of words and their way of explaining things, so might have favoured the usage of the Western concept of "6/8 rhythm." However, I avoided being the first to mention it in any interview. A few musicians also brought up the fact that I am a Western trained musician and therefore familiar with Western music theory.

Before looking in detail at the musicians' individual perspectives and conceptualisations of the "6/8 rhythm" and analysing the ways in which different layers of identity are constructed through the use of it, I will first briefly return to the origin of the concept of "6/8 rhythm". How is it rooted and how is it used in the Western musicological context?

The "6/8 rhythm" as Used in Western Musicology

The Western understanding of a "6/8 rhythm" is rooted in the idea of musical notation. As already discussed in chapter 2, it was during the Renaissance that it became common practice for Western composers and musicians to divide and measure music (Van Leeuwen 1999: 37). Measuring music and grouping it into rhythmic entities such as, for example, 3/4 or 6/8 implies a distinction and alternation of strong and weak beats that still forms part of the basis of all definitions in dictionaries as well as of education at music schools and conservatories (Arom 1991: 180). When the bar line was first introduced, around the early fifteenth century, it did not necessarily always coincide with a strong beat. The rule that main beats are preceded with bar lines only developed after the mid-seventeenth century.[1] As Dudley (1996) explains, the notion of measure in music lets Western musicians and music-listeners assume a consistent accentuation of metric pulses, which would be the first and fourth note in a 6/8 metre (Dudley 1996: 272). In order to make this point clearer, I would like to give a typical example of the usage and notation of a "6/8 rhythm" in the Western context. This will later help to explain my experiences of learning through the *lova-tsofina*, i.e. of learning without using any written notation, to be explained in chapter 6.

A very well-known piece of Western classical music in a "6/8 rhythm" is the "*Andante graziose*" in the piano sonata in A major by Wolfgang Amadeus Mozart. The 6/8 is indicated at the beginning of the piece and the assumed accentuation on the first and fourth eights in each bar is even more emphasised by the phrasing curves, which group together the first three eights in each of the first two bars:

Fig. 4-1: Excerpt from Wolfgang Amadeus Mozart's piano sonata A major, K 331 (300i).[2]

The fact that the Western understanding of a "6/8 rhythm" is so closely linked to or even based on musical notation becomes a matter of special importance considering that all of the musicians I worked with are autodidacts, many of them eager to tell me how they learned to play or compose music by listening to the radio, watching and listening to fellow musicians or just "hanging around" in the streets of the city. These learning experiences are often reflected in song lyrics; songs are dedicated

---

[1] Hiley (2007-2012).

[2] Mozart. 1955. *Klaviersonaten Band 2*, 160, Urtext-Ausgabe von Walther Lampe, München-Duisburg: Henle-Verlag.

to other musicians or to places of learning.[3] The musicians actually often describe their inability to read music as an asset, referring to Madagascar as a country of oral culture, often proudly referring to the Malagasy concept of *lova-tsofina*. The importance of learning by ear is emphasised by almost all Malagasy musicians. Rajery (alias Germain Randrianarisoa) is based in Antananarivo and one of the few musicians who is internationally well known. He is also one of the few who makes a living through his music, and who has produced a number of albums that are distributed internationally. He plays the *valiha* but also sings, mainly his own compositions, and is currently directing his own recording studio and label "Valimad" in Antananarivo through which he supports other Malagasy artists.[4] Rajery considers the "musical ear" to be something given to all persons. However, he sees differences in how it is used and whether a person acquires the habit of using it. He mentions rhythm in this context, arguing that without using the "musical ear," one will never achieve a sense of rhythm:

> *Chacun a leurs manières de voir des choses. En plus aussi, d'adopter et ça aussi, ça dépend aussi d'oreille. Tout dépend d'oreille évidement. Parce que si on n'a pas d'oreille, on n'aura jamais le sens du rythme. Mais de toute façon, l'oreille musicale, c'est naturelle, tout le monde l'a! Tout le monde a cette oreille musicale, mais c'est juste la manière de l'utiliser. Oui, l'habitude!* (Interview Rajery, 17.12.2007)

> Everyone has his own way of seeing things. But also of adopting things. And this also depends on one's ear. Obviously everything depends on the ear. Because if you don't use your ear, you'll never get a sense of rhythm. But anyway, having a 'musical ear' is a natural thing, everyone has it! Everyone has a 'musical ear,' it's all about the way you're going to use it. Yeah, about the habit! (Interview Rajery, 17.12.2007)[5]

---

[3] For example: Erick Manana's song "*Vakoka*" is dedicated to all the "traditional musicians" ("*musiciens traditionels*") in Madagascar he learnt with and his song "*Revirevinay taloha*" tells the story of a little wall in front of his friends' house where he used to sit with his friends (with whom in the 1970s he founded the group "Lolo sy ny tariny"); there, they played their guitars and composed new songs.

[4] Rajery also initiated the festival "Angaredona. Le festival des musiques vivantes à Madagascar," which first took place in 2004. For further information, see Angaredona (2008). In December 2007, I went to Mahajanga, at the island's North-West coast, with Rajery, where in the building of the "Alliance Française" he had organised a competition open to all local musicians through which he then chose groups and solo musicians to take part in the 2008 festival in Antananarivo.

[5] Please note that these are my own translations. They are verbatim, rendering the text as closely as possible to the original rather than attempting to achieve stylistic perfection.

His argument here mirrors a very famous debate within ethnomusicology initiated by John Blacking (1973) with his book *How musical is man?*, in which he argues that all men are musical and that it is wrong to speak of the "musical" and the "un-musical" in terms of talent. Rakotomavo (alias: Germain Rakotomavo) is director of a boys' high school in Antananarivo. He plays *valiha* and guitar, though not regularly on-stage; he mainly plays at home or with fellow musician friends. He is very interested in research, has collected a number of books and has also asked me to send him ethnomusicological literature which is difficult to find in Madagascar. Rakotomavo argues that for him Malagasy rhythm is not measured as in Western music; he talks about an "experiential rhythm," claiming that it is through experience that people master rhythm:

> *C'est très libre. Donc, notre rythme-là, c'est pas du rythme mesuré comme dans la musique occidentale. C'est des rythmes expérimentaux. C'est à partir d'expériences qu'ils ont ce rythme-là.* (Interview Rakotomavo, 1.8.2008)

> It's very free. Our rhythm, it's not a measured rhythm like in Western music. It is rather experiential rhythms. It is from experiences that they get this particular rhythm. (Interview Rakotomavo, 1.8.2008)

The notion of "experience" will continue to be a central theme within this and following chapters. It appears within the musicians' discourses and becomes of crucial importance with regard to their musical practices, my own, and those we share.

The Musicians' Usage of the Term: Identification or Taking Distance?

When looking at the musicians' individual usage and understanding of the concept of "6/8 rhythm," different trends emerge: some musicians identify with the term and use it without verbally reflecting upon it; others take distance from it, identifying it as something "foreign." The latter group can be further divided into musicians who do not use the term at all (as they do not see its applicability for Malagasy music) and those who use it while treating it as something imposed from the outside. There are also musicians who use the term "6/8 rhythm," but who adapt it in some way to the Malagasy context by transforming it or giving it another meaning; for example, some used it in plural form as "6/8 rhythms" in order to stress the variety of rhythms as well as the common rhythmic base in Madagascar.

In the following I will analyse various examples and explain how they can be distinguished in terms of these different trends, focussing on issues of identity, including the musicians' perceptions of "Self" and "Other," or their search for collective musical identity.

Some musicians use the term "6/8 rhythm" without questioning its meaning or its applicability for Malagasy music. Sammy (alias Samoela Andriamalalaharijaona) is a multi-instrumentalist, singer, instrument-maker and composer from Antananarivo. He has been a member of several music groups, such as "Tarika Sammy" (with whom he toured internationally) and in 2010 released the CD "Tsara Madagasikara," produced by German producer Birger Gesthuisen.[6] Sammy describes the "6/8 rhythm" as the rhythm that unites all Malagasy music, claiming you can find it everywhere on the island:

> *On a un rythme qui nous unit là. Ce rythme, c'est toujours... Moi, je vois toujours le 6/8 quoi. Tu vois? Tu trouves ça partout dans toute l'île!* (Interview Sammy, 23.11.2007)

> We have a rhythm that unites us. This rhythm, it's always... I always see the 6/8. You see? You find this everywhere on the island! (Interview Sammy, 23.11.2007)

Bilo (alias Dana Ramahaleo Bilo) is a *salegy* musician and singer, originally from the North but currently based in the capital. Much like to Sammy, Bilo regards the "6/8 rhythm" as the rhythm that unites all Malagasy music. He explains that there are differences with regard to the tempo but that all the musical styles of the different regions are in "6/8 rhythms," (note the plural):

> Bilo: *Le vrai rythme en malgache c'est le 6/8. Mais il y a des 6/8 qui sont un peu lents, ça dépend des régions, qui sont un peu lents, il y a des rythmes qui sont un peu excitants qui est un peu plus rapide que l'autre.*
> Jenny: *Donc c'est le tempo qui varie.*
> Bilo: *Oui, c'est le tempo qui varie, mais le rythme c'est 6/8. Et c'est ça qui réunit toutes les musiques malgaches. Mais chacun a sa manière de...*
> Jenny: *Ça veut dire que le 6/8, on le trouve vraiment partout, même au Sud...*
> Bilo: *Même au Sud jusqu'au Nord. Tu vois, il y a le kilalaka, c'est le 6/8. Il y a aussi le hira gasy de Tananarive, c'est le 6/8. Il y a aussi le kidogo de Fianarantsoa, c'est le 6/8. Il y a aussi le salegy, le malesa du Nord. Tout ça, ce sont des 6/8.* (Interview Bilo, 19.8.2008)

---

[6] Samy Izy (2010).

Bilo: The real rhythm in Malagasy is the 6/8. But there are also 6/8 that are
a bit slow, it depends on the regions, that are a bit slow, there are rhythms
that are a bit exciting, a bit faster than the other.
Jenny: So it is the tempo that varies.
Bilo: Yes, it's the tempo that varies, but the rhythm is the 6/8. And that's
what reunites all Malagasy musics. But everyone has his way of…
Jenny: That means that the 6/8, you can find it really everywhere, even in
the South…
Bilo: Even in the South to the North. You see, there is the *kilalaka*, it's the
6/8. There is also the *hira gasy* from Tananarive, that's the 6/8. There is
also the *kidogo* from Fianarantsoa, that's the 6/8. There is also the *salegy*,
the *malesa* from the North. All these are 6/8. (Interview Bilo, 19.8.2008)

Justin Vali (alias Justin Rakotondrasoa) is another famous and
internationally-renowned *valiha* player, who has recently become very
successful with his group "Ny Malagasy orkestra," the first "national
Malagasy orchestra" as he calls it. The aim of this group, according to
Justin Vali, is to fuse different Malagasy regional styles to create music
that can represent the country as a whole. I will return to this group later in
the chapter, when I look at musicians' discourses related to marketing
strategies. Justin Vali is also member of the group "Madagascar AllStars"
and has produced a number of albums, both solo and with his different
groups. Justin is based in France, but plans to move back to Madagascar
and is already spending more and more time on the island. Justin Vali also
speaks of the "6/8 rhythm" with regard to the musical styles of the
different regions of Madagascar. Speaking about his "Ny Malagasy
Orkestra" project, he explains that the "6/8 rhythm" is the base of all
Malagasy musics and that because of this common base all musicians can
easily join in with their individual musical styles:

*Bon, nous, notre idée, si vous avez écouté les morceaux tout à l'heure,
c'est vrai que dans un morceau on a vu un petit peu de tout, mais c'est
pour cela que pour moi, le rythme 6/8 ici à Madagascar, la même cadence,
en fait avec la même cadence, on peut faire tout rentrer là-dedans, tous les
accents de tsapiky, de salegy, de basesa, etc. Donc, c'est ça qui est nous.
C'est pour cela que tous dans un morceau, tous les musiciens de région,
chaque région peuvent exprimer leur style, en fait. C'est ça.* (Interview
Justin, 23.11.2007)

Well, we, our idea, if you have listened to the pieces earlier, it's true that in
one piece we have seen a bit of everything, but that is why for me, the 6/8
rhythm here in Madagascar, the same cadence, in fact with the same
cadence, you can integrate everything, all the accents of the *tsapiky*, the
salegy, the *basesa* etc. So, that's us. That is why everything is in one piece;

in fact all the musicians of all the regions can express their style. That's it.
(Interview Justin, 23.11.2007)

Sammy, Justin Vali and Bilo speak on a more general level, using the
idea of the shared "6/8 rhythm" to create a common musical identity. Jean-
Claude (alias Jean-Claude Vinson) is a half-French half-Malagasy guitarist
who lives in Antananarivo. He primarily talks about the "6/8 rhythm" as
part of his personal experience. Like the others, he uses the term without
further commenting on it, saying that everything he plays immediately
turns into a "6/8 rhythm," as this forms part of his inspiration. He
mentions foreign musical styles, such as hip-hop or blues, explaining that
although he is capable of playing them in the usual way, he would
normally play them in a "6/8 rhythm." In saying this, he identifies the "6/8
rhythm" as an important feature of Malagasy music and stresses his own
"Malagasiness." This is especially interesting because of Jean-Claude's
half-French origin:

> Mais c'est bizarre quand j'écoute une chanson qu'elle soit pop, qu'elle soit
> techno, qu'elle soit hip hop, qu'elle soit blues, et si je prends toute de suite
> une guitare et que je rejoue la chanson, elle sort en 6/8. J'arrive plus à...
> Je peux la jouer en 4/4, mais c'est pas de mon inspiration. C'est pas un
> problème si je joue, mais je trouve plus sympa si... [Tout le monde rit].
> (Interview Jean-Claude, 18.7.2008)

> It is strange, when I listen to a song, be it pop, be it techno, be it hip-hop or
> be it blues, and if I immediately take my guitar to play that song, it comes
> out as 6/8. I can't anymore...I can play a 4/4, but it's not my inspiration.
> It's not a problem if I play, but I think it's nicer if... [Everyone laughs].
> (Interview Jean-Claude, 18.7.2008)

As explained earlier, it is important to reflect upon the particular
research context, including my being a Western trained musician, a fact
that all the musicians I worked with were aware of. This might have
influenced the musicians' choice of words and their way of explaining
their music. This becomes evident, for example, in Jaojoby's (alias Eusèbe
Jaojoby) argument. Jaojoby is probably the most famous *salegy* musician
and is often called the "king of *salegy*."[7] Like Bilo, Jaojoby is originally
from Northern Madagascar, but has lived in the island's capital for a few
years and frequently travels to both Europe and North America for
concerts. Jaojoby represents what I have identified as another trend, that of
musicians using the concept of "6/8 rhythm," but distancing himself from

---

[7] See for example Eyre (2002).

it at the same time. Jaojoby emphasises that it is the "theoreticians" who call the rhythm in Madagascar a "6/8 rhythm." His understanding of a theoretician includes someone's ability to notate music. He explains that when writing down the metre of Malagasy music, it would be in a "6/8 rhythm," emphasising the structure of overlapping binaries and ternaries.[8] Jaojoby identifies me as a theoretician and although he is laughing while referring to me as one of these theoreticians, I felt that he wanted to make clear that he himself was not one. He confirmed this suspicion later by telling me that he is not a theoretician, referring to his way of learning music through practice:

Moi, je ne suis pas théoricien, juste quelques notions de solfège quand j'étais jeune. Moi, je joue comme ça. C'est dans la pratique. Alors, je crois que c'est un peu difficile pour moi d'expliquer. (Interview Jaojoby, 21.8.2008)

Me, I am not a theoretician, just some bits of music theory when I was young. I play like this. It's in the practice. So, I think it's a bit difficult for me to explain. (Interview Jaojoby, 21.8.2008)

Furthermore, he does not speak of Malagasy music in general, but only of the music that he himself plays, namely *salegy* music:

Oui, bon écoute, déjà il y a le... Oui, la musique que je fais, le salegy, pour les théoriciens... comme Jenny... quand on écrit, la mesure rythmique c'est le 6/8. Ouais, mesure composée. Il semble qu'à la base c'est du carré, 1, 2, 3, 4, mais au fait c'est 1, 2, 3, 4, 5, 6, 1, 2, 3, 4, 5, 6. (Interview Jaojoby, 21.8.2008)

Yes, well listen, already there is...yes, the music that I play, the *salegy*, for the theoreticians...like Jenny...when you write it, the rhythmical metre is the 6/8. Yeah, a compound metre. At the base it appears to be 'square' 1, 2, 3, 4, but in fact it is 1, 2, 3, 4, 5, 6, 1, 2, 3, 4, 5, 6. (Interview Jaojoby, 21.8.2008)

Hajazz (alias Haja Mbolatiana Tovo Rasolomahatratra) is an electric guitar and electric bass player keenly interested in jazz music. He often performs with his brother Mendrika (alias Mendrika Rasolomahatratra), a percussionist. In Antananarivo, where he comes from and lives, he is well known for having developed a special technique of playing the electric bass and guitar that resembles *valiha* and *marovany* sounds and playing

---

[8] Interview Jaojoby, 21.8.2008.

styles. Similarly to Jaojoby, Hajazz also assumes some distance from the
concept of "6/8 rhythm," arguing that it is the "music teachers" and the
"connoisseur musicians" who define things this way. He himself seems to
juggle with terms such as 4/4 or 6/8 and says that it is not very common
among Malagasy musicians to give names or definitions, indirectly
referring to the concept of *lova-tsofina*:

> Hajazz: *En général, ce sont des profs de musique qui disent 6/8. Mais c'est
> un peu mélangé, on peut dire aussi même 4/4. [Il montre][9] (...) Ou 6/8 ou
> 12/8, je sais pas. C'est entre les trois.*
> Jenny: *Mais, par exemple, si tu répètes avec des autres musiciens
> malgaches et vous parlez... si jamais ça arrive que vous parlez...*
> Hajazz: *Non non, c'est rare de trouver des... Ce sont des musiciens
> connaisseurs qui disent toujours 6/8 comme ça.* (Interview Hajazz,
> 12.8.2008)

> Hajazz: In general, it is the music profs who call it 6/8. But it's a bit mixed,
> you can also say 4/4. [He demonstrates][10] (…) Or 6/8 or 12/8, I don't
> know. It's between the three.
> Jenny: But, for example, when you rehearse with other Malagasy
> musicians and you talk…if ever it happens that you talk…
> Hajazz: No no, it's rare to find the… It is the connoisseur musicians who
> always call it 6/8 like this. (Interview Hajazz, 12.8.2008)

A conversation I had with three musicians (Ricky, Jean-Claude and
Mendrika) supports Hajazz's argument that it is rare for Malagasy
musicians to give musical definitions. At some point during our discussion
I insisted on asking how they, between musicians, communicate about
rhythm, as for example during a rehearsal. When I asked, all of them burst
out in laughter, explaining to me that my asking about it already reveals a
difference between us. They argue that Malagasy musicians do not
verbally communicate about this:

> Jenny: *Mais il y a quand même... Je sais pas si il y a une répétition, et vous
> parlez du rythmes dans ce sens, est-ce que vous utilisez des mots pour...
> [Tout le monde rit] Ou on ne discute pas ?*
> Ricky: *Ouais, c'est ça le problème.* (Interview Ricky, 18.7.2008)

> Jenny: But there is still…I don't know when there is a rehearsal and you
> talk about rhythm in that way, do you use words for…[Everyone laughs].
> Or you don't talk?

---

[9] Sound example 2 on DVD.
[10] Sound example 2 on DVD.

Ricky: Yes, that's the problem. (Interview Ricky, 18.7.2008)

These three examples show how the musicians, indirectly or directly, argue that there is no agreed terminology for "rhythm" in Madagascar. They also express a certain discomfort with the term "6/8 rhythm," emphasising that it is a term used by others, i.e. by foreigners. This attitude also shines through in their way of explaining their music. For example, Hajazz added *"Ou 6/8 ou 12/8, je sais pas. C'est entre les trois."* Throughout their explanations, they draw a very clear line between "us," the Malagasy musicians and "them," the foreigners, including me as a researcher. The same can be seen in the following example, which is a discussion I had with the two musicians Bebey and Papay. Bebey (alias Mathurin Rakotomanga) is a singer and member of the legendary group "Lolo sy ny tariny" that I mentioned in the previous chapter. Papay (alias Papay Raveloaris) is a farmer from outside the capital, a rock musician who sings and plays bass guitar. He has his own rock band called "Iraimbilanja" (meaning "One Franc") and also founded the group "Sivy Mahasaky" ("The nine who dare"). I will come back to this group and Papay's ambitions for it later in this chapter. In the discussion I had with Bebey and Papay, they explicitly excluded me from the shared experience all Malagasy musicians have with regard to rhythm. In contrast to the examples above, they use the term "6/8 rhythm" without identifying it immediately as something foreign. However, by juggling a set of different terms, such as "rhythm," "accents," or "tempo," they point out a general terminological confusion:

Bebey: *Mais le rythme qu'on dit chaque fois que c'est le 6/8 ça étonne Jenny quand on [il tape le pied], quand on fait la rythmique.*
Jenny: *Par exemple j'ai filmé beaucoup des pieds pendant des concerts, si c'est un public vazaha/malgache et tu regardes les pieds, c'est jamais pareil.*
Bebey: *Jamais! C'est jamais pareil. Nous, on a notre truc. Et en fait, nous, on a tout le temps des accents sur le 6/8. En fait c'est ce que... elle, elle cherche ça. Et moi, je lui dis 'Tu peux pas faire ça, Jenny' [tout le monde rit] 'Parce que c'est malgache et c'est un esprit en fait.' Et là, elle me tire la langue quand je dis ça. Mais en fait, ça doit être vrai dans quelque part, même Radonné, Donné, on lui a expliqué ça. Et on a appelé l'autre là...*
Jenny: *Fanaiky.*
Bebey: *Fanaiky. Il était là, donc moi, j'ai dit 'Fanaiky, viens ici, fais-moi du 6/8.' Et lui était là et Jenny aussi... en fait Donné, Fanaiky et moi, quand on fait le 6/8, on a toujours le même...*
Papay: *Tempo.*
Bebey: *... Accent. En fait, c'est des accents, parce que...*

Jenny: *Non, je crois que, si j'ai bien compris, en fait je crois que c'est pas le 6/8, mais on l'appelle 6/8.*
Bebey: *Nous, on appelle ça 6/8, mais en fait c'est pas du 6/8 en fait.*
Papay: *C'est vraiment bizarre aussi le tempo et puis la façon de compter.*
(Interview Papay and Bebey, 21.7.2008)

Bebey: But the rhythm, every time we say that it's a 6/8, it strikes Jenny, when we [he taps his feet], when we play the rhythm.
Jenny: I have filmed, for example, people tapping feet during concerts and in a *vazaha*/Malagasy audience, if you look at the feet, it is never the same...
Bebey: Never! It is never the same. We, we have our thing. And in fact, we, all the time we have our accents on the 6/8. In fact that's... that's what she is searching for. And I tell her 'You can't do this, Jenny' [everyone laughs] 'Because that's Malagasy, in fact it's an *esprit*.' And then, she sticks her tongue out at me when I say this. But in fact, it must be true, somehow. Even Radonné, Donné, we explained it to him and then we called the other one...
Jenny: Fanaiky.
Bebey: Fanaiky, he was there, so I said 'Fanaiky, come and show me a 6/8.' And he was there and Jenny as well.... in fact Donné, Fanaiky and me, when we play the 6/8, we always have the same...
Papay: Tempo...
Bebey: ... accent. In fact, it's the accents, because...
Jenny: No, I think, if I have understood well, in fact I think it is not a 6/8, but we call it 6/8.
Bebey: We, we call it 6/8, but in fact, it is not a 6/8.
Papay: It is really bizarre, also the tempo and then the way of counting.
(Interview with Papay and Bebey, 21.7.2008)

The discussion with Bebey and Papay is another example of the way many of the musicians engaged in the ethnomusicological research and their perception of themselves as researchers. Many of the musicians have told me that they see a need for this research, as they need to be able to explain their music and foreigners need to be able to understand Malagasy music. This "researching" aspect often appears within the musicians' discourses, reinforced by the absence of a shared indigenous terminology, as well as a certain discomfort with the foreign concept that some musicians resort to. Rajery, for example, explains that he is still not sure how to define in technical terms what he calls the "Malagasy rhythmic symbiosis." He expresses a need to find an answer to this, as well as the discomfort he feels when using technical terms such as "6/8" or "12/8 rhythm:"

La symbiose rythmique malgache ! Moi, je pose aussi la question, pour le moment, est-ce que c'est le 6/8 ou le 12/8? Donc, nous, on continue, quelle est la différence exactement et quelle est la particularité du 12/8 malgache par rapport au 12/8 européen? Quelle est la particularité de 12/8 malgache au rapport aux africains? Donc, c'est toute une recherche. Ça se dit pas comme ça! Moi, je pense, donc, je fais attention à tout ce que je dis, parce que c'est vraiment, c'est très très musical, très technique. Donc, il faut faire attention [il rit]. On peut pas dire, c'est comme ça le rythme malgache. On peut pas dire ça, parce que des fois ça varie d'une région à l'autre. (Interview Rajery, 17.12.2007)

The Malagasy rhythmic symbiosis! Me, at the moment I also ask the question, is it the 6/8 or the 12/8? So we go on, what is exactly the difference and what is the particularity of the Malagasy 12/8 in comparison to the European 12/8? What is the particularity of the Malagasy 12/8 in comparison to the Africans? That's quite a research. You can't just say it like this! I think, I am really careful with everything I am saying, because it's really, it's very very musical, very technical. You have to be careful [he laughs]. You can't say the Malagasy rhythm is like this. You can't say that, because it varies from one region to the other. (Interview Rajery, 17.12.2007)

Terminological Confusion

All examples that I have analysed not only show how the concept of "6/8 rhythm" is used in many different ways by the musicians but also how their different uses and understandings lead to even more terminological confusion. This implies not only confusion around the specific concept of "6/8 rhythm," but also around "rhythm" and other terms related to music. I will demonstrate this argument in more detail with the following example.

Example *Salegy*

Salegy music is one of the Malagasy musical styles most represented on the international music market. As mentioned above, the best-known representative of it is probably Jaojoby. As music journalist Banning Eyre writes in his article on *salegy* music in the "froots magazine," Jaojoby performed his first international show in Paris in 1989. His album *Salegy!*, produced by Ben Mandelson for the label Rogue, was recorded in Madagascar in 1992. It was first released in Europe and then later licensed to Xenophile in the US (Eyre 2002: 41). Eyre describes *salegy* music as follows:

Salegy is rowdy, 6/8, electric pop music from Madagascar's north east coast, far from the hubbub of Tana… These days, *salegy* has more or less arrived as the national dance-pop music (Eyre 2002: 40).

This short extract already includes some of the confusing and contentious issues within the musicians' discourses on *salegy* that I will analyse. First, Eyre describes *salegy* as a "6/8 rhythm." The majority of the musicians agree with this, using the term themselves. However, there is also some confusion, as *salegy* is itself often used as a synonym for "6/8 rhythm" by some musicians. Second, Eyre also describes *salegy* as a musical style. Within the discourses of the musicians, the term *salegy* is also used differently and is more specific; it can for example be used to refer to a dance or a rhythm. Third, Eyre writes on the one hand that *salegy* is related to the Northern region of Madagascar; on the other hand he describes it as "the national dance-pop music." To what extent *salegy* represents Madagascar at the national level is another controversial issue discussed by the musicians. This issue relates to the origin, history and development of *salegy*.

Jaojoby explains that the word *salegy* did not exist until the 19th Century. When thinking of *salegy*, he argues, one needs to think of "Malagasy folklore in a 6/8 metre that is accompanied by instruments coming from the Occident." Based on this definition, he explains that it was with the arrival of the accordion in Madagascar that *salegy* really assumed its current form. The origin of *salegy* can be found in traditional songs across the island, as well as in 6/8 metre, that previously went by names referring to the different regions and ethnic groups of the island:

On n'a pas parlé du mot salegy avant le 19ième siècle. Quand on parle salegy, il faut avoir dans la tête: folklore malgache, à la mesure 6/8, accompagné par des instruments venus de l'Occident. On a commencé de parler du mot salegy dans le 19ième siècle quand l'accordéon était arrivé ici. Moi, je n'étais pas là. Donc, quand le musicien malgache là, il joue de l'accordéon, il a essayé de jouer son folklore avec et là le mot salegy est né. Parce qu'avant l'arrivée de l'accordéon… eh ben, les Malgaches, ils jouaient a capella. Ils battaient des mains ou il y avait des tambours, cithare tubulaire là, valiha, à l'époque on ne parlait pas encore du salegy. On avait l'habitude de dire "chant Sakalava" ou bien "osiky Tsimihety", "hira Betsimisaraka" ou "hira Merina". On appelait comme ça. Mais depuis l'accordéon est venu dans le 19ième siècle donc, on a commencé à entendre le mot salegy. (Interview Jaojoby, 21.8.2008)

We didn't speak of the word *salegy* before the 19th century. When you speak of *salegy*, you need to think: Malagasy folklore, in a 6/8 metre, accompanied by instruments that come from the West. We started to use the word *salegy* in the 19th century when the accordion arrived here. I wasn't there. So, when the musicians at the time played the accordion, they tried to play their folklore with it and that's where the word *salegy* was born. Because before the arrival of the accordion... well, the Malagasies, they played a capella. They clapped their hands or there were drums, the tube zither *valiha*, at the time you did not speak of the word *salegy*. You would say *"chant Sakalava"* or *"osiky Tsimihety," "hira Betsimisaraka"* or *"hira Merina."* That's how it was called. But when the accordion arrived in the 19th century, you started to hear the word *salegy*. (Interview Jaojoby, 21.8.2008)

In an interview with Jaojoby (conducted by Bernard Terramorsi and Elie Rajaonarison in 1999),[11] he explains that there are also traditional songs that are in a 4/4 metre. He uses *salegy* as a synonym for "6/8 rhythm" by saying that here he is talking about *salegy* only (and not about 4/4 metre). He further explains that in other regions, the word *salegy* is not used and the music is named differently, even if it is exactly the same:

Il y a aussi d'autres rythmes traditionnels, d'autres chants traditionnels à mesure 4/4 par exemple. Mais là, nous parlons de salegy. Par exemple à l'Est, ils l'appellent basesa, mais c'est la même chose bien sûr. Dans le Sud, ils ne l'appellent pas salegy, et pourtant les Vezo de Tuléar, les Antandroy, ils jouent de la musique pareille à celle des ancêtres du salegy, avec le marovany, valiha, accordéon. Ils appellent ça jihé. C'est la même chose. (Jaojoby, quoted in Terramorsi and Rajaonarison 2004: 173)

There are also other traditional rhythms, other traditional songs in a 4/4 metre for example. But here, we speak of *salegy*. In the East, for example, they call it *basesa*, but it's the same of course. In the South, they don't call it *salegy*, and the Vezo from Tuléar, the Antandroy, they play the same music as the ancestors of the *salegy*, with the *marovany*, *valiha*, and accordion. They call it *jihé*. It's the same thing. (Jaojoby, quoted in Terramorsi and Rajaonarison 2004: 173)

In the interview with me he describes *salegy* specifically as a rhythm that is played everywhere in Madagascar. He even goes so far as to call *salegy* the "federal rhythm of all Malagasy people." His argument is that all Malagasy know how to play *salegy*. At the same time, he says that it is

---

[11] The interview was conducted in 1999 in Antananarivo and published in 2004 (Terramorsi and Rajaonarison 2004).

right to claim that *salegy* has its origin in Madagascar's North. For him, *salegy* seems to be both regional and national:

> Jaojoby : *Oui, oui, puisque... je m'excuse... puisque le salegy est vraiment le rythme fédérateur de tous les Malgaches. Tous les Malgaches savent jouer du salegy.*
> Jenny: *Et tous les Malgaches appellent ça salegy ?*
> Jaojoby: *Pas forcément. Mais quand on dit que le salegy ça vient du Nord, c'est aussi vrai !* (Interview Jaojoby, 21.8.2008)

> Jaojoby: Yes, since... I'm sorry... since the *salegy* is really the federal rhythm of all Malagasies. All Malagasies know how to play the *salegy*.
> Jenny: And all Malagasies call it *salegy*?
> Jaojoby: Not necessarily. But if you say that the *salegy* comes from the North, that's true as well! (Interview Jaojoby, 21.8.2008)

Bilo agrees with him on the special role *salegy* holds within Madagascar; he sees *salegy* as the most successful music in Madagascar because of its spread across the island:

> *Oui oui, c'est le salegy qui a voyagé partout à Madagascar, parce que maintenant c'est une musique roi à Madagascar, maintenant sur notre temps, c'est une musique roi à Madagascar.* (Interview Bilo, 19.8.2008)

> Yes, it's the *salegy* that has travelled everywhere in Madagascar, because now it is one of the most successful musics of Madagascar, at our present time, it's the most successful music of Madagascar. (Interview Bilo, 19.8.2008)

Sammy, however, regards *salegy* as something regional, something belonging to the North. Although he does not use the word *salegy* in the context of other regions, he nevertheless explains that the rhythm is everywhere the same. Only the name for it changes:

> *Non, tu sais, le salegy, ça... ça vient d'une région, c'est vrai. Par exemple si tu parles de Mahajanga, le salegy ça vient du Nord quoi. Mais dans le Sud on s'appelle ça tsapiky. C'est la même chose ! Tu vois ? Si tu prends le [il montre][12], tu vois, c'est la même chose ! Tu comprends ce que je veux dire ? Tu prends les Hauts Plateaux, il y a une chose qu'on appelle le vakisaova. Le vakisaova c'est à peu près avec le clap de main, il fait [il montre][13]. C'est toujours comme ça.* (Interview Sammy, 23.11.2007)

---

[12] Sound example 3 on DVD.
[13] Sound example 3 on DVD.

No, you know, the *salegy*, it… it comes from one region, that's true. For example if you speak of Mahajanga, the *salegy* comes from the North. But in the South you call this *tsapiky*. It's the same thing! You see? If you take the [he demonstrates],[14] you see, it's the same thing! Do you understand what I mean? You take the High Plateaux, there is something which is called *vakisaova*. The *vakisaova* it's similar with the hand clapping, it goes [he demonstrates].[15] It's always like this. (Interview Sammy, 23.11.2007)

At first glance, Rajery seems to agree that every region has a similar rhythm, a type of "6/8 rhythm." Talking about one of his current musical projects, he says that he is working with the musical style called *vakodrazana*, "the 6/8 of the High Plateaux" as he calls it. Whereas he first emphasises that *vakodrazana* is not *salegy*, only a little later he also calls it the "*salegy* of the High Plateaux," using *salegy* as a synonym for "6/8 rhythm:"

> *Donc, là, avec le style là, j'ai exploité un peu le style de vakodrazana des Hauts Plateaux. Ça veut dire, c'est à peu près le 6/8 des Hauts Plateaux, c'est pas le salegy… Mais, ça c'est vraiment du 6/8 des Hauts Plateaux, du salegy des Hauts Plateaux en quelque sorte. Parce que chaque région a leur style de salegy.* (Interview Rajery, 17.12.2007)

> Well, with this style here, I have used a bit the style of the *vakodrazana* of the High Plateaux. It means that it is more or less the 6/8 of the High Plateaux, it's not the *salegy*… But, this is really the 6/8 of the High Plateaux, in a way it's the *salegy* of the High Plateaux. Because every region has its style of *salegy*. (Interview Rajery, 17.12.2007)

In another moment, Rajery argues that *salegy* is not a genre of music but a way of dancing. He explains that when *salegy* is understood from a historical perspective, the genre should be called "*antsa;*" "*salegy*" is the way of dancing to it:

> *En fait, ça dépend, déjà, le salegy, c'est pas du genre de musique. L'antsa, c'est ça le genre de musique. Le salegy, c'est une manière de danser, en général. Historiquement, c'est comme ça.* (Interview Rajery, 17.12.2007)

> In fact, it depends, already the *salegy*, it's not a musical genre. *L'antsa*, that's the genre. In general, the *salegy*, that's a way of dancing. Historically, it's like this. (Interview Rajery, 17.12.2007)

---

[14] Sound example 3 on DVD.
[15] Sound example 3 on DVD.

According to Rajery, *antsa* is a musical genre which has its origin in the North-West of Madagascar, where the Sakalava people live. It implies singing and hand-clapping and up to three accompanying instruments, including for example the *kabosy*. A characteristic of this genre is the call-and-response singing. Rajery further talks about an evolution that took place when people started to use the musical genre of *antsa* to animate for dancing: it was then that drum kits and electronic instruments were added and that *salegy* as a dancing style was born.[16]

This is completely contrary to what Bilo says. He argues that *salegy* signifies the rhythm and that there is a special dance that goes along with it, called *kawitchi*. At the same time he explains that although *salegy* is first of all the rhythm, it includes many different things at the same time:

> *Il y a la musique salegy, bon. Si tu écoutes une musique salegy qui est là et tu veux danser, donc, tu danses le kawitchi. C'est la façon de danser le salegy. Donc, le nom de la danse c'est kawitchi ... Mais le salegy, ça reste un rythme, mais dans le salegy là, il y a beaucoup des choses.* (Interview Bilo, 19.8.2008)

> Well, there is the *salegy* music. If you listen to a *salegy* music which is there and you want to dance, you dance the *kawitchi*. That's the way you dance the *salegy*, the name of the dance is *kawitchi*... But the *salegy* stays a rhythm, but within the *salegy*, there are many things. (Interview Bilo, 19.8.2008)

In another part of the interview, Bilo says that *salegy* is in general a song, a traditional song from the North of Madagascar. At the same time, he argues, that many things form part of *salegy*, and that *salegy* is first of all dancing and singing:

> *En fait... le salegy en général c'est une chanson. C'est une chanson traditionnelle du Nord de Madagascar. Donc, dans le salegy, il y a beaucoup des choses. Le salegy veut dire, façon de parler, façon de vivre. La façon de vivre. On vit dans le salegy. Donc, en tant que chanson, il y a des chants, des chants traditionnels, il y a des percussions, il y a de la danse, la danse surtout. Donc, chanter et danser, c'est le salegy.* (Interview Bilo, 19.8.2008)

> In fact... in general the *salegy* is a song. It's a traditional song from the North of Madagascar. So, within the *salegy*, there are many things. The *salegy* is a way of speaking, a way of living. The way of living. We live within the *salegy*. So as a song, there are songs, traditional songs, there is

---

[16] Interview with Rajery, 17.12.2007.

percussion, there is dance, especially dance. So singing and dancing, that's the *salegy*. (Interview Bilo. 19.8.2008)

When I told him that I was often slightly confused by the different ways people use the term *salegy*, he assured me again that *salegy* was only the name of the rhythm:

Bilo: *Oui, les gens utilisent ça dans des sens différents, parce que quand on dit salegy, c'est seulement le rythme. Tu vois ?*
Jenny: *C'est le nom du rythme ?*
Bilo: *Le nom du rythme.* (Interview Bilo, 19.8.2008)

Bilo: Yes, the people use it in different ways, because if you say *salegy*, it's only the rhythm. You see?
Jenny: It's the name of the rhythm?
Bilo: The name of the rhythm. (Interview Bilo, 19.8.2008)

In the same way that I do not aim to find out or judge whether the concept of "6/8 rhythm" suits the Malagasy context, my aim is not to find the right definition of *salegy*. The analysis above of the musicians' discourse on *salegy* shows that the word is used in numerous ways. Musicians often use it, as well, in different and somewhat contradictory ways; they slightly change the usage depending on the context in which they are talking about it, or even depending on the question they have been asked. It also shows, once more, the presence of the concept of "6/8 rhythm" within the musicians' discourses and their search for musical identity. There is no shared understanding or usage of *salegy* as a term among the musicians; the terminological confusion here confirms a more general terminological confusion, one that also applies to "rhythm." Musicians like Bilo and Jaojoby, who are known as *salegy* musicians, and who are fairly successful in the music market, tend to emphasise the representative role of *salegy* as a national music style. To them, *salegy* seems to integrate both usages: the potential of representing Madagascar as a whole combined with an element of regional pride. But other musicians, such as Rajery (himself from the High Plateaux region), say that every region has its style of *salegy*, using it as a synonym for "6/8 rhythm." Others again do not identify with *salegy* in that way and do not use it on this general level, but instead mention it as one of many regional musical styles. Everyone agrees the origin of *salegy* lies in the North of the island. However, musicians feel different towards the role of *salegy* within the country's music scene. The musicians' discourse on *salegy* therefore becomes interesting with regard to identity issues, as it brings together two

major trends: the longing to find a common musical identity and attempts
to manifest the musical diversity of the different regions of the island.

One element that all musicians share is their aim of gaining access and
becoming successful on the international "world music market." Their
discourses on the "6/8 rhythm" here come into play because "rhythm"
seems to be an important part of the musicians' individual experiences and
ideas concerning marketing strategies.

The Challenge of the International "World Music Market" and Musicians' Individual Experiences: Perspectives and Strategies

According to Stoke (2004), with the coining of the term "world music"
in the 1980s a complex discourse emerged that was primarily intended

> to energize and enthuse compact disk (CD) buyers, and is living its own
> unruly life in music journalism... and on the fringes of academia in
> conferences, artist-in-residence programs, concert tours, workshops, and
> academic publications (Stoke 2004: 52).

Exactly because of this complexity in which "the global dimensions of
the local product" are often understood in different ways by different
actors, including record companies, studio technicians and musicians
(Stoke 2004: 53), many scholars have focused on analysing discourses
about "world music" (e.g. Taylor 1997, Frith 2000, Théberge 2003). Stoke
(2004), for example, argues that many musicians who have been labelled
as "world music artists" actually have difficulties with this definition or
even refuse it as a label for themselves (Stoke 2004: 52)—an experience
shared by some of the Malagasy musicians.

It is beyond the scope of this book to go into much detail about studies
of "world music" discourses.[17] What scholars identify as key notions
within the discourses on "world music"—"authenticity, roots, hybridity,
and the local" (Stoke 2004: 59; see also Taylor 1997)—also appear in the
musicians' individual perspectives on how to best access the international
market. The notions of "authenticity" and "hybridity" at first glance seem
to be opponents, but the situation, especially from a discursive point of

---

[17] For further reading on this topic see Taylor (1997), Frith (2000), Bohlman
(2002), Théberge (2003) and Stoke (2004).

view, is much more complex; the two terms are often complexly entangled (Stoke 2004: 59).[18] This also manifests in the musicians' own experiences.

All musicians agree that Malagasy music has not yet been really successful on the international music market. However, they differ in their opinions on why this is the case and how it could be changed. Again, "rhythm" seems to play a crucial role in the musicians' ideas and suggestions. The lack of proper international success for Malagasy music is a topic that regularly comes up; musicians reflect often upon the reasons for it. Here, the research context is important as well. As already discussed in chapter 1, some musicians are likely to have seen in me a potential helper in gaining access to the Western music market, a fact that I must take into consideration in my analysis of the musicians' discourses about this particular topic.

Two major trends appear within the musicians' discourses. First, that most musicians still see an obstacle in their inability to properly explain their music to a foreign audience. They argue that Malagasy music would be much more successful and internationally appreciated once it becomes more accessible and understandable for foreign audiences. Second, other musicians take the contrary view; they think it is actually an asset for the marketing of Malagasy music that it is difficult for foreigners to understand and play the music. They argue this creates curiosity and some sense of "exoticism." In both cases, "rhythm" seems to be the central theme. Whereas in the first trend musicians describe "rhythm" as the element in need of proper explanation to make it accessible to the outside world, the others see an advantage in the confusion that it creates. Another important argument and contentious issue concerns the actual musical sound and the arrangements and compositions. Some musicians argue that it is important to open up musically to the foreign world and integrate non-Malagasy musical elements and styles to approach foreign audiences and create an interest in Malagasy music; others argue that it is more important to make Malagasy music as "pure" as possible. In the following, I will analyse some of the musicians' arguments in more detail. Again, I will focus on identity issues, including the musicians' perceptions of "Self" and "Other" in this context.

Most musicians see a great marketing potential in Malagasy rhythm and at the same time the need to make it accessible for the international public. Sammy, for example, highlights the importance of rhythm to make people dance. He draws a comparison with the music of African stars,

---

[18] Frith (2000) even goes so far as to say that in world music circles hybridity is "the new authenticity" (Frith 2000: 312).

such as Baaba Maal, and says that he tries to change the Malagasy rhythm in the way these musicians do so that his own music is danceable as well:

> *Mais là, on a changé un peu le rythme des fois comme Youssour N'Dour, Baaba Maal et les autres là qu'on arrive à danser avec. Mais si tu écoutes vraiment comment ils font, (il rit) waouh ! C'est dur ! Et là, dans la musique malgache, moi je fais ça aussi. J'essaie de le trouver.* (Interview Sammy, 23.11.2007)

> But here, we have changed the rhythm a bit like Youssour N'Dour, Baaba Maal and the others with whom you can dance. But if you really listen to how they are doing it [he laughs] wow! That's difficult! And in Malagasy music, I do this as well. I'm trying to find it. (Interview Sammy, 23.11.2007)

The comparison to African music stars is interesting because of the tendency—especially in the High Plateaux region where most of the musicians (including Sammy), come from—to emphasise that they are *not* African, but Malagasy. I have mentioned this conflict between the High Plateaux people and the Côtiers already in chapter 2. For Sammy, the challenges of the international music market actually seem to create or encourage a certain collective African identity among musicians.

The relation of Malagasy music to African music is also an issue that comes up in the following examples. Jean-Claude and Ricky compare the rhythm in Madagascar with a precious stone that has not yet been polished to make it attractive on the market. Two arguments shine through in this metaphor: first, they see an immense potential in Malagasy music, particularly in rhythm that has not yet been properly utilised; second, a certain adaptation of Malagasy music is necessary in order to spark interest in Malagasy music:

> Ricky: *C'est quoi l'histoire du rythme à Madagascar ? Peut-être c'est à cause de ça qu'on est bloqué par rapport aux Maliens, aux Sénégalais, aux Brésiliens...*
> Jean-Claude: *C'est peut-être ça effectivement que... une fois on m'a demandé, mais pourquoi la musique malgache a du mal à sortir? Parce qu'elle trop riche mais attends, qu'est-ce que tu racontes, elle est trop riche? [Tout le monde rit].*
> Ricky: *C'est peut-être ça.*
> Jean-Claude: *Tu vois, tu prends une pierre précieuse dans la terre, il y en a beaucoup ici à Madagascar. Exemple, prends une pierre, il y a plein de bouts, c'est cassé de partout, il y a des trucs, mais c'est une pierre précieuse. C'est un peu comme le cas de l'émeraude de 550 kilos qui est sortie de Madagascar. Une pierre précieuse. Alors, on va au marché, on*

trouve des gens qui achètent des bijoux et ils, eux ils voient ça, oh la la, il y a pleins de bouts, c'est mal foutu, j'achète pas. Alors que là on peut faire des milliers bijoux. Alors, la musique malgache elle est comme ça. Le rythme malgache. Il faut la prendre et puis la tailler pour que les gens puissent la prendre. (Interview Ricky and Jean-Claude, 18.7.2008)

Ricky: What is the history of rhythm in Madagascar? Maybe that's why we are stuck in comparison to the Malians, the Senegalese, the Brazilians…
Jean-Claude: Maybe that's it, indeed…once I was asked, why does Malagasy music have difficulties to get out there? Because it is too rich, but wait, what do you mean, it's too rich? [Everyone laughs].
Ricky: Maybe that's it.
Jean-Claude: You see, you take a precious stone from the earth, there are many here in Madagascar. For example, take a stone, there are many bits and pieces, it's completely broken, there are bits, but it's still a precious stone. It's a bit like the 550kg emerald that was found in Madagascar. A precious stone. So we go to the market, we find people who buy jewellery and they, oh la la, there are plenty of bits and pieces, it's a mess, I don't buy it. Even though you could make thousands of jewellery pieces with it. Well, Malagasy music is like that. The Malagasy rhythm. You need to take it and then cut it so that the people appreciate it. (Interview Ricky and Jean-Claude, 18.7.2008)

Whereas here, Jean-Claude draws a clear distinction between Malagasy and African music, describing them as in competition, he later considers Malagasy rhythm an African rhythm, although he hesitates to do so. He explains that he thinks that Europeans have not yet understood that rhythm is the most important element in African and Malagasy musics. He concludes that if African rhythm or Malagasy rhythm had melodies as beautiful as the Beatles, they would be much more successful:

Parce que pour l'instant en Europe peut-être on n'a pas encore compris ça. Mais une fois ça va.... Le rythme en Afrique c'est ce qui est le plus important, c'est très très riche. Si le rythme africain, malgache... bon, c'est africain, avait des mélodies aussi belles que les Beatles et les autres... c'est ici que ça va se passer la musique. C'est simplement la mélodie à mettre sur ce rythme. Et voilà... tout est ouvert. (Interview Jean-Claude, 18.7.2008)

Maybe in Europe for the time being we have not yet understood this. But once it works…the rhythm in Africa, that's what is most important, it's very, very rich. If the African, Malagasy rhythm… well, it's African, had as beautiful melodies as the Beatles and others… music would be happening here. It's only about putting the melody onto that rhythm. And there we go…everything is open. (Interview Jean-Claude, 18.7.2008)

Papay has a similar idea of the need to adapt Malagasy music to some extent for an international audience. In the 1990s he founded a group called "Sivy Mahasaky" ("the nine who dare"), bringing together three jazz musicians, three rock musicians and three *mpihira gasy*. Papay explains that despite the group's success within Madagascar, it did not exist for very long due to a lack of financial support. The initial idea of the group was to fuse different musical styles and thereby add something to Malagasy music to give it a more powerful sound. In contrast to most other musicians, Papay speaks of "the monotony" of Malagasy rhythm; he regards it as an obstacle, as something that needs to be changed in order to make the music more successful:

Papay: *J'ai imaginé pourquoi la musique malgache ça n'arrive jamais à percer...*
Jenny: *Sortir vraiment?*
Papay: *De faire du showbiz vraiment coûteux quoi. Peut-être c'est à cause de cette monotonie, parce que des gens, il y a des gens qui aiment le coté de la bonne mélodie. Et il y a des gens qui aiment bien... comment ça... des chorus ou bien c'est comme ça. Et peut-être à cause de cette monotonie ... J'ai espéré avant avec Sivy Mahasaky... J'ai entendu beaucoup de musique malgache et ça m'a beaucoup plu. Mais ce que j'ai remarqué c'est qu'il manque du punch. Ça veut dire que les vakisaova et le hira gasy font...*
Bebey: *Voilà, cette pêche! C'est vrai ce qu'il dit!*
Papay: *Et c'est pour cela que j'ai essayé de regrouper ces gens de hira gasy, les vakodrazana, bon parce qu'il y a des gens qui font la musique malgache à leur façon, c'est pas mal. Mais ce qu'ils leur manquent, c'est la pêche quoi!* (Interview Papay and Bebey, 21.7.2008)

Papay: I have thought about why Malagasy music never manages to break through...
Jenny: To really get out there?
Papay: To make proper expensive showbiz. Maybe it's because of this monotony, because people, there are some people who like the melodic side in music. And there are people who like...what can I say... choruses or things like that. And maybe it's because of that monotony... Before I had hopes with Sivy Mahasaky... I've listened a lot to Malagasy music and I really liked it. But what I realised is that there is some energy missing. I mean what the *vakisaova* and the *hira gasy* do...
Bebey: Here we go, that energy! It's true what he is saying!
Papay: And that is why I have tried to group together *hira gasy* and Vakodrazana people, well, because there are people who play Malagasy music in their own way, that's not bad. But what they are missing is the energy! (Interview Papay and Bebey, 21.7.2008)

Bebey, who also participated in my interview with Papay, knows the group "Sivy Mahasaky" and had by then heard them play. He sees a great marketing potential in such a group, exactly because of their approach of fusing Malagasy music with musical styles like jazz and rock. He argues that international audiences would immediately get something out of this music and understand something as the music has something "of theirs" as well:

> *En fait c'est ça qui doit se vendre en plus et ça c'était une bonne idée. Ça, ça doit être... Tu sais, quand les gens vont regarder ça dans un festival en Allemagne, ils vont comprendre quelque chose. Ils sont pas... ils font pas cet effort de comprendre. Ils vont tout de suite comprendre, parce qu'il y a un peu de 'leurs' dans le truc.* (Interview Papay and Bebey, 21.7.2008)

> In fact that's what should really work and that was a good idea. This must be... you know, when the people watch this at a festival in Germany, they will understand something. They are not... they don't have to make an effort to understand. They will immediately understand, because there is something of 'theirs' in this thing. (Interview Papay and Bebey, 21.7.2008)

A similar idea inspired one of Erick Manana's musical projects in which I participated as a violinist and to which I will return in chapter 6. By arranging standard jazz tunes such as Louis Armstrong's "All of me," in a Malagasy version, Manana hoped to spark interest in Malagasy music. He argues that although the Malagasy rhythm becomes the basis for the song, it still appeals to a wider public because it retains elements familiar to each listener.[19]

In contrast to these examples, Jaojoby does not see any need to adapt Malagasy music or make it more accessible for an international audience. Rather, he advises Malagasy musicians to make Malagasy music as "purely" as possible because this is what is expected and appreciated:

> *D'ailleurs, je conseille toujours ceci à mes collègues malgaches: 'si vous voulez percer, il faut faire gasy-gasy, malgacho-malgache,' parce que c'est ce que le reste du monde aime, c'est ça qu'il attend des artistes malgaches.* (Jaojoby, cited in Terramorsi and Rajaonarison 2004: 185)

> Besides, I always advice my Malagasy colleagues the following: 'if you want to break through, you need to make it *gasy-gasy*, as Malagasy as you can,' because that's what the rest of the world likes, that's what they

---

[19] Discussion with Erick Manana, 20.12.2009.

expect from the Malagasy artists. (Jaojoby, cited in Terramorsi and Rajaonarison 2004: 185)

When he was asked about advice for younger musicians in Antananarivo who dream of going to Europe, he also emphasised the importance of making one's own music, i.e. Malagasy music:

> *Eh bien, je leur ai toujours conseillé: 'Faites la musique malagasy, faites-la bien, ça sera votre passeport, votre billet d'avion.'* (Jaojoby, cited in Terramorsi and Rajaonarison 2004: 187)

> Well, I always advise them: 'make Malagasy music, make it well, that will be your passport, your flight ticket.' (Jaojoby, cited in Terramorsi and Rajaonarison 2004: 187)

This was already true for him in the 1970s in Madagascar. In an interview with *Froots* journalist Banning Eyre, Jaojoby recalls how at the time he had performed with his group "Players" and how they had adopted other African rhythms into Malagasy rhythms:

> We made more African and Malagasy rhythms: *kwassa-kwassa*, *sigoma*, and also rhythms from the Indian Ocean, like *sega*. We played most of the African rhythms, but we made them Malagasy (Jaojoby, cited in: Eyre 2002: 41).

Jazz saxophone player Seta (alias Seta Ramaroson) is one of the few musicians reading and writing music and also gives music classes and teaches musical notation in Antananarivo. He is convinced that transcription is the way to make Malagasy music approachable and accessible for foreign people. He gives the example of Salsa music, which has become particularly popular through different means: the spread of Salsa dancing classes and parties as well as Salsa music books and music scores. As Seta puts it, Salsa music has become reproducible and approachable to foreign people.[20]

Seta's idea that transcription holds the key for international success becomes especially interesting with regard to the musicians' emphasis on the *lova-tsofina*. This will be the focus of the next chapter, in which I will analyse the musicians' own theories and ideas about the origin and meaning of "rhythm" in Madagascar. As I have followed the *lova-tsofina* myself, I will also come back to the issue of transcribing music in chapter 6. There, I will also analyse my own experiences with "rhythm," gained

---

[20] Interview Seta, 22.7.2008.

through both the analysis of discourses and of musical practices, explaining how these experiences relate to the concept of "6/8 rhythm."

Conclusion

The central presence of the Western concept of "6/8 rhythm" in the idea of musical notation within the musicians' discourses raises questions. At first glance it seems contradictory, especially as the musicians emphasise the importance of oral tradition and the concept of *lova-tsofina* for Malagasy music. However, I have argued that instead of studying seemingly contradictory discourses and trying to judge what seems right or wrong, it is useful to look at when, how and in what circumstances individual musicians make use of this concept. Therefore, I looked at the particular research context and have given examples of circumstances that have definitely influenced the use of this foreign concept, such as the musicians' bond to the capital Antananarivo, with its role as "cultural hub" and its cultural infrastructure, as well as the musicians' aim of reaching the international world music market and the usage of the language French, all of these aspects being interrelated and interdependent.

The usage and understanding of the concept of "6/8 rhythm" varies amongst the musicians; contestation and terminological confusion occurs. I have therefore analysed the musicians' *individual* uses and understandings, looking at different parts of discourse in which "6/8 rhythm" seems to play a significant role for musicians whereas some use the term without reflecting further on it, others use it but call it a foreign concept, often declaring it inappropriate for Malagasy music. Some argue that it is non-Malagasy people, especially "music theorists," who use this concept to describe Malagasy rhythm. These two trends—on the one hand the musicians who accept the concept and on the other those who distance themselves from it—clearly point at the terminological confusion around the "6/8 rhythm" and around "rhythm" and musical terminology in general within the musicians' discourses. This also becomes clear in my example of the discourses on *salegy* music and "6/8 rhythm:" e.g. there is discord among the musicians about whether *salegy* defines a musical style, a dance or a rhythm. Further, whereas some musicians use the word *salegy* as a synonym for "6/8 rhythm," often seeing the *salegy* as important at the national level, others emphasise its regional bond to the North-East of Madagascar.

The concept of "6/8 rhythm" furthermore plays a significant role in the musicians' discourses about their strategies to reach the international world music market. Again, musicians' opinions and experiences vary, with two major trends coming to the fore. Some musicians see a need to improve their ability to explain their music to foreign audiences; here, many also argue that it is useful to integrate foreign musical elements into their music, so that it becomes easier for non-Malagasy people to understand and identify with the music. Others, though, see more potential in the confusion that rhythm in Malagasy music creates for international audiences; they say that playing the music "as Malagasy as possible" would make it more interesting and "exotic" for foreign listeners.

The next chapter will focus on the seeming counterpart of the "6/8 rhythm," the musicians' experiences of the *lova-tsofina* that shine through in their discourses on the origin and meaning of "rhythm" in Madagascar.

CHAPTER FIVE

EXPLORING THE *LOVA-TSOFINA*:
MUSICIAN'S THEORIES ON THE ORIGIN
AND MEANING OF "RHYTHM"
IN MALAGASY MUSIC

Introduction

The previous chapter has shown that, although the concept of "6/8 rhythm" is used constantly by the majority of Malagasy musicians, individual understandings and uses of it vary a great deal. Whereas in its original Western context the concept of "6/8 rhythm" is based on the idea of musical notation and understood as a means to measure music, in the Malagasy context it takes on very different meanings. Musicians—directly and indirectly—emphasise its relation to the indigenous concept of oral transmission, the *lova-tsofina*. With only one or two exceptions, all the musicians I worked with are autodidacts who neither read nor write music. Although some regret the lack of institutional infrastructure for music education in Madagascar, most musicians explain with pride and confidence that their "music schools" are the streets of their home villages and cities, the radio, or musicking neighbours, friends and relatives. This side of their musical lives is evident in songs dedicated to and glorifying these persons or places.[1]

This chapter now takes a closer look at the *lova-tsofina* by analysing the diverse discourses of the Malagasy musicians on the origin and meaning of "rhythm" in their country's music. It follows on from the previous chapter to investigate how identity is constructed through the

---

[1] For example: Erick Manana composed the song "*O Rakoto*" as a tribute to the legendary flute player Rakoto Frah with whom he played for many years. He also composed his own Malagasy version of the song "Crying in the rain," called "*Tamboho*," telling the story of a small wall in Antananarivo where he used to sit with his musician friends in the 1970s as they composed their very first songs.

musicians' discourses about the meaning and origin of "rhythm" in Madagascar. "Rhythm" is explained, understood and experienced in many ways that touch upon different *topoi*, such as the country's natural environment and Malagasy everyday life. All of these *topoi* are interrelated; almost all of them are also deeply rooted within Madagascar itself. References concerning the meaning of "rhythm" or its origin always point to the "land of the ancestors" and rarely mention influences from outside the island.

This interplay establishes the kinds of question this chapter can answer. How and through what kind of images or metaphors do the musicians create their ideas of what is typically "Malagasy"? What kind of characteristics and symbols do they use to depict their nation or their own communities, even if it is an "imagined community" (Anderson 1991) of some sort?

The analysis of the musicians' discourses will show that ideas of being similar or dissimilar, as well as the general debate on sameness and difference appear as persistent topics. However, there are different geographic levels at which this is expressed: Madagascar versus the Western world; Madagascar versus African mainland; or High Plateaux region versus coastal regions.

The Importance of Listening to the Musicians' Own Concepts

In chapter 3, I argued for the importance of listening to the musicians' own concepts and ideas of music and musicking, with regard to Agawu's "presumption of sameness" (Agawu 2003): In order to avoid merely relying on prevalent Western analytical discourses on music and music-making, we need to listen carefully to and fully integrate the voices of the people we work with.

The discourses about the origin and meaning of "rhythm" analysed in the following all relate to the musicians' ideas and understandings of the indigenous concept of oral transmission, the *lova-tsofina*. Even if the concept of "6/8 rhythm" appears in the discourses analysed below, the use of this particular term is not the focus of this chapter. However, some arguments from the previous chapter remain relevant for this chapter's analyses, including the importance of the particular research context, my double role as a researcher and (Western trained) musician, or the musicians' aim to reach the international "world music market."

The *Topoi*

In order to investigate the different ways in which the musicians conceptualise the origin and meaning of "rhythm," I have searched for recurring *topoi* in their discourses. The division into different fields may seem artificial at some points; all the *topoi* involved are interrelated. However, a framework is needed to systematise the enormous range of perspectives and the constant debate on unity and diversity (or sameness and difference). Organising this around subject areas will produce the clearest presentation.

There are two dominant *topoi* within the musicians' discourses on "rhythm." First is that of the environment, including such aspects as the actual physical environment of the island, the peoples' orientation and movements within it, or their association with and sensibility towards the environment. This includes their treatment of animals, especially of the all-important *zebu* cows that play a central role in Malagasy culture. This *topos* of the environment is closely related to another very prominent theme, that of everyday life and its constitutive activities, such as working, eating and walking. Activities such as speaking and singing link up with another important *topos:* that of the Malagasy language. Many musicians see a close relation between several aspects of the country's language and "rhythm." Musicians also express ideas about moving, often related to dance, mentioning the styles of dancing, its developments and inspirations for choreographies. Yet another *topos* is that of emotions, or of spiritual ideas that some musicians have towards "rhythm." It embraces the personal views and feelings likely to be most personal to the musicians. As mentioned above, almost all the musicians' ideas are rooted in Malagasy culture and come from within the borders of the island. There are, however, a few musicians who mention influences from outside, especially as regards the origin or history of the "Malagasy rhythm."

The concept of "rhythm" is highly contested, as we have seen in chapters 2 and 4 and will also see in the musicians' discourses discussed below. I will primarily analyse the musicians' perspectives on the origin and meaning of "rhythm." However, there isn't a strictly defined concept of "rhythm" so, I will also include broader ideas and reflections, including some related to music more generally.

Environment

Considering the vast body of literature on Madagascar's nature and various discourses glorifying the island's flora and fauna—in tourism adverts and TV documentaries, most obviously—it might not be completely surprising that the environment has turned out to be so important within the musicians' discourses. Environmental topics often appear in the musicians' self-presentation on stage. The need for environmental awareness is something musicians talk about when they present their country of origin and their music to foreign audiences, as the example of the "Voajanahary" project by Dama Mahaleo and Ricky given in chapter 1 shows.

With regard to "rhythm," there is a strikingly broad range of environmental aspects the musicians reflect upon. They talk about the geographical environment, as it appears in landscape or climate; they mention people's attitudes towards the environment, such as their relationship with particular animals or their knowledge of particular natural phenomena; and they reflect upon people's movements and orientation within the environment, including in relation to both cosmic structures and local infrastructure.

The interconnectedness of environment and music has been mentioned and researched in other parts of the world, as in Zemp's work with the Are'are people on the Solomon Islands (Zemp 1978, 1979). There is also Turnbull (1965), who lived and worked with the Mbuti "Forest people" in former Zaire, and Feld (1981), who conducted research on the Kaluli people in New Guinea. The latter writes about the particular connection between environment and rhythmical aspects in the music of the Kaluli people. Although melody in the verbalisation of Kaluli theory on music is more prominent than temporal aspects, they use terms deriving from water movements as part of their musical terminology for pacing (Feld 1981:32-33).

One connection often drawn by the Malagasy musicians is between the materiality of the musical instruments and the environment which provides the raw material. There are for example different types of the Malagasy zither, the *valiha*. While the *valiha* in the High Plateaux region is built out of a long bamboo with the strings attached all around it, bamboo does not grow in the South of Madagascar. There is a different type of *valiha*—the *marovany*—there, which is constructed of a wooden (or sometimes metal) box with strings attached to each side of it. The *lokanga bara*, a type of violin played among the Bara people living in the South of the island, has strings made out of vegetable fibre or goats' gut.[2] It seems sensible to think the material, or the way of playing an instrument, has an effect on

---

[2] For a further detailed description of Malagasy instruments, see Randrianary (2001): 109-114.

the sound of the music. Many Malagasy musicians even argue that the playing style, which is related to the way an instrument is built, also relates particularly to "rhythm." This is something I will explain further in the next chapter, as this is also an experience that I have had myself.

The majority of musicians share the idea of a rhythmic base that is present everywhere on the island. However, what they call it and how they refer to it varies greatly (as covered in the previous chapter). This basic assumption is also present in their ideas about environment and rhythm. The persistent discourses about sameness and difference that I discussed earlier also come through clearly as part of this theme, as the following examples will show. Difference and sameness are negotiated within Madagascar, as for instance between different ethnic groups or the long-established often critical attitude towards people from the High Plateaux and people from the Coast, as well as between Madagascar and the outside world, especially the Western industrial countries.

Jean-Claude, for instance, regards the environment as the reason for the Malagasy 6/8 rhythm's specific character when compared with the same rhythm played outside Madagascar, especially in jazz music:

C'est l'environnement, parce que le 6/8 on le retrouve aussi dans le jazz des Etats-Unis, Miles Davis, il le fait depuis depuis, tous les grands du jazz, Hendrix, Carlos Santana fait du 6/8 jusqu'à aujourd'hui. Mais leur vision, c'est différente aux Malgaches, et c'est l'environnement à Madagascar qui fait que le 6/8 est particulier et c'est ce qu'il fait qu'un type comme Santana qui est un maître du 6/8 s'en rêve de venir ici. (Interview Jean-Claude, 18.7.2008)

It's the environment, because you can also find the 6/8 in American jazz, Miles Davis, he's been playing it ever since, all the big stars in jazz, Hendrix, Carlos Santana plays the 6/8 until today. But their vision is different to that of the Malagasies, and it is the environment in Madagascar which makes the 6/8 specific and makes that a guy like Santana, who is a master of the 6/8, dreams of coming here. (Interview Jean-Claude, 18.7.2008)

Others emphasise instead regional differences in Madagascar that the environment creates with regard to music and rhythm. Sammy, for example, is convinced that the rhythm in Madagascar is unique and compares its different appearances with a chameleon:

Mais ça vient de Madagascar. C'est-à-dire qu'on est dans une île qu'on appelle les Malgaches et comme je t'avais expliqué, ça dépend de chaque région où il est. C'est comme un caméléon. Tombe le caméléon dans une

plante verte, et il sera vert. Quand il sera dans une plante marron, il sera
marron. C'est à dire, ça dépend de la région, de la terre, de son village
natal où il est. Et c'est là qu'il rentre l'inspiration. C'est à cause de la
terre Ça leur donne l'inspiration. (Interview Sammy, 23.11.2007)

But it comes from Madagascar. That means that we are on an island that
we call the Malagasies and as I explained to you, it depends on each region
where it is. It is like a chameleon. If the chameleon falls onto a green plant,
it will become green. If it is on a brown plant, it will become brown. That
means that it depends on the region, on the soil, on its home village, where
it is. And that is where inspiration comes in. It is because of the soil. It
inspires them. (Interview Sammy, 23.11.2007)

On a more concrete level, Ricky and Rakotomavo make a similar
statement. Ricky talks about the same "groove" that exists everywhere in
Madagascar. He argues that the environment determines the people's
sensibility towards the environment, just as it influences their relation to
animals. At the same time he argues that the physical environment also
influences the rhythm of each region and therefore produces different
"grooves." He once explained to me that the distance to the sea or to the
forest makes a big difference to the individual's own sensibility towards
the environment.[3] This example reveals that it is actually not only the
environment that matters but also one's position within it. Ricky not only
speaks about the Southern landscape, vast and monotonous, but also
describes the image of having the *zebu* cows "behind you." He positions
himself as someone from the High Plateaus region; with regard to all the
mountains and stairs, he describes the environment as "quieter" and
"wavy" in comparison to the South. However, despite these differences
within the environment, he claims all Malagasy people share the same
sensibility towards it:

Parce que si c'est Antandroy, par exemple, si un Antandroy joue quelque
chose rythmiquement et mélodie et harmoniquement, c'est pas la même
chose même de Fianarantsoa, juste à côté de Tuléar et Fort Dauphin,
parce que là-bas l'environnement c'est un peu...un peu vaste et grand, tu
vois? Donc, eux ils ont la possibilité de faire des différents rythmes... Et en
même temps de créer quelques mélodies avec les rythmes... Oui, parce que
c'est pas le même groove [il clappe les mains au même temps]. C'est pas
le même groove. Là-bas, tu vois...quand t'as vu des zébus, des trucs comme
ça derrière toi et le rythme ça symbolise les bêtes comme les zébus quoi.
Mais ici c'est plutôt calme et très ondulé. Donc, à mon avis, c'est par
rapport à tous les montagnes, les escaliers, des trucs comme ça... Tous les

---

[3] Interview Ricky, 18.7.2008.

*Malgaches: [il montre].⁴ Et ça, ça fait bouger tout le monde, même...
même groove, même sensibilité. Mais si on va rentrer dans la spécificité
d'environnement, là tu verras que ça c'est plutôt Antanosy, même si eux ils
font de kilalaka, même chose, mais il y a une expression différente par
rapport à la sensibilité et à l'environnement.* (Interview Ricky, 18.7.2008)

Because if an Antandroy, for example, if an Antandroy plays something
rhythmically and melody and harmonically, it is not the same as from
Fianarantsoa, just next to Tuléar and Fort Dauphin. Because there the
environment is a bit...a bit vast and big, you see? So, they have the
possibility to make different rhythms... and at the same time to create
some melodies with the rhythms... Yes, because it is not the same groove
[he claps his hands at the same time]. It's not the same groove. There, you
see...when you watch the zebus, things like that behind you and the
rhythm that symbolises the cattle and the zebus. But here it is rather calm
and very wavy. So, in my opinion, it is in relation to the mountains, the
stairs, things like that... All Malagasy people: [he demonstrates].⁵ And
this, this makes everybody move, same... same groove, same sensibility.
But if we enter into the specificity of the environment, there you see that it
is rather Antanosy, even if they play *kilalaka*, same thing, but there is a
different expression in relation to the sensibility and the environment.
(Interview Ricky, 18.7.2008)

Rakotomavo has a similar view, emphasising that it is a common
phenomenon, even worldwide, for the environment to become the people's
source of inspiration on various levels. He argues that there are therefore
differences from region to region. Ricky likewise compares the High
Plateaux region with the South of the island. He stresses the impact of the
mountains in the High Plateaux region, which make it possible for people
to play with echoes; this then results in both a prevalence of call-and-
response singing forms and the monotonous character of the songs from
the South. He gives a further example of how the relation with animals in
the environment impacts on the music, arguing that even the actual sounds
of them are integrated into the people's songs:

*Et je rentre là, là la région tu sais où ils habitent ces gens ? C'est leur
source d'inspiration, l'environnement. Leur source d'inspiration. Ils
utilisent donc de façon acoustique, l'air d'environnement. Ils construisent
aussi des instruments de cet environnement-là. Donc, ça va dépendre de
l'environnement là. Comme les gens disent, ils aiment des chansons
responsoriales, qui se répondent quoi. Parce que les Hauts Plateaux, c'est*

---

⁴ Sound example 4 on DVD.
⁵ Sound example 4 on DVD.

une région une région avec un relief très accidenté, il y a beaucoup des montagnes. Et ils jouent de l'écho. Il y a un qui commence et le reste qui répondent. Donc, ça c'est l'environnement qui fait ça. Par contre quand tu vas dans le Sud, c'est le bush, il y a la savane, la brousse, c'est plutôt des chansons monotones... Ça dépend de l'environnement quoi. Ça c'est une base connue. Je crois que c'est un peu dans le monde partout quoi. Pour les gens de la forêt, bon, c'est plutôt, dans leurs chansons on entend le gazouillement des oiseaux. (Interview Rakotomavo, 1.8.2008)

And I start there, you know in this region where these people live? It is their source of inspiration, the environment. Their source of inspiration. So they use the climate of the environment acoustically. They also build the instruments from this environment. So it depends on the environment. As the people say, they like responsorial songs, songs that respond to each other. Because the High Plateaux, it is a region with a highly uneven terrain, there are many mountains. And they play echo. There is one who starts and the rest who responds. It's the environment that does that. In contrary, if you go to the South, it is bush, you have the savannah and the bush, and there the songs are rather monotonous... It depends on the environment. It is a base that is very well known. I think it is a bit like everywhere in the world. For the people of the forest, well, it is in their songs that you hear the chirping of the birds. (Interview Rakotomavo, 1.8.2008)

Some of the musicians are also convinced that the environment has an effect on the people's moods and characters, which will then in turn also influence their music and rhythm. Interestingly, comparisons are always drawn between the "Côtiers" and the people of the High Plateaux region. This might have to do with the conflict-ridden relations between the two groups, the result of various historical and political issues (see also chapter 2). The musicians, however, avoid political terms, talking instead about such factors as temperature difference. *Salegy* star Jaojoby assumes that temperature has an impact on people's character and that people from the High Plateaux region are therefore calmer than people from the hotter coastal regions. He neither positions himself specifically as someone from the Coast, nor from the High Plateaux region. However, positioning within the environment again comes through in his description of the long vistas visible from the High Plateaux region—an image I have come across a few times:

Disons que sur les côtes, il fait plus chaud, on est plus... Eh ? [Il rit] Ah oui! Sur les Hauts Plateaux, on est là donc sur les Plateaux, on est plutôt donc dans la méditation. Oui, on regarde loin. Je ne dis pas que c'est vrai, eh ? C'est mon avis quoi [il rit]! (Interview Jaojoby, 21.8.2008)

Let's say that on the Coast it is hotter, and we are more...he? [He laughs]
Oh yes! In the High Plateaux, we are there on the Plateaux, we are rather
into meditation. Yes, you can look far. I don't say that this is right, eh? It's
my opinion [he laughs]! (Interview Jaojoby, 21.8.2008)

Ariry (alias Ariry Andriamoratsiresy) is a choreographer who also works
and gives dancing classes in the Rarihasina Culture Centre in
Antananarivo.[6] He has collaborated on projects with Ricky and travelled
abroad, including to West Africa and France, where he performed and
gave dancing workshops. Ariry, much like Jaojoby, stresses the impact of
temperature. He explains that he has experienced different ways of
learning and of understanding rhythm among people from the Coast and
people from the High Plateaux region:

> *Je sais pas. Peut-être c'est une question de température.... C'est ça. Et je
> me suis demandé que peut-être c'est à cause de... Je sais pas. J'ai pas
> encore fait l'analyse, mais seulement déduction comme ça. Mais peut-être
> il y a un impact à propos de la température, et l'altitude et position du
> soleil. Je sais pas.... Ça donne, ça donne... un impact psychologique et
> fonctionnement intellectuel ou spirituel ou sensationnel surtout. Donc, le
> rythme c'est ça.* (Interview Ariry, 26.7.2008)

I don't know. Maybe it's a matter of temperature... That's it. And I have
asked myself if it was maybe because of this...I don't know. I have not
made an analysis, but just a conclusion like this. But maybe there is an
impact in terms of temperature, and the altitude and position of the sun. I
don't know...this has, this has...an impact on how our brain works and
how we feel. That is rhythm! (Interview Ariry, 26.7.2008)

Self-positioning and the question of orientation and movement within
the environment seem very important to Ariry, as his memories of two of
his journeys abroad clearly show. The first trip was to West Africa, where
he was struggling to understand the rhythm, a difficulty he explains is
closely related to his own habits of orientation, as for instance with regard
to the rhythm of daylight and darkness:

> *Mais quand j'étais en Afrique, Afrique de l'Ouest, il y avait aussi un
> rythme que j'arrive pas à capter. Ils ont un certain... des compositions
> rythmiques, et contretemps que j'arrive même pas à écouter ou entendre.
> Donc, l'explication que moi, je pourrais apporter c'est que... c'est question
> d'orientation, orientation spatiale... A quelle heure le soleil se positionne
> et ce positionnement... c'est par rapport cosmique et spatiale. Ça*

---

[6] For more information on the Rarihasina Cultural Centre, see Fuhr (2006).

engendre pleins des réactions... réactions dans la coordination et dans la réflexion de la personne. (Interview Ariry, 26.7.2008)

But when I was in Africa, West Africa, there was also a rhythm that I didn't get. They have certain... rhythmical compositions, off-beats that I don't even manage to listen to or to hear. So, the explanation that I have come up with... it's a question of orientation, spatial orientation... at what time the sun positions itself and this positioning... this has to do with something cosmic and spatial. This generates many reactions...reactions within the person's coordination and reflection. (Interview Ariry, 26.7.2008)

His second trip was to France; it was again the environmental differences, especially the differences in sunrise and sunset that troubled his sense of rhythm:

Voilà. Parce que le soleil c'est dans le rythme. La fréquence qu'il revient et tout ça. Et quand j'étais en France la première fois en été, j'étais à Montpellier... J'étais désordonné tout de suite quoi. En voyant le soleil à dix heure du soir, j'étais complètement perdu quoi, à l'époque la première fois quand j'ai vu ça, parce que ça trouble mon habitude rythmique, voilà. Et donc, la danse et la musique c'est la déduction et le résultat de tout ça, je pense. (Interview Ariry, 26.7.2008)

Because the sun is in the rhythm. The frequency in which it returns and everything. And when I was in France for the first time in summer, I was in Montpellier... I was immediately confused. Seeing the sun at ten o'clock in the evening, I was completely lost, at the time when I saw this for the first time, because it troubled my rhythmical habit. And so, dance and music is the conclusion and result of all this, I think. (Interview Ariry, 26.7.2008)

In summary, these musicians agree that the environment has an enormous influence on music, particularly rhythm. The range of different aspects that are part of the environment is very diverse; the geographical nature or physical landscape is mentioned as well as peoples' attitude towards the environment they live in. This also includes the people's relation to animals, such as to the all-important *zebu* cows so often mentioned as part of working the land. Animals also appear as metaphors, such as the chameleon's use as representative of the simultaneous unity and diversity of the Malagasy rhythm. Further, the environment is often described as a source of both inspiration and food. Many musicians argue that it also influences people and therefore music-makers because it has an impact on people's characteristics of life style habits. Here, it is interesting to notice that differences between the High Plateaux region and the Coastal regions are most often stressed. This is not, however, expressed in any terms related to politics, but instead through the idea that temperature has an impact on people's mood. For many musicians the question of how one is positioned within the environment plays an important role. This embraces physical positioning, as with the long vistas possible in the High Plateaux region, as well as leading towards an idea of positioning in relation to other people. A debate about sameness and difference persistently informs the musicians' discourses; it takes place on different levels, as musicians make comparisons within Madagascar as well as between Madagascar and the outside, especially the Western world. If compared with the outside world, the "same groove" or Madagascar's common rhythmical base is stressed; within Madagascar, the emphasis lies instead on regional differences seen as responses to the natural environment. The constant shift between in-groups and out-groups is quite a well-known factor in processes of constituting identities. Meinhof and Galasinski, for example, argue that it is through narrativisation in particular that "[w]e position ourselves within and against the spaces and the people whom we see as belonging or not belonging to our own groups" (Meinhof and Galasinski 2005: 102). Whereas some musicians speak from a very personal or individual point of view, as when Ariry talks about his personal experiences while travelling, others speak instead from a wider angle; for instance, they might present their views as those of someone from the capital or the High Plateaux region or even, as simply as those of a Malagasy person. Questions about "who I am" and "who I am not" are constantly touched upon and the interweaving comparisons at and of different levels show that identities are constantly renegotiated in the course of the musicians' discourses.

Everyday Life

Malagasy everyday life cannot really be separated from the *topos* of the environment, as many of the musicians' arguments and ideas clearly show. Many of them state that the environment we live in influences or even determines our everyday activities. It makes an enormous difference, for example, whether a person lives in a city or in the countryside; whether they live in coastal areas near harbours and ships (offering work, trade etc.), and where fishing is important or in very dry and hot savannah-like areas where water is rare. Many musicians argue that in everyday life we accustom ourselves to the environment we live in; it definitely affects aspects of our life, including food, work, our movements and our other habits. The musicians also say it has a strong effect on music, rhythm in particular; they argue that music and rhythm are already present for them in various aspects of everyday life.

The diversity of examples that the musicians give for rhythm being inherent to Malagasy everyday life is astonishing. The majority of the musicians tend to emphasise the inseparability of everyday activities and music. Samy (alias Samuelson Rabenirainy) lives in Antananarivo and in the 1970s was a member of the group "Lolo sy ny tariny" (already mentioned in chapter 2), in which he played the violin. He performs only occasionally, in so-called "cabarets" (smaller concerts, often in restaurants or bars), but is interested in music research. Samy used to work as a journalist for the MBS television.[7] Over many years, he has collected musics from all around the island, gathering a valuable collection of recordings. Samy once explained to me that you can actually hear the "6/8 rhythm" in the jiggling of coins by the little boys who sell sweets on the Avenue de l'Indépendance in Antananarivo.[8] Another example comes from Erick Manana, who has worked for a long time with the famous *sodina* player Rakoto Frah (who died in 2001). In conversation, he told me that when Rakoto Frah was eating, you could actually see him playing the flute and that when watching him play the flute you could easily imagine him eating.[9] I will come back to flutist Rakoto Frah in the next chapter.

There are two symbols or themes that tend to appear more often than others: *zebu* cows and rice, along with the various activities surrounding these two themes. Another connection often drawn by musicians is that rhythm is also inherent in the everyday speaking habits of Malagasy people. In the same conversation mentioned above, Samy also told me that the "6/8 rhythm" could be heard in the bus drivers' shouts to gather people for journeys in Antananarivo.[10] Others persist in stressing the important role singing has in everyday contexts. Bilo for example, explains that singing itself is a "way of living:"

> *Le salegy c'est... comment on dit aussi? C'est la façon de vivre. Tu vois, le salegy c'est la façon de vivre. Donc, on vit avec le salegy... chez nous, tu es heureux, tu chantes. Tu es malheureux, tu chantes. Tu fais ta cuisine, tu*

---

[7] Madagascar Broadcasting System; affiliated with the party Marc Ravalomanana who at the time of writing is still in exile in South Africa. The building of MBS was burned down, destroyed and closed during the riots in 2009 by supporters of Andry Rajoelina.

[8] Conversation with Samy, Antananarivo, December 2007.

[9] Conversation with Erick Manana, Paris, 28.2.2008.

[10] Conversation with Samy, Antananarivo, December 2007.

chantes. Tu chantes toujours le salegy. Donc c'est la façon de vivre. (Interview Bilo, 19.8.2008)

The *salegy* that's... how do you say? It's a way of living. You see, the *salegy* is a way of living. So, we live the *salegy*... for us, if you are happy, you sing. You are upset, you sing. You cook, you sing. You always sing the *salegy*. So it's a way of living. (Interview Bilo, 19.8.2008)

These ideas are grounded in the musicians' assumption that there is a close relation between rhythm and the Malagasy language, as we will see in the next part. The *topos* of dance already appears in the musicians' ideas about everyday life. Although I will discuss this later on as a *topos* in its own right, it shows again how all these *topoi* are in fact interconnected. On a very general level, there are two further assumptions that are shared among some of the musicians. First, that in some way all Malagasy people are musicians and second, that the Malagasy "6/8 rhythm" is a rhythm everyone could easily adapt to and identify with. Sammy for instance is convinced that all Malagasy people are musicians and explains that as soon as someone starts making a rhythm, others immediately join in:

Moi, je dirais que, je dirais vraiment que les Malgaches, ce sont des gens tous musiciens. On est né pour la musique là. Parce que tant que tu vois quelqu'un donner un début du rythme, trrrrr! (Interview Sammy, 23.11.2007)

I would say, I would really say that Malagasies are all musicians. We are born for the music! Because as soon as someone starts playing a rhythm, trrrrr! (Interview Sammy, 23.11.2007)

Samy speaks of the "universality" of Malagasy music and argues it is a music that everyone can easily identify with, not at least because he regards this rhythm as a "synthesis of civilisation," as a metre that "composes itself" in reality:

Tout le monde peut se retrouver dans cette structure musicale. Pour tout le monde, c'est très facile à s'adapter... En réalité cette universalité de cette musique, ce n'est pas une lecture... ethnocentriste comme disent certaines hypothèses. Mais c'est justement le résultat d'une synthèse de civilisation... Parce que c'est un temps qui se compose en réalité qui s'adapte à tous les temps. (Interview Samy, 7.12.2007)

Everyone can identify with this musical structure. It is very easy for everyone to adapt... In reality the universality of this music, it is not an ethnocentric interpretation as certain hypothesis suggest. But it is just the result of a synthesis of civilisation... Because it's a metre composed in reality and that adapts to all other metres. (Interview Samy, 7.12.2007)

He gives further evidence for his idea of the "6/8 rhythm" as a "universal metre," drawing several examples from everyday life. He argues that everything works according to a "biological clock," starting each day with the cockcrow and sunrise. However, most examples for the expression of this "biological clock" he mentions are movements, such as marching, running, or the *zebu* cows pulling the cart:

Oui le 6/8, parce que là je vais t'expliquer un phénomène. La vie des Malgaches là, est réglée par l'horloge biologique. Donc, c'est rattaché intimement à la vie quotidienne. L'horloge malgache, c'est quand le coq chante et le soleil lève la tête, c'est ça. Donc, tout est... Comment on peut dire ça... Tout est régulé par rapport à ce qu'on appelle l'horloge biologique. Donc, c'est au rapport qu'ils sentent, les Malgaches sentent et ce qu'il fait dans la vie quotidienne, c'est l'expression de tout ça. Quand tu entends le 6/8, tu peux utiliser le 6/8 comme la marche, marche militaire... Le 6/8, c'est vraiment ça, même si tu fais le jogging, c'est le 6/8... La marche normalement c'est en 2 ou 4 temps, mais quand tu cours, quand tu... par exemple poursuives les bœufs et tout ça, la charrette, même si tu vois la charrette dans le Sud, quand les zébus tirent la charrette, c'est 6/8. C'est vraiment un temps universel. (Interview Samy, 7.12.2007)

Yes the 6/8, because I will explain a phenomenon to you. The life of the Malagasies, it is regulated by the clock of nature. So, it is intimately affiliated with everyday life. The Malagasy clock; that's when the cock crows or when the sun raises its head, that's it. So everything is... how can I put it... everything is regulated in relation to what we call the clock of nature. It's in relation to what they feel, what the Malagasies feel and what they do in their everyday life, it's an expression of all this. When you hear the 6/8, you can use it for marching, a military march... the 6/8, it's really that; even if you go running, it's the 6/8... Normally the march is in a metre of 2 or 4, but if you run, if you... for example follow the cattle and all this, the cart, even if you see the cart in the South, when the zebus pull the cart, that's 6/8. It is really a universal metre. (Interview Samy, 7.12.2007)

He argues that everything in everyday life is "rhythmacised" and that this rhythm often has a function, such as supporting work or lulling children to sleep. He says therefore that it is related to the tempo of everyday life. People use, play and compose this rhythm that inherits their everyday life, as his example of the Antandroy people shows: even when walking they do not feel or think in a binary rhythm, but the "6/8 rhythm" which is always present and related to their everyday life:

> *Même la façon de marcher, on sent un peu le 6/8. Les Antandroy vont pas marcher 1, 2, 1, 2, 1, 2... c'est un peuple marcheuse si on peut dire [il rit] qui joue des temps composés en marchant quoi. C'est lié, c'est lié vraiment au tempo de la vie, de la vie quotidienne. Même si on fait quelque chose, il y a un chant adapté à ça, si on transporte des pierres par exemple, il y a quelqu'un qui dit 'Alefa!' C'est pour rythmer, conjuguer l'effort en même temps. Et ça se forge petit à petit, cette pratique rituelle en réalité... Même pour bercer les enfants, c'est rythmé par rapport à la... par rapport au chant. C'est rythmé, c'est toujours rythmé, rythmé, rythmé.* (Interview Samy, 24.11.2007)

> Even in the way of walking, you can feel the 6/8 a bit. The Antandroy people wouldn't walk in 1, 2, 1, 2, 1, 2... they are walking people, if one can say so (he laughs) who play metres that are composed while walking. It is related, it is really related to the tempo of life, of everyday life. Even if you do something, there is a song adapted to it, when you transport stones for example, there is someone saying '*Alefa!*' This is to give rhythm and to join forces at the same time. And this ritual practice builds up slowly in reality... Even in order to lull children to sleep, it's rhythmical in relation to... in relation to the singing. It is rhythmical, always rhythmical, rhythmical, rhythmical. (Interview Samy, 7.12.2007)

Jazz saxophonist Seta agrees that Malagasy everyday life is always "rhythmic." He explained to me that this is a big difference to life in Europe, where people lost the rhythm of everyday life to some extent; this, he says, can be seen in the way that modern European trains now make no more noise and therefore are "giving no more rhythm."[11]

Ratovo (alias Ratovonirina Ranaivovololona) is a *valiha* player from Antananarivo who builds instruments himself; he works at the Ministry of Culture and has opened a very small private museum that holds a collection of instruments from across the island. Ratovo shares Samy's idea that rhythm and work are related. He explains that it was common to sing during work to co-ordinate movements, such as moving heavy stones, or create a nice atmosphere. This singing, sometimes even shouting, also created rhythm:

> *Je sais pas, mais d'après qu'on fait des travaux, les travaux dans le champs, il n'y a pas de musique, mais on chante, et en même temps on chante pour arriver pour faire glisser les gros pierres, pour arriver à un*

---

[11] Conversation with Seta, Antananarivo, 22.7.2008.

tel mètre ou pour pousser, pour travailler, ou pour créer... pendant les colonisations ou avant comme ça, il y a un travail d'équipe et dans le travail d'équipe, on chante et on fait des cris pour animer du travail et on crée des chanson comme des esclave... et on crée des rythmes. Parce que les proverbes malgaches, on chante et on chante en même temps dans le travail et on ne sent pas que le travail est très dur et très fort quelque chose comme ça. Et on pouvait avec le chant et le rythme et on arrive à créer une bonne ambiance dans le travail. Et c'est là que naît les rythmes. (Interview Ratovo, 26.7.2008)

I don't know, but then we work, the work on the fields, there is no music, but we sing, and at the same time we sing in order to shift big stones, to make them reach a certain level, or to push, to work, and to create... during colonisation and before this, there was team work and there, they would sing or shout and they created songs like the slaves... and created rhythms. Because there is a Malagasy proverb, you sing and you sing and at the same time during work, you don't feel that the work is very difficult and very hard, something like this. And thanks to the songs and the rhythm you manage to create a nice atmosphere during work. And that's where the rhythms were born. (Interview Ratovo, 26.7.2008)

The claim that rhythm is related to movements features in almost all the musicians' statements regarding everyday life, whether they talk about movements as part of work or about walking and dancing.

Rakotomavo argues that the Malagasy rhythm is formed of a structure of overlapping binaries and ternaries. He calls the ternary structure its "analytical metre" and the binary structure its "synthetic metre." He thinks the "synthetic metre" is based on walking and the "analytical metre" is related to language (we will see this in more detail in the next part). He explains this with an example of the Betsileo region, a region with a dialect he considers very close or perhaps even inseparable from singing:

Là, c'est, je pense bien que c'est très primitif. Qu'est-ce qu'il est basé de ce temps? La marche alors. C'est pas la marche militaire, eh? C'est la marche. Et comme il y a des gens qui font toujours le trajet à pied, ils sont toujours en train de marcher, ils ont toujours ce rythme-là... Là, il faut pas oublier, je reviens à ce que j'ai dit en avant... il faut pas oublier qu'on utilise la langue dans la mélodie. Et les mots dans la langue. Il y a des gens, même quand ils parlent, il y a des régions, je prends l'exemple de la région de Betsileo, quand ils parlent on dirait qu'ils chantent. Ils parlent comme ça [il montre].[12] On dirait qu'ils chantent. Dans la vie courante. Donc, il n'y a pas cette notion de mélodie à part! C'est déjà dans la vie

---

[12] Sound example 5 on DVD.

quotidienne quoi! Même quand ils se parlent, on dirait qu'ils chantent entre eux. (Interview Rakotomavo, 1.8.2008)

Well, it's, I do think that it is very primitive. What is the base of this metre? The walk. It's not the military march, eh? It's the walk. And as there are people who always make their way on foot, they are always walking, they always have this rhythm... Well, you shouldn't forget, I come back to what I said before... you shouldn't forget that we use the language in the melody. And the words in the language. There are people, even when they speak, there are regions, I take the example of the Betsileo region, when they speak you'd say they sing. They speak like this [he demonstrates].[13] You'd say they sing. In actual life. So, there isn't this separate notion of melody! It's already in everyday life! Even when they talk to each other, you'd say they sing to each other. (Interview Rakotomavo, 1.8.2008)

As mentioned above, dance movements also appear in the musicians' ideas about rhythm in everyday life. Interestingly, they often refer to the Malagasy *zebu* cows, which also relate to the other reoccurring theme, namely that of rice. Jaojoby remembers how French tourists once compared *salegy* dance with the movements of *zebu* cows:

Oui, il y avait des Français des années 70, moi j'étais jeune, je jouais dans une boîte de nuit, quand on joue le salegy là, ils arrivent, ils ont plaisanté : 'on va faire la danse de zébus.' C'est un peu comme les zébus qui piétinent la rizière. Ça tourne en rond comme ça le salegy. (Interview Jaojoby, 21.8.2008)

Yes, there were these French people in the 70s, I was young, I played in a night club; when we played the *salegy* there, they came and they were joking: 'we will dance the dance of the *zebus*.' It's a bit like the *zebus* which tramp the rice field. It moves in circles like this, the *salegy*. (Interview Jaojoby, 21.8.2008)

The idea that people copy the *zebu* cows in their movements and their dances is also present in Rakotomavo's example from the Bara region in the South of Madagascar. He explains that it is often movements in everyday life, such as the pounding of rice in the High Plateaux region, that create rhythm. The Bara people are always with their *zebu* cows and in their dances imitate the movements of these animals. He also gives an example from the Vezo people, fishers who live on the Southwest coast of

---

[13] Sound example 5 on DVD.

the island. In their dances, you can easily hear the casting of the fishing net:

> *Non, mais le rythme c'est plutôt à partir de leur condition de vie, ce qu'ils font tous les jours. Tu sais, les gens des Hauts Plateaux, comme ils pilent le riz, comme ils pilent le riz, ils font du riz, et on pile le riz... C'est pas un seul qui va piler ou une seule, c'est trois, quatre. C'est là qu'ils acquièrent de temps en temps ce rythme. Egalement les zébus. Il y a une semaine, deux semaines là, un festival dans le Sud... dans la région d'Isalo, dans la région des Baras. Et comme les Baras ne se séparent jamais des bœuf, leurs danses ce qu'ils font les bœuf quoi. Ils copient ce qu'ils font les bœufs, parce que...qu'est-ce qu'ils font tous les jours? Ils gardent les bœufs, donc ils sont toujours en contact avec ces animaux-là. Ils les gardent, ils observent, ils essaient de copier ce qu'ils font. Qu'est-ce qu'ils font, quand ils dansent, quand ils dansent, les bœufs, ils font comme ça et les danseurs ils font comme ça. Et comme les bœufs donnent des coups de patte, ils font comme ça et c'est ça le karetsaka. Donc, à partir des choses de tous les jours, de ce qu'ils font tous les jours, ils apprennent aussi. A part l'environnement donc, il y a aussi ce qu'ils font tous les jours. C'est leur vie quotidienne, c'est ça. Les Vezo qui sont des grand pêcheurs, c'est le coup de... de fivoy, on appelle ça le fivoy. Et quand ils dansent, tu entends ça toujours dans les danses.* (Interview Rakotomavo, 1.8.2008)

No, but the rhythm it's rather in relation to their life condition, to what they do every day. You know, the people of the High Plateaux, when they pound the rice, when they pound the rice, when they make rice, and you pound rice...it is not one person alone who pounds, it's three, four. That is where they sometimes gain knowledge of rhythm. Likewise the *zebus*. One week or two weeks ago, there was a festival in the South... in the region of Isalo, in the region of the Bara people. And as the Bara people never separate from their cattle, their dances are what the cattle do. They copy what the cattle do, because...what do they do the whole day? They look after the cattle, they are always in contact with these animals. They look after them, they observe, they try to copy what they do. What they do when they dance, when they dance, the cattle, they do like this and the dancers do like this. And as the cattle kick out they do like this and that's the *karetsaka*. So, from the things that they do every day, from what they do every day, they also learn. Beside the environment there is also what they do every day. That's their everyday life. The Vezo people are great fishermen. And it's the hit of the... the *fivoy*, you call this *fivoy*. And when they dance, that is what you hear in their dances. (Interview Rakotomavo, 1.8.2008)

Ariry mentions another everyday activity related to the theme or "symbol" of rice: using feet to dig the rice fields. As people do this work every day, it also gives rhythm:

> Ariry: *Il y a une certaine...une certaine explication et interprétation, quand tu tapes le sol par le pied, ça veut dire quelque chose. Ça veut dire quelque chose dans le rite, dans la tradition, dans le... la vie quotidienne. Par exemple, si jamais tu vas dans la rizière, les formes... les formes de... comment on dit ça ? De bêcher la terre, il y avait pas encore les bêches, les trucs tracteurs comme ça. Mais c'est par les pieds, par des bois. Donc, on utilise les pieds, on tape sur le sol. Donc, c'est cette forme quotidienne que quand ils dansent les gens dans les villages, ça revient automatiquement.*
> Jenny: *Et ça donne aussi déjà...*
> Ariry: *Le rythme, bien sûr. Et c'est automatique, parce que tous les jours, il fait comme ça.* (Interview Ariry, 26.7.2008)

> Ariry: There was a certain… a certain explanation and interpretation, when you stamp the soil with the feet, it means something. It means something within the rite, within the tradition, within the… within everyday life. For example, if ever you go into the rice fields, the ways… the ways to… how can I put it? In order to dig the soil, there were not yet any spades, things like tractors and all this. But it is with the feet, with wood. So, you use the feet to stamp the soil. So, this everyday movement automatically returns when the people dance in the villages.
> Jenny: And this already also gives…
> Ariry: The rhythm, of course. And it's automatically, because every day, they do this. (Interview Ariry, 26.7.2008)

In summary, all musicians share the idea that rhythm is inherent in everyday activities or movements like working, speaking, walking and dancing. Two themes appear often and often in relation to each other: *zebu* cows and rice. Various activities surrounding these two themes are mentioned in relation to rhythm, such as the *zebu* cows pulling the cart or the *zebu* cows ploughing the rice fields. Musicians also give attention to the relation of both themes to the people themselves, noting for example that people imitate the *zebu* cows in their dances and that they need these animals to produce their daily rice.

Except for the examples of the bus drivers shouting in the "6/8 rhythm" and the boys' jiggling coins in Antananarivo's streets, all examples of everyday activities depict life in the countryside. This identification with the rural population of Madagascar is striking as all of the musicians represented in this work live in or come from the capital. Most of them do not work daily on the rice fields, go fishing or have direct contact with *zebu* cows. However, the musicians take these things to be "typically Malagasy" because for the vast majority of Malagasy people these activities are part of a daily routine. Most of the musicians also have family in the countryside; some have even lived in rural areas before moving to Antananarivo, often with the hope of improving their chances of starting a musical career. Therefore, even if they all live in the capital now, many of them have experienced life in the countryside and often retain considerable stores of knowledge about farming, harvesting, fishing and similar activities.

Let us now revisit the debate on sameness and difference. Within the *topos* of everyday life, the musicians tend to emphasise sameness rather than difference, even within Madagascar. Regional differences are mentioned, such as the idea of the Antandroy as "walking people" and the Vezo's close links with fishing. However, these examples are not mentioned in a way that stresses differences. The Malagasy rhythmical structure (whether referred to as 6/8 or not) is understood instead as a unifying element. Musicians describe it as a result of the mixture of cultures and influences present in Madagascar that have formed a synthesis. Similar discourses about musical syntheses and the fusion and mixture of musical styles can also be found in ethnomusicological literature on Madagascar (see for example Schmidhofer 1995 or Harison 2005). Scholars, including Malagasy scholars Rakotomalala (2003) and Randrianary (2001), have also emphasised the close relation of music to everyday life. Some musicians also characterise the rhythmical structure as very flexible; they argue that everyone, including non-Malagasy people, can easily identify with it. I will come back to this argument in the next chapter, when I describe in detail how I personally experience and understand this structure when musicking.

Language

Another *topos* that has been extremely relevant to my own learning and playing of Malagasy music—one I will therefore revisit in the next chapter—is that of the Malagasy language. Most Malagasies, musicians included, stress the fact that they all share the same language, even if it is one with various dialects. The spread of Malagasy throughout the island can be described as a "continuum of dialects (...) with mutual comprehensibility (...) estimated at no less than 60% of the lexicon even at the extreme ends of the continuum" (Rasolofondraosolo and Meinhof 2003: 130).

The idea that all Malagasy people can understand each other wherever they come from is often emphasised by the musicians. Samy, for example, regards language as the foundation of all the common musical structures he identifies in Malagasy musical styles, such as the "6/8 rhythm," polyphony and the call-and-response singing style called *antsa* (already mentioned in the discussion of *salegy* music in the previous chapter).[14] Bilo also emphasises the fact that they all share one official language and even concludes that Malagasy people are therefore always able to recognise each other easily:

> *J'arrive pas à expliquer comment, mais ça ce qu'on appelle malgache, parce que nous, on est différent des autres... oui, des autres gens. Donc, peut-être ça vient de cela, parce qu'on a tous les rythmes, on a tous les rythmes, mais le rythme essentiel c'est le 6/8 et on a une langue... notre langue officielle. On a notre langue officielle. C'est pas la langue des Imerina, mais c'est une langue officielle et on se connaît... pas comme les Africains ou les... tu vois les Congolais. Ils ont des différentes ethnies et ils se parlent en français pour se faire connaître, mais pas leur langue. Mais nous, les Malgaches, même tu viens du Sud, du Nord, de l'Ouest on se connaît toujours.* (Interview Bilo, 19.8.2008)

> I can't explain how, but what we call Malagasy, because we, we are different from others...yes, from other people. So, maybe it comes from there, because we all have rhythms, we all have rhythms, but the essential rhythm is the 6/8 and we have one language... our official language. We have our official language. It is not the language of the Merina people, but it is an official language and we recognise each other... not like the Africans or... you see, the Congolese. They have different ethnicities and they speak French in order to get to know each other, but not their language. But we, the Malagasies, even if you come from the South, the North, the West we always recognise each other. (Interview Bilo, 19.8.2008)

Personally, I have experienced a few situations that showed me this wished-for possibility of boundless communication is not guaranteed always to work; differences in dialect can present some challenges. I was present at the very first rehearsal of Justin Vali's "Ny Malagasy orchestra," a group introduced in the last chapter. The different members of this group come from many different regions of the island and they had difficulties understanding each other's dialects. The most obvious communication problems were between the musicians from the Southern

---

[14] Conversation with Samy, Antananarivo, 7.12.2007.

regions and those from the capital.[15] Erick Manana told me that he was
once asked to translate one of his songs from Malagasy to French; to do
so, he first had to speak to his friend who had written the lyrics. This
friend was from the Northwest coast, so there were many expressions
Erick Manana himself could not easily translate from this particular
dialect.[16]

The *topos* of language has already come up within the *topoi* discussed
above, as singing is for example regarded as an everyday activity, one
closely related to speaking.

What follows is a presentation of the musicians' ideas of the direct
connection between language and rhythm that shows some musicians go
even deeper into the analysis of the structure of the Malagasy language.

Rakotomavo is definitely the biggest advocate among the musicians of
the idea that music and language are inseparable, which he explains by
referring to the close relationship between singing and speaking. Malagasy
music always means singing; there are also different forms of semi-
singing:

> *Bon, comme nous avons la langue d'un côté, l'unicité de la langue, on peut
> parler également de l'unicité de la musique malgache. Il faut pas oublier
> que la musique malgache, est toujours chantée. Donc, on utilise la langue
> dedans. On réplique la langue dans la musique. Il y a des formes semi
> chantées qu'on appelle le jijy,[17] le saova, quelque chose comme ça. Ce
> sont des formes semi chantées. Donc, la base c'est la langue.* (Interview
> Rakotomavo, 1.8.2008)

> Well, as we have the language on the one hand, the unity of the language,
> you can equally speak of the unity of the Malagasy music. You shouldn't
> forget that Malagasy music is always singing. We use the language in it.
> The language is replicated in the music. There are forms of semi-singing
> that we call *jijy*,[18] *saova* and things like that. These are forms of semi-
> singing. So, the base is the language. (Interview Rakotomavo, 1.8.2008)

He gives an example of the Betsileo region in the Southern High
Plateaux area, where rhythmical speaking is often part of a musical
performance:

---

[15] Personal observation during the rehearsal of Justin's "Ny Malagasy Orkestra,"
Mahabo Andoharanofotsy, 22.11.2007.
[16] Conversation with Erick Manana, France, February 2009.
[17] See sound example 1 on DVD for an example of the *jijy*.
[18] See sound example 1 on DVD for an example of the *jijy*.

Les Betsileos ils appellent ça le kipotsaka, quand ils chantent, quand ils chantent, tout d'un coup ils s'arrêtent à chanter et avant de danser ils font ce qu'on appelle kipotsaka, ils parlent comme ça et de façon rythmée [il montre].[19] Ils parlent, mais le rythme est toujours là. (Interview Rakotomavo, 1.8.2008)

The Betsileo people call this *kipotsaka*, when they sing, when they sing, suddenly they stop singing and before dancing they do what is called *kipotsaka*, they speak like this in a rhythmical way [he demonstrates].[20] They speak, but the rhythm is always there. (Interview Rakotomavo, 1.8.2008)

As already mentioned, Rakotomavo always sees a structure of binaries and ternaries in Malagasy music, distinguishing "synthetic metre" from "analytic metre," with the latter based on the language. Interestingly, although making such a general statement, here he describes it with a particular regional example, namely the dialect of the High Plateaux region. In this dialect, words are often trisyllabic. Once they are integrated into the music, the emphasis of the words—i.e. which syllable is stressed—remains the same. This is the same reason he argues there are no strong or weak beats in the music itself but that it is the emphasis of the words that is important:

C'est la mesure synthétique qui est toujours à deux temps, et là, c'est la mesure analytique qui se rapproche, donc, toujours de la langue. C'est ça. Et c'est la superposition de ces deux... Bon... moi, j'avance une hypothèse, mais c'est une hypothèse qui est à moi là. Ça part de la langue. La plupart des mots là, surtout pour nous, les gens des Hauts Plateaux, c'est des mots trisyllabiques. Tanana, tongotra... ce sont des mots trisyllabiques. Et ce sont ces mots, donc, une fois intégrés dans la musique, on doit encore garder l'accent, c'est pourquoi il n'y a pas des temps forts ou des temps faibles. C'est l'accent des mots même, l'accent qu'on... Parce que deux mots, je prends un exemple de tànana et tanàna. Tànana, c'est la main et l'autre c'est la ville, le village. (Interview Rakotomavo, 1.8.2008)

It's the synthetic metre that is always in two, and then, the analytical metre that always approaches the language. That's it. And the two overlap... Well... I propose a hypothesis, but it's my own hypothesis. It's about the language. The majority of words, especially for us, the people of the High Plateaux, are three-syllabic words. *Tanana, tongotra...* these are three-syllabic words. And these are words, once they are integrated into the

---

[19] Sound example 6 on DVD.
[20] Sound example 6 on DVD.

music, you still have to keep the accentuation, that's why there are no strong and weak beats. It's the accentuation of the words themselves, the accentuation that you...because two words, I give an example of *tànana* and *tanàna*. *Tànana* means hand and the other one town, or village. (Interview Rakotomavo, 1.8.2008)

The issues of accentuation and of strong and weak beats will be central to the next chapter when I look at my own musical practices. The close relation of music and language with regard to accentuation has also been researched in other parts of the world. Ethnomusicologist Henry Stobart and music psychologist Ian Cross (2000) in a joint research project have undertaken studies on the so-called "Easter songs" in the Bolivian Andes. Having performed listening and clapping exercises with subjects from different cultural and linguistic backgrounds, they found that Bolivian subject who all spoke Quechua or Aymara as their mother tongue—in contrast with all European subjects—clapped in time with the performer's footfalls, even though many did not know this specific music before (Stobart and Cross 2000: 81). They see a possible explanation for this in the prosodic structure of both Quechua and Aymara, the languages in which the "Easter songs" are sung (Stobart and Cross 2000: 83-84). Therefore, they argue, language is significant for the understanding of rhythmic structure and rhythmic perception in Andean music (Stobart and Cross 2000: 88).[21]

Ricky is also convinced that the "6/8 rhythm" is inherent in Malagasy language and sees the accentuation of words as an important factor within the music. In contrast to Rakotomavo, he speaks of strong and weak beats as a result of this and explains that he always experienced the "strong beats" in Madagascar as different to those of the African mainland. His explanation for this is that he felt a sense of "future" in the sound and emphasis of Malagasy words, such as *andrandràina* (meaning "to give value to something").[22]

For *valiha* player and singer Rajery, music and text also go together. He explains this by means of his own composition techniques, in which it varies whether he first composes the music and adds the lyrics later or vice

---

[21] They warn however, that Spanish and Quechua music, for example, should not be seen as neatly isolated spheres. Also, the "Easter songs" studied incorporate a number of Spanish loan words, and Quechua words have often been set to melodies derived from Spanish prosody and vice versa.

[22] Interview Ricky, 18.7.2008.

versa. He describes the process of composing as finding a collage of both text and music:

> *Bon, je t'explique d'abord, parce que moi, la musique, c'est très lié aussi avec les textes. Parce que moi, j'imagine, quelquefois ça m'arrive les textes et après, je fais la musique après. Des fois, ça m'arrive aussi la musique et les textes après. Mais j'essaie toujours, comment dirais-je, de trouver ce collage, par exemple, je veux la musique adéquate avec les textes. Et les textes, c'est pareil. Et aussi l'esprit de la chanson, le thème de la chanson.* (Interview Rajery, 17.12.2007)

> Well, first let me tell you, because for me, music is very much related to texts. Because for me, I imagine. Sometimes it is the texts that come to me first and I create the music afterwards. And sometimes, it's the music that comes first and afterwards the texts. But it's always about, how can I say, finding this collage, for example, I really want the music to suit the texts. And for the texts, it's the same. And also the esprit of the song, the theme of the song. (Interview Rajery, 17.12.2007)

One question certainly then comes up as not all Malagasy music is accompanied by texts or singing. How does language relate to instrumental music? Rakotomavo argues that instrumental music should be understood as "songs that are no longer sung." He says people who play instrumental music always have the lyrics on their mind:

> Rakotomavo: *La musique instrumentale, c'est un peu le secret de la musique instrumentale malgache. La plupart de la musique instrumentale, ce sont des chansons qu'on ne chante plus. Moi, ce que...*
> Jenny: *Ça veut dire que la langue est toujours là, même si...*
> Rakotomavo: *Elle est toujours là. Elle est toujours là. Et tu arrives à bien jouer cette musique instrumentale quand tu connais... quand tu as dans ta tête les paroles. Tu chantes pas, mais tu les as dans ta tête. C'est mieux.*
> (Interview Rakotomavo, 1.8.2008)

> Rakotomavo: Instrumental music, it is a bit the secret of the Malagasy instrumental music. The majority of instrumental music is songs that are no longer sung. What I...
> Jenny: That means that the language is always there, even if...
> Rakotomavo: It is always there. It is always there. And you manage well to play this music if you know...if you have the lyrics in your head. You don't sing them, but you have them in your head. That's better. (Interview Rakotomavo, 1.8.2008)

Similar ideas about playing techniques and different ways of thinking while musicking, especially concerning rhythm, will be discussed further in the following chapter.

Another topic that has already been touched upon, although only indirectly within the discussion of the other *topoi* is that of tempo. Some musicians think that the environment or life style has an effect on people's mood, characteristics, dancing or speaking habits which will, in turn, influence the music, tempo in particular.

Hajazz, however, sees a direct link between language and tempo, even using the strong metaphor of a "marriage." He explains that it is not the rhythm that differs from region to region, but the dialect that people speak:

Hajazz: *Parce qu'on pense que ça c'est déjà longtemps que ça existe. Quoi dire ? Le mariage du tempo et le langage malgache. Ça fait longtemps. Ça fait longtemps que ça existe.*
Jenny: *Mariage, ça veut dire que le tempo est lié...*
Hajazz: *Lié à la langue.*
Jenny: *Ça veut dire aussi que c'est ça qui fait la différence entre, par exemple, les Hauts Plateau et les autres régions ? Parce que le dialecte ici c'est différent?*
Hajazz: *Non... c'est le dialecte... Donc, la signification est toujours pareille, mais le dialecte, c'est le dialecte qui est un peu différent. Mais le sens... quoi dire? Le sens des mots et tout ça, c'est pareil... sauf dans le Sud, les Antandroy ils ont un peu...*
Jenny: *Et là aussi le rythmique est différent?*
Hajazz: *Non non, pas trop... C'est ça qui est toujours identique, au niveau rythmique.* (Interview Hajazz, 12.8.2008)

Hajazz: Because we think that this exists already for a very long time. How can I put it? The marriage of the tempo and the Malagasy language. That was long ago. That exists already for a long time.
Jenny: Marriage, that means that the tempo is related to...
Hajazz: Related to the language.
Jenny: Does it also mean that this also creates the difference between, for example, the High Plateaux and other regions? Because here the dialect is different?
Hajazz: No...it's the dialect...well, the meaning is always the same, but the dialect, it's the dialect that is a bit different. But the meaning...how can I put it? The meaning of the words and all this, that's the same...except in the South, the Antandroy people are a bit...
Jenny: And there the rhythm is also different?
Hajazz: No no, not very much...that is what is always identical, on the rhythmical level. (Interview Hajazz, 12.8.2008)

In summary, the relation of rhythm and language is experienced and understood through a set of very different aspects. Speaking habits—such as the tempo of speech—and regional dialects are mentioned as well as the structure of Malagasy language, the role that language plays as song lyrics and how this influences techniques of composition. Language is generally seen as a unifying element in Malagasy culture and all musicians tend to emphasise the possibility of understanding each other regardless of their regional origin. In some of the musicians' explanations, understanding is meant in a wider than merely linguistic sense, i.e. there is some claim that recognition can also imply "being different from others" (outside Madagascar) as in Bilo's description. This idea of sameness shared via the language also mirrors the public and academic discourses on the Malagasy language. Regional examples are mentioned in the musicians' discourses but not—as is the case within the *topos* of the environment—to describe difference. Rakotomavo, for example, speaks of the unity of Malagasy language but also points out that the people of the High Plateaux region are set apart by their use of many trisyllabic words. In my own observations, I have also recognised communication problems between people from different regions. However, the dominant discourse suggests that the Malagasy language tends to foster a pan-Malagasy identity as it is regarded and experienced as a unifying element and a shared tool.

Dance

Another *topos* that has already come up because it is strongly related to movements is that of dance (for example, dances that imitate the Malagasy *zebu* cows). Most musicians share the idea that dance is something which, similarly to language, is inseparable from music. Concerning rhythm in particular, the musicians' ideas again touch upon different aspects, such as choreography and how certain dancing styles have developed. They also link it to the particularity of the Malagasy "6/8 rhythm" and how this influences Malagasy dancing styles.

Rakotomavo considers rhythm to be the basis of everything in Malagasy music, something which one "must have" for dancing as well:

Avant de danser, il faut avoir le rythme. Sinon, c'est pas la danse, c'est la chorégraphie. Il y a une différence entre chorégraphie et la danse. Donc, c'est la base. (Interview Rakotomavo, 1.8.2008)

Before dancing, you need to have the rhythm. If not, it's not dance, it's choreography. There is a difference between choreography and dance. So, that's the base. (Interview Rakotomavo, 1.8.2008)

Ricky is convinced that one of the characteristics of the Malagasy "6/8 rhythm" is that it "always" makes people dance. He explains that when performing, as soon as the group enter the "6/8 rhythm" all dancers are really at ease and completely identify with it. If they take it out, people still dance but it will become "plain:"

> *Quand je fais le truc avec Ariry, par exemple, on n'a pas des normes, des rythmes, mais on tape, on tape, on tape et quand tu donnes le 6/8, tous les danseurs ils sont vraiment à l'aise quoi. Ils se retrouvent vraiment dans le.... 'Ouf, on est là!' Mais si tu enlèves le rythme 6/8, ils dansent, mais c'est pas la même chose. Et là, je sais pas comment on va expliquer ça, mais des fois, c'est comme ça et ça chauffe, eh? Dès que tu mets le truc en 6/8, tout le monde est parti et quand tu enlèves le 6/8, ça reste plat.* (Interview Ricky, 18.7.2008)

> When I do this thing with Ariry, for example, we don't have any norms, rhythms, but we tap, we tap and when you give the 6/8, all the dancers they are really at ease. They really find themselves in the… 'Phew, there we are!' But if you take the 6/8 rhythm away, they dance, but it's not at all the same. And there, I don't know how to explain this, but sometimes, it's like it is heating up, eh? As soon as you turn the thing into a 6/8 rhythm, everyone starts and as soon as you take it out, it's all flat. (Interview Ricky, 18.7.2008)

Samy emphasises the fact that the "6/8 rhythm" can easily be adapted to other rhythms and that Malagasy people like to play with this in the way that they "adopt" foreign dances in classical metres, such as the waltz, to the Malagasy "6/8 rhythm:"

> *Ça veut dire, si tu veux danser le valse, tu peux le jouer avec le 6/8, tu peux danser le valse avec le 6/8… Si si si. Pour la marche, ça va encore. Quelle danse aussi? Bon, tout ce qui est en 2 temps, 3 temps, 4 temps. Les temps classiques.* (Interview Samy, 7.12.2007)

> It means that if you want to dance a waltz, you can play it with a 6/8, you can dance the waltz with the 6/8… Yes, yes, yes. For the walk, it still works. What kind of other dance? Well, everything that is in 2, 3, or 4. The classical metres. (Interview Samy, 7.12.2007)

Jaojoby's reflection on the development of *salegy* dancing style mirrors Samy's idea that the Malagasy "6/8 rhythm" is flexible; *salegy* nowadays is danced in whichever way people want to dance it, whereas for a long time the *salegy* had been danced a certain way. Jaojoby even speaks of the "dance of liberty." One general characteristic is that people move a lot within the room where they dance:

Mais la danse -là, quand on tape les pieds, au sol là, ça c'est depuis tous les temps, nos ancêtres ils dansaient comme ça. Ils tapaient du sol des pieds, donnant le rythme. Eh ben aujourd'hui on danse aussi comme ça. On danse comme ça le salegy. Les années 60, on danse le salegy un pas en avant, un pas en derrière, on avance comme ça. C'est un peu comme ça. Aujourd'hui on peut danser libre! Ou on marche comme ça, on fait ce que l'on veut. En fait, tout ce qu'on veut, oui oui. Ah oui, le salegy, c'est la danse de la liberté ! Eh écoute, ça c'est du moi... C'est vrai! Toi aussi, tu peux dire ça, puisque quand tu regardes les gens danser, ils font ce qu'ils veulent. A single, ou à deux personnes, ou à trois ou à plusieurs! Mais en général, ils tournent en rond dans la salle, en général. Je sais pas si tu as remarqué ça. Par exemple quand il y a un bal dans une grande salle, quand on fait le salegy, en principe, ils tournent en rond dans la salle. (Interview Jaojoby, 21.8.2008)

But this dance, when you tap your feet, on the soil, that has been like this all the time, our ancestors danced like this. They tapped the soil with their feet, giving the rhythm. And well, today we also dance like this. We dance the *salegy* like this. In the 60s, you danced the *salegy* going a bit forward, a bit backward, a bit forward like this. It's a bit like this. Today you can dance freely! Or you can walk like this, you do what you want. In fact, everything you want, yes yes. Oh yes, the *salegy*, that's the dance of liberty! And listen, that's from me... it is true! You as well, you can say this, because if you regard the people dancing, they do what they want. All alone, or with two, three or more people! But in general, they move in circles in the room, in general. I don't know if you have realised this. For example, if there is a great ball in a big hall, when we do the *salegy*, in principle, they move in circles in the hall. (Interview Jaojoby, 21.8.2008)

Ratovo is also convinced that rhythm is related to dance and has observed changes in dancing styles. He describes the new dances, as very creative and even calls one, the *kilalaka*, a "revelation." The causes he identifies for these changes in dance are influences from abroad, especially from the African mainland:

Ratovo: *Les danses aussi c'est lié avec, oui, parce que même si vous avez bien remarqué maintenant avec des générations de 2007 ou 2006 ou 2005 avec le kilalaka, ils ont créé une danse un peu bizarre, ils ont créé d'une certaine façon une chorégraphie à partir de son style, comme Tsilivy. Ça, ça existe...*
Jenny: *Bizarre dans quel sens pour vous?*

Ratovo: *Le bizarre c'est... c'est comme une créativité, mais c'est propre façon... On danse pas comme ça avant, mais ça c'est une créativité, une révélation...*
Jenny: *Une créativité qui va dans la direction que malgache ou influencée par...*
Ratovo: *Influencée par les Africains, d'autres influencées par les Africains, d'autres influencés... à partir des vidéos, tout ça... tout ça, je pense qu'il y a une partie influencée par des vidéos, des clips internationales. Surtout des Africains... Avant, on ne danse pas comme ça.*
(Interview Ratovo, 26.7.2008)

Ratovo: Dances as well are related to, yes, because even if you have noticed, now with the generations of 2007 or 2006 or 2005 with the *kilalaka*, they have created a dance which is a bit weird, they have created somehow a choreography based on a style like that of Tsilivy. That exists…
Jenny: Weird in what way for you?
Ratovo: What is weird is… it is like creativity, but it's in a particular way… you didn't dance like this before, but this, this is creativity, a revelation…
Jenny: Creativity related to being Malagasy or influenced by…
Ratovo: Influenced by the Africans, other influenced by the Africans, others influenced by… by videos and all this…all this, I think that there is a part that is influenced by videos, international clips. Especially the Africans… before, we didn't dance like this. (Interview Ratovo, 26.7.2008)

Choreographer Ariry explains a new project in which he wants to create something inspired by the music of the ancestors and "traditional dances." For him this implies work that is always related to the particular Malagasy rhythmical structure of binaries and ternaries:

C'est pas que moi je vais coder la danse traditionnelle de mes ancêtres, mais je vais essayer de créer une danse qui est codée à partir de la danse traditionnelle, ça s'inspire de la danse traditionnelle. Donc, c'est pourquoi c'est toujours lié au rythme. J'aime toujours toujours toujours les binaires et ternaires et tout ça! (Interview Ariry, 26.7.2008)

It's not that I will encode the traditional dances of my ancestors, but I will try to create a dance that is inspired by traditional dance, it is inspired by traditional dance. So, this is why it is always related to rhythm. I always always always love binaries and ternaries and all this! (Interview Ariry, 26.7.2008)

In summary, as already seen in the discussion of the previous *topoi* and as the statements of the musicians here confirm, the musicians regard dance as something inseparable from music. Similar to the other *topoi*, a variety of aspects concerning dance appear in the musicians' discourses. Dance is depicted as an everyday activity and also is linked closely to the environment; there are for example dances inspired by the movements of *zebu* cows. In terms of inspiration for dances and its developments, two directions are mentioned: one is influences from outside Madagascar, such as from the African mainland or from the Western world (mainly through music videos); the other is influences or inspiration from within Madagascar, as with the ancestors' role in inspiring choreographer Ariry's new project. In this context, the structure of binaries and ternaries in Malagasy music comes into play. The specificity of the Malagasy rhythm is mentioned by many musicians and with regard to dance; they suggest several characteristics of this rhythmical structure or "6/8 rhythm," including its flexibility and openness, its ability to make people dance and the ease with which it adapts to other rhythms. Regional differences do not seem to play a very important role, nor is dance—unlike language—particularly emphasised as a unifying element.

Influences From Outside

The tendency throughout all these *topoi* related to the origin and meaning of "rhythm" is to mention the rootedness of it in Madagascar and Malagasy culture. But some musicians make some rather vague assumptions about both influences from abroad and historical intercultural encounters that have made their impact on the music and rhythm. Interestingly, these assumptions are often followed by the explicit explanation that the Malagasy rhythm already had its particularities, that it was perhaps not completely the product of outside influences. The most common idea, however, is that the rhythm "comes from everywhere," just as Malagasy people say of themselves that they come from everywhere.[23]

Jaojoby explains that Malagasy people came from all the different continents and brought the rhythm with them. He is eager to emphasise that he is not himself a historian:

> *Les Malgaches, ils viennent d'Afrique, de l'Asie, ou de l'Arabie, de l'Inde et même aujourd'hui il y a des métisse de l'Europe, de l'Occident, comme tu dis. Voilà déjà. Donc, les Malgaches sont arrivés ici avec ce rythme.*

---

[23] This idea was often expressed in many of the interviews I conducted, but also in many conversations I had with people in an everyday context. For an overview of the history of the different waves of immigration in Madagascar's history, see Brown (1979).

Moi je ne suis pas historien, donc, je fais déjà une réserve. (Interview Jaojoby, 21.8.2008)

The Malagasies, they come from Africa, from Asia, from Arabia, from India, and even today there are *métisses* from Europe and the Occident as you say. So, the Malagasies arrived here with this rhythm. I am not a historian, it's only my opinion. (Interview Jaojoby, 21.8.2008)

Rajery follows up on Jaojoby's explanation, describing the particularity of the Malagasy "6/8 rhythm" and emphasising that its richness comes from the many different sources of influence. Like Jaojoby, he also stresses that he is not an academic or an expert on this:

En fait, d'après tout ce que j'ai vécu, tout ce que j'ai vu et tout ce que je sais, je suis pas ethnomusicologue, mais c'est vraiment riche, parce que c'est mélangé des différentes origines, je pense. Parce que là, le 6/8 on trouve aussi en Afrique, au Maroc, au Mali, donc, c'est extrêmement riche, mais on a notre particularité quand même. (Interview Rajery, 17.12.2007)

In fact, after everything that I have experienced, that I have seen and according to what I know, I am not an ethnomusicologist, but it's really rich, because there is this mixture of different origins, I think. Because the 6/8, you find as well in Africa, in Morocco, in Mali, so it's extremely rich, but we nevertheless have our particularity. (Interview Rajery, 17.12.2007)

Ratovo on the one hand much emphasises the mixture of cultures in Madagascar and speaks of an *"influence planetos"* and a "metamorphose of rhythms" that has come to Madagascar during the 20th century, including rhythms from Europe (like the waltz) and from Brazil. But he also stresses the particularity of Malagasy rhythm; he argues that there are also rhythms "that have not been influenced:"

Ratovo: *Mais il y a une influence planetos, c'est là... il y a une influence planetos, même si dans l'île, ils se sentent qu'une autre musique, même si c'est important... il y a d'autres musiques, parce qu'il y a une métamorphose... C'est quoi la musique de l'Afrique... des rythmes très... comme des Zoulous ou... il y a des styles qui sont lié à des rythmes malgaches. Parce qu'on a des Zoulous qui étaient déjà ici à Madagascar, ils ont pensé, les enfants c'est ici.*
Jenny: *Ça veut dire, vous voulez dire que le rythmique est surtout aussi influencé par des rythmiques africains?*
Ratovo: *Oui oui. Il y a une partie qui est influencée, il y a d'autres influencées par des Brésiliens... Il y a déjà une métamorphose de rythme qui arrive à Madagascar maintenant, dans le 20ième siècle. Mais par*

avant il y a des rythmes qui n'est pas influencés par des... par les autres Africains... Mais quand même, 1800, vers 1800 je pense, il y a déjà des étrangers européens qui arrivent à Madagascar, qui ont déjà apporté le valse. Donc, c'est là qui commence le... surtout dans les Hauts Plateaux, ils ont utilisé des rythmes de valse. Mais les rythmes très traditionnels, pas des valses. (Interview Ratovo, 26.7.2008)

Ratovo: But there is an influence '*planetos,*' it's there... there is an influence '*planetos*', even on the island, they feel like it's another music, even if that's important... there is other music, because there is a metamorphose ... What is the music of Africa... rhythms that are very... like the Zulus... there are styles that are related to Malagasy rhythms. Because there were Zulu people who had been already here in Madagascar, they thought, the children that's here.
Jenny: That means, you are saying that the rhythm is also especially influenced by African rhythms?
Ratovo: Yes, yes. There is a part that is influenced, others are influenced by the Brazilians... there is a metamorphose of rhythm that now arrives in Madagascar in the 20th century. But before, there were rhythms that have not been influenced by... by the other Africans... but still, in 1800, about 1800 I think, there were already European foreigners who had arrived in Madagascar, who already had brought the waltz. So, that when they started... especially in the High Plateaux they have used waltz rhythms. But very traditional rhythms, not waltzes. (Interview Ratovo, 26.7.2008)

However, not all musicians regard these influences as enriching the Malagasy rhythm. To some musicians at least, this sheer number of different influences grounded in the island's history (as well as present influences from abroad) almost seem like a danger against which the Malagasy rhythm has to fight. Jean-Claude explains that there will always be areas of Madagascar to which no foreign influences will find their way. This is reminiscent of the *topos* of everyday life, in which many of the musicians show their identification and sympathy with the rural population of Madagascar. He speaks therefore of the strength and survival of this rhythm. In his example, the national electricity company of Madagascar symbolises the dangerous influences the rhythm faces. He argues that there are still remote parts in Madagascar without electricity, which implies that foreign influences will not reach these areas:

Moi je pense que ce rythme malgache est suffisamment fort, suffisamment ancré que même s'il y a des influences extérieures, elle va survivre, elle va vivre. Elle va vibrer toujours. Et ces influences, au contraire, vont enrichir ce rythme. Mais la base elle est là. Et si tu regardes la 'Jirama' comme disait Ricky, 'Jirama' assure 18% en électricité de la population de

Madagascar. Ça veut dire qu'avec les 18% il y a toujours des délestages. Donc, la population elle n'a pas à s'inquiéter de la perte du 6/8, parce que dans les villages, des coins de Madagascar, il n'y a pas d'électricité. Donc, on joue des instruments traditionnels et on joue cette musique traditionnelle, donc le 6/8 est là, en permanence. Donc, on doit pas avoir peur. (Interview Jean-Claude, 18.7.2008)

I do think that this Malagasy rhythm is sufficiently strong, sufficiently ingrained so that even if there are external influences, it will survive, it will live. It will always vibrate. And these influences, in contrast, will enrich this rhythm. The base, it is there. And if you regard 'Jirama' as Ricky said, 'Jirama' provides for 18% of the electricity of the population of Madagascar. That means that with 18% there are lots places without electricity. So, the population doesn't have to worry about losing the 6/8 because in the villages, in the corners of Madagascar, there is no electricity. So, we play traditional instruments and we play traditional music, so the 6/8 is permanently here. So we don't have to be afraid. (Interview Jean-Claude, 18.7.2008)

In summary, the musicians' ideas about influences from abroad and the history of the country and of the rhythm, tend to be vague. However, the emphasis on the Malagasy rhythm's particularity is explicit and this stresses difference from the outside world. This is also mirrored in allusions to the Malagasy "6/8 rhythm" being in danger (because of influences from outside) or in the statement that there are rhythms on the island that have not been influenced at all. Different regions seem not to play a role; differences in terms of historical events are not mentioned with regard to specific regions. The rhythm is instead again experienced as a pan-Malagasy unifying element.

Emotions and Spiritual Ideas

The last *topos* contains ideas and assumptions that deal with emotions and spirituality. Again, I want to emphasise that the division into these different *topoi* is not always clear-cut; there are so many interconnecting elements. Especially regarding emotions within musical experiences, one often encounters symbols or metaphors that people use to embrace these emotional aspects, as the example of the Kaluli people shows. Feld (1981) explains:

Sa can stand alone to mean 'waterfall,' can prefix verbs of sound making and textual organization. As it generally stands for 'waterfall' in its usual context, it generally stands for intervals of the descending minor third in sound terminology. This is found in the calls of the fruit doves, and stands alone as a symbol of sadness, isolation, and loss (Feld 1981: 30).

Sadness is also inherent in the music in another way; Feld explains that for the Kaluli people weeping and shedding tears often form part of the music itself—they "weep in the melody" (Feld 1981: 28). Many Malagasy musicians regard rhythm as something to do with—or even based on—"feeling." Whereas some instead consider aspects of communication and reflect upon a more general "Malagasy soul," others emphasise the personal and sensitive aspects of it. I will pick up the aspect of personality and individuality again in the next chapter, as my own musical experiences indicated the *lova-tsofina* implies or is in itself something individual and personal.

In a way that links two *topoi*, one of dance and the other of influences from abroad, Justin Vali explains the spirituality of Malagasy rhythm. He uses opposing features, such as "body and soul," "rhythm and melody," and "Africa and Asia." He sees a combination of two sides in Malagasy music, crediting this as a result of the voyages of Malagasy ancestors. He associates Africa with rhythm and body[24] and Asia with melody and soul:

Je pense que ça c'est le fait des voyages des ancêtres malgaches qui étaient partis de loin, qui passent par l'Afrique et qui viennent de l'Indonésie ou l'Asie et ils passent par l'Afrique après, arriver ici à Madagascar. Parce que moi, je pense qu'il y a le 6/8. Si on écoute ça, c'est vraiment le rythme spirituel. Mais le rythme qui est très posé par l'Afrique, on est là aussi, les racines africaines. On est là aussi, les racines asiennes, indonésiens. Et moi je pense que c'est à cause de ça que le 6/8 était créé, parce qu'en même temps, c'est spirituel. Mais en même temps, il est corps quoi, rythmique aussi... Parce que quand on écoute les musiques africaines, par exemple, c'est vrai que ça fait danser. C'est le corps qui manifeste tout de suite. C'est le corps qui manifeste. Mais quand écoute ici un peu la musique malgache, c'est vrai qu'il y a une mélodie qui suit le rythme. Donc, on se rappelle quand même qu'il y a la mélodie asiatique là-dedans, les côtés asiatiques. Mais on a aussi le rythme. En même temps, on a aussi le rythme. Ça se prouve que les ancêtres malgaches, il fait voyager, on part l'Afrique et on arrive ici à Madagascar... Voila. C'est la combinaison de les deux, je pense, qui crée vraiment notre rythme ici. C'est un petit peu en l'air et spirituel, en l'air mais pas vraiment posé quelquefois. Parce que les musiciens, quand ils jouent le 6/8, le rythme était en l'air. (Interview Justin Vali, 23.11.2007)

---

[24] Justin's idea mirrors Agawu's critique that Africa is always associated with rhythm which I have discussed in detail in chapter 2; see Agawu (2003).

I think that this is the fact of the travels of the Malagasy ancestors who had left from far, who passed via Africa and who came from Indonesia or Asia and they later passed via Africa, arriving here in Madagascar. Because I think that there is the 6/8. When you listen to this, it is really the spiritual rhythm. But the rhythm is very much influenced by Africa, there we are, the African roots. We also have the Asian roots, Indonesian. And I think it is because of this that the 6/8 was created, because at the same time it is spiritual. But at the same time it is body, rhythmical as well… Because when you listen to African musics, for example, it is true that it makes people dance. It's the body that immediately reacts. It's the body that expresses. But when you listen to Malagasy music a bit, it is true that there is a melody that follows the rhythm. So, we still remember that there is an Asian melody within it, an Asian side. But we also have the rhythm. And at the same time, we also have the rhythm. That is the proof that the Malagasy ancestors travelled, you leave Africa and you arrive here in Madagascar… So, it's the combination of the two, I think, that really creates our rhythm here. It's a bit in the air and spiritual, in the air but sometimes not really set. Because the musicians, when they play the 6/8, the rhythm is in the air. (Interview Justin Vali, 23.11.2007)

Feld (1981) also mentions the image of "in the air" in Kaluli theory on music; for them, all composition starts with melody, which is always "'in the air' with the sound of the birds, or actually vocalized as one sings a melody" (Feld 1981: 29).

Erick Manana, however, explained to me that the Malagasy musicians' use of the image of the rhythm being "in the air" derives from the image of tapping feet; for *vazahas* the strong beat in Malagasy music always seems to match the moment the musicians' tapping foot is up.[25] I will come back to discussions of strong and weak beats in the next chapter.

Interesting again, is the relation mentioned to other *topoi*, such as the environment. Samy, like Justin, takes up the idea of Madagascar as a place where different "worlds" emerge and describes it from a very positive point of view, describing the "6/8 rhythm" as the result of a successful "melting pot" of cultures. One reason for this, he says, is the ease with which Malagasy people learn by ear and their ready adaptability to any new musical styles and situations in general:

Parce que moi personnellement je me tiens encore l'idée que Madagascar, c'est une zone de convergence de la civilisation, c'est une zone tampon donc. Et c'est pour ça que les Malgaches en réalité arrivent très très facilement à s'adapter. Et la réponse au 6/8, c'est justement ça… Non, c'est parce que les Malgaches peuvent s'adapter à créer à partir de cette,

---

[25] Discussion with Erick Manana, 17.10.2010.

de faire la synthèse en réalité de civilisations, de tempos, de tempéraments et tout ça pour créer, et c'est ça que Tsilavina a dit la dernière fois, c'est un 'melting-pot' réussi en réalité. Et tout le monde se retrouve ici. Les Malgaches ont une facilité étonnante d'oreille musicale, de s'adapter à tous les types de musique et à toutes les situations. C'est ça. Et le 6/8 c'est justement la synthèse de tout ça. (Interview Samy, 7.12.2007)

Because personally I still stick to the idea that Madagascar, it's a zone of convergence of civilisation, so it's a buffer zone. And it's because of this that the Malagasies in reality manage very easily to adapt. And the answer to the 6/8, it's exactly this... No, it's because the Malagasies can adapt themselves to create from, in reality to make this synthesis of civilisation, of tempo, of character and all this in order to create, and that's what Tsilavina said the other day, it's a melting pot succeeded in reality. And everyone can identify with it here. The Malagasies have an astonishing ability of a musical ear to adapt to all sorts of music and to all situations. That's it. And the 6/8 is exactly the synthesis of all this. (Interview Samy, 7.12.2007)

He mentions the influences from a range of continents and nations that have shaped the rhythm in Madagascar, explaining that rhythm has a very spiritual aspect to it which he thinks is based on "Oriental cultures:"

Samy: *Ça c'est ... à mon avis, il faut chercher ça à partir de la fusion malayo-polynésienne et africaine. Parce que avec l'histoire de peuplement ce qu'on a dit tout à l'heure, il y avait donc, les Africains, et après l'arrivée de malayo-polynésiens, il y avait les Africains arabisés, islamistes donc. Après... ce sont des grandes tendances, moi, je parle pas des Indiens, des Chinois [il rit]. Il y a l'arrivée des Européens. Et ainsi de suite. Ça, c'est l'aspect rythmique, ça c'est l'aspect spirituel, la dimension spirituelle de la musique.*
Jenny: *C'est quoi par exemple?*
Samy: *La dimension spirituelle, c'est un peu l'Orient quoi. Si tu fais l'étude sur la culture orientale, c'est... il y a cet aspect spirituel.* (Interview Samy, 24.11.2007)

Samy: This... in my opinion, you must look for this in the Malayan-Polynesian African fusion. Because with the history of the people, what we just said, there are the Africans and afterwards the arrival of the Malayan-Polynesians, there were Arabianised Africans, Islamists. Later... these are the big tendencies, I don't speak about the Indians, the Chinese [he laughs]. There is the arrival of the Europeans and so on. This is the rhythmical aspect; this is the spiritual aspect, the spiritual dimension of the music.
Jenny: What is it, for example?

Samy: The spiritual dimension, that's a bit like the Orient. If you study the
Oriental culture, it's… there is this spiritual aspect. (Interview Samy,
24.11.2007)

Bilo shares this idea that Madagascar is shaped by different cultures.
However, when asked why they all shared the same rhythm, as he had
argued before, he said that he was not sure. He describes Madagascar as a
"country of colours," a "globe" formed of all the different cultures:

*Là… je sais pas à cause de quoi [il rit]. Mais ce que je sais, tu vois, nous
les Malgaches, on est un pays des couleurs. Tu vois, on trouve toute la
couleur. Moi, je sais pas, même jusqu'à maintenant d'où vient la racine
malgache, parce qu'on est dans une île. Peut-être ça vient de l'Afrique,
peut-être ça vient de l'Europe. Il y a des Européens, il y a des Asiatiques, il
y a partout et ça se forme dans un globe qui s'appelle Madagascar, tu
vois? [Il rit]* (Interview Bilo, 19.8.2008)

There… I don't know it's because of what [he laughs]. But what I know,
you see, we the Malagasies, we are a country of colours. You see, you find
all colours. Even until now I don't know where the Malagasy root comes
from, because we are on an island. Maybe it comes from Africa, maybe it
comes from Europe. There are Europeans, there are Asians, there is
everything and that becomes a globe that is called Madagascar, you see?
[He laughs] (Interview Bilo, 19.8.2008)

Despite or perhaps because of these mixtures, influences and fusions
that people mention, many musicians tend to emphasise the "Malagasy
soul" that one needs in order to play and understand the music and rhythm.
I myself was often told I would never be able to understand the music fully
or play it exactly as Malagasy people do; the "Malagasy soul" would
always be missing. Some, however, encouraged me, saying that if I
continued to play with Malagasy musicians and stayed a long time in
Madagascar, learnt the language properly, listened to a lot of the music
etc., I might have the chance to learn it. I return to this as part of the
reflection of my personal experiences in the next chapter.

However, musicians even have different opinions about this "soul;" for
instance, Ratovo sees "soul" as something related to ethnicity, something
that is not merely a "unifying factor" for all Malagasy people. However,
he claims all Malagasies share a certain sadness and melancholy grounded
in living on an island. So when abroad, Malagasies tend to show solidarity
towards their compatriots, including those from other regions:

Ratovo: *Ça c'est... j'ai pas l'idée tellement l'idée ça vient d'où, parce que je pense que l'âme malgache... il y a toute une âme très différente... dans l'ethnie, je pense l'ethnie... chaque ethnie a sa façon d'exprimer l'âme... Même si c'est quand même solidaire, parce que c'est une île. Donc, il y a toujours une mélancolie qui est basée de tout ça.*
Jenny: *Mélancolie?*
Ratovo: *Mélancolie, la tristesse d'être une île. On est très solidaire. C'est là que se repose tout le temps les Malgaches. Pourquoi? Parce que quand on allait de loin, c'est en Angleterre ou en Allemagne ou quelque part, on se reconnaît quand on rencontre, même si d'autres musiques de l'Est, de l'Est de Tamatave, du Sud, eh? On se reconnaît que c'est notre musique, même si c'est l'âme de l'Est ou l'âme des Hauts Plateaux.* (Interview Ratovo, 26.7.2008)

Ratovo: This is... I don't really have an idea where it comes from, because I think that the Malagasy soul... there is a soul that is very different...in ethnicity, I think ethnicity... every ethnicity has its way of expressing the soul... Even if it is still solidly united, because it is an island. So, there is always a melancholy that is based on all this.
Jenny: Melancholy?
Ratovo: Melancholy, the sadness of being an island. We show a lot of solidarity. That is what the Malagasies rely on all the time. Why? Because when we are far away, in England or in Germany or somewhere else, we recognise each other when we meet, even if the music is another in the East, in the East in Tamatave, in the South, eh? We always recognise that it is our music, even if it is the soul of the East or the soul of the High Plateaux. (Interview Ratovo, 26.7.2008)

Ratovo also mentions another aspect of "soul:" it can be the propulsive element while playing music. When doing recordings, for example, people sometimes do not play exactly on the beat because their soul does not work according to strict timing:

Ratovo: *Et c'est là, le problème malgache! Même moi, je me sens très bien, mal à l'aise à partir de... Il y a des moments forts de l'âme, il y a des sentiments... Même si c'était carré, je ne respecte pas le carré [il rit]. Je me pose la question... Il y a toujours quand on fait des enregistrements, ça c'est une faute grave, mais c'est pas une faute grave ça, mais c'est l'âme qui me pousse... à aller au-delà! C'est pas le mesure qui manque, s'il manque quelquefois ou ça dépasse, c'est pas juste sur le...*
Jenny: *Beat?*
Ratovo: *Sur le tempo [il tape le pied].* (Interview Ratovo, 26.7.2008)

Ratovo: And that's it, the Malagasy problem! Even me, I feel really good, not at ease when...there are strong moments of the soul, there are

feelings... even if there are rules I don't respect them [he laughs]. I ask myself... always when you make recordings; that's a big mistake, it is not a big mistake, but it's the soul that pushes... go there! It is not the metre that is missing, if it is missing sometimes or if it exceeds sometimes, it is not exactly on the...!
Jenny: Beat?
Ratovo: With the tempo [he taps his feet]. (Interview Ratovo, 26.7.2008)

Ratovo's idea of the "soul" as driving force when playing music leads towards regarding rhythm to be something personal. The choreographer Ariry speaks of an "interior rhythm." When creating choreographies it is not always the music that pushes him towards new movements; often this "interior rhythm" and what he calls "already lived rhythms" propel his work:

Bien sûr que des fois j'utilise pas de support musicale pour mes chorégraphies, mais je pense que c'est le rythme intérieur et le souvenir des différents rythmes que moi, j'ai vécu à coté et tout ça qui me poussent à faire des mouvements. (Interview Ariry, 26.7.2008)

Of course, sometimes I don't use musical support for my choreographies, but I think that it is the interior rhythm and the souvenir of different rhythms that I have experienced besides and all this that pushes me to make movements. (Interview Ariry, 26.7.2008)

Ricky also describes the personal side to rhythm. Everyone has his or her own rhythm and it is therefore a question of sensibility:

Oui oui et là, Jenny, je ne parle pas de techniques par rapport à ça. 6/8, 3/4, 4/4, 12/8... Ça, moi je trouve que c'est le fait du rythme, chaque personne, chaque individu a son rythme. Et ça c'est une question de sensibilité et cette sensibilité qui explique, qui explique vraiment le rythme. (Interview Ricky, 18.7.2008)

Yes yes, and there, Jenny, I don't speak about technique with regard to this. 6/8, 3/4, 4/4, 12/8... I think that it is a matter of rhythm, each person; each individual has his/her rhythm. And it's a question of sensibility and it is this sensibility that explains, that really explains the rhythm. (Interview Ricky, 18.7.2008)

But he also sees a universal side to rhythm and regards the "6/8 rhythm" as in some sense a universal one. What makes the difference is the sensibility towards this rhythm:

Mais moi, je pense que c'est universel. Comme Santana fait, quand il joue le 6/8, c'est 6/8, c'est universel. Mais la sensibilité, c'est ça qui est différente. C'est ça qui est différente, la sensibilité, parce que c'est... là, on ne parle pas de technique, là on parle vraiment.... de respiration, tu vois? (Interview Ricky, 18.7.2008)

But I think that it is universal. Like Santana does, when he plays the 6/8, it's 6/8, it's universal. But the sensibility, that's what is different. That's what is different, the sensibility, because it is... there, we don't talk about technique, there we really talk about... about breathing, you see? (Interview Ricky, 18.7.2008)

For Ricky, rhythm is always about communication, which also relates to sensibility; there is some element of rhythm he thinks one just cannot explain. He defines rhythm as the "communication within human sensibility," for which he gives a few examples. When playing, it is often via looks that he communicates with other musicians. They do not need to talk to understand each other. Ricky also interprets Santana's dream of coming to Madagascar as a search for spiritual aspects in music:

Oui, mais moi, Jenny, je te dis que 'ça sonne pas malgache,' c'est faux! Mais ça rentre pas dans la sensibilité, parce que le rythme, dès que tu l'as, tu peux faire tout ce que tu veux, même avec un Brésilien, même avec... Je sais pas quoi! Mais c'est une question vraiment complicité, sensibilité et ça c'est le rythme quoi. Et c'est ça qui définit le rythme... Même moi, quand je joue avec lui, on fait comme ça et on se comprend et là, toi tu regardes, mais toi tu comprends pas, mais ça veut dire quoi ça? Pourquoi ils se regardent par rapport à ce rythme-là? Mais nous, on se regarde comme ça... regarde, tu vois?... On se regarde et on se comprend. On se comprend, mais on n'arrive pas à s'expliquer [il rit]. C'est quoi ce regard-là? On se comprend, mais on n'arrive pas à s'expliquer et là, pour toi c'est vraiment important d'expliquer ça dans tes recherches que le rythme là-bas, c'est... spirituel quoi! Moi je pense comme ça. C'est spirituel. Et peut-être c'est à cause de ça que Santana, peut-être il voulait vraiment venir pour sentir les choses, parce qu'on n'arrive pas à expliquer ça... C'est ça. Et le rythme c'est vraiment la communication dans la sensibilité humaine. Définition [il rit]! Ça, c'est ma définition [tout le monde rit]. Si on arrive à se communiquer... parce qu'on parle tout le temps, mais on joue pas. Mais un jour j'ai dit à Jean-Claude, on va jouer! Comme ça, eh? Et là, on est resté, on est resté, parce que tu vois, c'est comme ça. (Interview Ricky, 18.7.2008)

Yes, but Jenny, I tell you that 'this doesn't sound Malagasy,' that's wrong! That's not about sensibility, because the rhythm, as soon as you have it, you can do everything you want, even with a Brazilian, even with... I

don't know! It's really a question of complicity, sensibility and that's
rhythm. And this is what defines rhythm... Even me, when I play with
him, we do like this and we understand each other and then, you, you
watch, but you don't understand, but what does that mean? Why do they
look at each other with regard to this rhythm?... We look at each other and
we understand each other. We understand each other, but we can't explain
it to each other [he laughs].What is it, this look? We understand each other,
but we can't explain it to each other and there, for you it is really important
to explain in your research that this rhythm there... it's spiritual! That's
how I see it. It's spiritual. And maybe it's because of this that Santana,
maybe he really wanted to come in order to feel these things, because we
can't explain it... That's it! And the rhythm, that's really the
communication within human sensibility. Definition [he laughs]! That's
my definition [everyone laughs]. If we manage to communicate... because
we talk all the time, but we don't play. But one day I said to Jean-Claude,
let's play! Like this, eh? And there, we stayed, we stayed, because you see,
that's how it is. (Interview Ricky, 18.7.2008)

Ricky also mentioned in a discussion with Jean-Claude and me that he
considers the heart to be the "centre of rhythm."[26] Reacting to this idea of
Ricky's, Jean-Claude suddenly remembered an anecdote from his trip to
the Mikea forest with a group of Italians. He told us that when these
Italians listened to music from the Mikea people for the first time, they
were surprised, especially by the rhythm that they had never heard before.
After thinking and listening for a very long time, one of them apparently
said that he had finally found out to what this rhythm corresponds to: the
heartbeat. Jean-Claude continued speaking:

*Ou alors, c'est le rythme cardiaque pris d'émotion, là on va en 6/8 [Ttout
le monde rit].* (Interview Jean-Claude, 18.7.2008)

Or otherwise, it's the cardiac rhythm affected by emotion; there we go with
the 6/8 [everyone laughs]. (Interview Jean-Claude, 18.7.2008)

In summary, the musicians' statements about emotional aspects and the
spirituality of rhythm seem almost like explanations or answers to the very
vague ideas of some musicians about influences from abroad and about the
historical development of this rhythmical structure. These influences are
described in basically positive terms this time, with Madagascar depicted
as a *"melting pot réussit en réalité,"* or as a "synthesis of civilisation" to
which the "6/8 rhythm" is the overall answer. Again, the debate on

---

[26] Interview Ricky, 18.7.2008.

sameness and difference that runs through the musicians' discourses is striking. It touches upon different levels—ranging from the personal to more general statements. For the first time within all these *topoi*, sameness is emphasised across the island's borderlines and the universality of the "6/8 rhythm" is stressed. Further, the idea that rhythm is at the end something very personal and that everyone has an individual rhythm also points to sameness; the musicians do not distinguish Malagasy from non-Malagasy people at this point, nor do they mention regional particularities. The metaphor of the "soul" also passes throughout this debate and appears at different levels. Interestingly, it functions as a pointer to sameness as well as to difference. Whereas many musicians carry the idea of a "Malagasy soul," claiming it necessary to understand it to properly play in the Malagasy rhythm, others speak of a "soul" that is different in each ethnic group. Others tend to emphasise individuality, as expressed in terms such as "interior rhythm." Difference is therefore created between Madagascar and the outside world, between different ethnic groups and also between each individual person.

Conclusion

The analysis of the musicians' own theories on the origin and meaning of rhythm in Madagascar has opened up a broad palette of topics and debates. It also shows that rhythm is understood, explained and experienced in many different ways. I have identified different subject areas—recurring *topoi*—within the musicians' discourses, through which they conceptualise "rhythm," *topoi* that all relate to the concept of oral tradition, to the *lova-tsofina*. These *topoi*, with one exception, are rooted within Madagascar itself: the environment, everyday life, language, dance, influences from outside, and emotional or spiritual ideas. Although sorting topics into these *topoi* has been the basis of my analysis, they are all closely interrelated. They should also be seen as very broad groupings; each *topos* contains very varied elements. The environmental *topos*, for example, deals with the physical environment as well as with people's relations to and movements within the environment. Language includes speaking habits but also the musicians' theories on the actual structure of their language and the role of language as song lyrics.

Questions of identity are negotiated throughout the musicians' discourses on the origin and meaning of "rhythm." This is expressed through a constant debate on sameness and difference that runs through all the *topoi*. However, this debate takes on different shapes as it appears on various levels. Comparisons are made between different pairs of regions:

in Madagascar, such as between the High Plateaux area and the Coastal regions; between Madagascar and the African mainland; or between Madagascar and the Western world. Here, looking at the different *topoi* reveals that identities and feelings of belonging are expressed differently. The *topoi* of language, of everyday life and of dance are experienced as shared elements that emphasise a pan-Malagasy identity; within the *topos* of environment, the musicians often distinguish regional specificities. However, the *topos* of environment also supports the idea of the "same groove" as a presence across the whole of the island. It therefore compares Madagascar as a whole with the "rest" of the world. Musicians often create images of what they consider typically "Malagasy." Especially in the *topos* of everyday life, it is apparent that all musicians—in spite of their bond to the capital Antananarivo—identify strongly with a rural lifestyle. This also explains the persistent appearance of two themes: *zebu* cows and rice, both literally as part of daily activity and as metaphors.

The *topos* of influences from abroad, again, stresses the particularity of the Malagasy rhythm taken as a whole, even if this is expressed through rather vague ideas about historical developments and influences. The balancing act between difference and sameness can probably be seen most obviously in the musicians' statements about emotional aspects of rhythm. The idea or even metaphor of a "Malagasy soul" again creates a pan-Malagasy feeling of belonging and a related expression of exclusion: musicians claim the ability to play this rhythm requires having this "Malagasy soul." On the other hand, "soul" is understood to be something personal and is associated with an "interior rhythm" that all human beings have. This is the only time sameness between Madagascar and the outside world is explicitly expressed.

I will refer back to many aspects of these *topoi* and the musicians' experiences in the following chapter, in which I focus on my own musical experiences, giving concrete examples of how I have linked discourses and musical practices and analysed the interrelation of both.

CHAPTER SIX

EXPERIENCING "RHYTHM"

Introduction

In the previous two chapters, I analysed discourses, first by looking at the musicians' discourses on the concept of "6/8 rhythm," and second, by exploring the concept of *lova-tsofina* and the origin and meaning of "rhythm" in Madagascar in the musicians' own discussions.

This chapter gives insight into my shared musical experiences with the musicians. I aim to show how engaging in discussions with musicians and listening to and analysing their discourses informed my musical practices. In turn, I will show how the experiences I gained through musicking informed my analysis of discourses.[1] Here, I should stress that my own musical practices and experiences are not in any way an instruction on how to learn and play Malagasy music. Furthermore, the examples I give aren't necessarily in chronological order—such an ordering would confuse the question of which was primary between theory and practice—but are examples of a constant interplay in which one informs the other. I will therefore often refer back to aspects and *topoi* from the last two chapters.

This chapter takes up the crux of my research and through concrete examples once more examines the issue of the "6/8 rhythm" and the *lova-tsofina*. In contrast to the last two chapters, which have focussed on these concepts, the experiences of our shared music-making emphasise the unity of these two discourses. As chapters 4 and 5 have already shown, individual understandings of both concepts vary a great deal in the Malagasy context and I have argued that instead of looking at seeming contradictions within these different discourses, we need to take the extra step of understanding them in close relation to our musical experiences.

The need to participate musically in research is a topic also raised by the Malagasy musicians themselves, mirroring the ongoing debate within ethnomusicology about the need to move towards more performative research (e.g. Baily 2008). During my encounters with Malagasy

---

[1] For a complementary assessment of this theme, see Fuhr (2011).

musicians, many often explained to me that the only way to learn and understand Malagasy music was to play it. Some musicians expressed regret that it was always non-musicians writing about and explaining their music whilst the musicians themselves were unable to do so.[2] Taking the musicians' arguments seriously, my study of experiences of "rhythm" presents research that has grown out of shared experiences that appear in our musical experiences and practices as much as in the ways in which we discuss them and our music-making.

Although many musicians emphasise the difficulty of expressing in words what they feel or sense when musicking—mirroring a debate prominent within ethnomusicology (see chapter 3)—three important topics have come to the fore within the musicians' discourses that directly concern their musical experiences of "rhythm:" first, that musicians reflect often on their methods of composing and many of them have an interest in "Malagasising" already-existing tunes and songs; second, that foot-tapping, counting and clapping to music are activities musicians especially concentrate on; this is closely related to the third topic, debates about intercultural musical encounters, as it is especially these activities that are often the cause of musical (mis-) understandings.

I will present an analysis of these three topics as an introduction to this chapter, once more taking identity as the key issue. As in the last two chapters, I will focus on the musicians' perceptions of "Self" and "Other," as well as on shifting identities, such as individual versus collective identity, regional versus collective, and Malagasy versus African versus Western.

Composing and "Malagasising" Tunes

Musicians often talk openly about their own personal ways of composing music. Within their reflections upon this topic, a trend comes to the fore: the drive to "Malagasise" already-existing music and songs, in other words, to create a Malagasy version of foreign musical tunes. When talking about composing, but even more so when talking about "Malagasising" music, musicians constantly refer to identity issues. This includes drawing clear boundaries between Malagasy and non-Malagasy, which I will analyse in the following examples that show again that

---

[2] This argument appeared in many conversations and discussions with various musicians. It was intensely discussed in my conversation with Rija Randrianivosoa, Erick Manana, and Rivo Razafindramanitra before our concert in Poitiers, France, 22.1.2010.

"rhythm" is a topic constantly reoccurring, one that matters to the musicians.

The first example that I would like to present in detail is from a discussion I had with *valiha* player Rajery. He often mentioned to me that he appreciates *tsapiky* music, which has its origin in Southwestern Madagascar, in the region of Tuléar.[3] In one interview with him, we talked about his album *Sofera*[4] and how he had worked on the opening song "*Tandremo*." In this song, he makes use of *tsapiky* music in a very particular way, i.e. by creating a very personal version of it. The title "*Tandremo*" in Malagasy means "Caution" and it is addressed to young people in particular. The song is a warning to the youth to think carefully before doing something. This theme of the song had been the starting point for Rajery's composition. He explains that this idea of reaching young people to pass on a message required him to find the right rhythm. He decided for the *tsapiky* because of its resemblance to reggae music, especially if you reduce the *tsapiky's* tempo just a little bit. He is convinced that young people are attracted by festive music such as reggae. When first hearing the song, listeners will think that it is reggae though it is actually *tsapiky* music. However, Rajery also points out that he and his musicians have their very own way of playing *tsapiky* which differs from the way it is played in its region of origin. They are not even in fact able to play *tsapiky* in its original way. The differences lie both in the melodies of the guitar and in their singing style. What stays the same is the "rhythmic root." Rajery also mentions that some listeners might be reminded of South African music by the song. He therefore describes the song as a kind of musical journey:

Rajery: *Donc, comment faire pour créer le rythme déjà? Parce qu'il y a le thème. C'est pour dire aux jeunes: attention! Donc il faut réfléchir avant de faire quelque chose. Donc, pour attirer l'attention des jeunes, pour que le message soit passé, donc quel rythme? Quel tempérament? Donc, ça c'est tout un travail. Donc là, j'ai choisi le tsapiky, mais en écoutant au premier, tu sens que 'Ah, c'est un reggae ça!' Tu vois? Mais effectivement si on fait le dérivé de tsapiky ou si on diminue un petit peu le tempo, c'est du reggae. Oui, c'est incroyable! Mais nous, on se rendait pas compte quand on a travaillé cette musique, on a fait comme ça et après... En fait, parce que là, tu sais... les jeunes ils adorent les trucs un peu festifs, tu vois? Qui bougent, en majorité, tu vois? Les jeunes, ils ont besoin de ça. Et là, on a travaillé le tsapiky. En première partie de la chanson, on se dit que*

---

[3] Detailed analyses of *tsapiky* music can be found in the works of French ethnomusicologists Julien Mallet. See Mallet (2000, 2004, 2007, 2008, and 2009).

[4] Rajery (2007).

bon, les gens ils vont croire que c'est du reggae. Mais déjà, la manière de jouer la guitare, c'est pas du reggae. Des fois aussi tu sens que 'Ah, c'est du Sud-Af.!' Donc, tu vois? C'est du voyage. Mais le fond de la chanson c'est du tsapiky. [Il montre][5] Ça, c'est le tsapiky. Mais il y a aussi une chose qui le dit que nous, on peut pas faire le tsapiky comme ils l'ont fait les musiciens du Sud. Donc, nous, on fait le tsapiky à notre manière à nous.

Jenny: *Et c'est quoi la différence si on compare ça avec le tsapiky au Sud?*

Rajery: *En fait, la différence, c'est par exemple, c'est la mélodie de la guitare.*

Jenny: *Mais le rythme est le même?*

Rajery: *Le rythme est le même.*

Jenny: *La différence est peut-être dans la mélodie...*

Rajery: *Dans la mélodie. Parce que là tu sais, les chanteurs du tsapiky, c'est pas comme je fais. C'est pas pareil. Mais on a essayé de garder cette racine rythmique. Que ce rythme c'est du tsapiky quoi... Donc, c'est notre manière aussi de montrer le tsapiky, de jouer le tsapiky. Donc, c'est nous, d'après notre petite analyse, notre petite recherche quoi. Parce qu'on ne peut pas faire pareil comme ils ont fait. Parce que nous aussi, on aimerait bien créer quelque chose, chercher quelque chose de nouveaux. Mais ça reste toujours dans l'esprit de tsapiky* (Interview Rajery, 17.12.2007)

Rajery: Well, how to create the rhythm? Because there is the theme. It's to tell the youth: Caution! You need to think well before doing something. So, in order to attract the youth's attention so that the message gets across, which rhythm? Which character? So that's hard work. Here, I have chosen the *tsapiky*, but if you listen to it, first you will feel 'Ah, that's reggae!' You see? But actually if we drift away from the *tsapiky* and if we reduce the tempo a little bit, it's reggae. Yes, it's incredible! But we didn't realise when we worked on that music, we just did it like that and later... In fact, because here, you see... the young people they adore festive things, you see? Things that make you dance, most of them do... you see? The young people, they need that. And here, we have worked the *tsapiky*. In the first part of the song, we have said, well, the people will think that it is reggae. But already, the way of playing the guitar is not reggae. Sometimes you also feel 'Ah, that's South African!' You see? It's a journey. But the base of the song is *tsapiky*. [He demonstrates][6] That's *tsapiky*. But there is also this thing that says that we can't play the *tsapiky* like the people from the South. So we play the *salegy* in our own way.

Jenny: And what is the difference if you compare it to the *tsapiky* in the South?

Rajery: In fact, the difference, it's for example the melody of the guitar.

Jenny: But the rhythm is the same?

---

[5] Sound example 7 on DVD.
[6] Sound example 7 on DVD.

Rajery: The rhythm is the same.

Jenny: The difference is maybe in the melody...

Rajery: In the melody. Because you know, the singers of *tsapiky*, it's not like I do it. It's not the same. But we tried to keep the rhythmical root. That this rhythm is, it's *tsapiky*... Well, it's also our way of showing the *tsapiky*, of playing the *tsapiky*. So, that's us, based on our small analysis, our small research. Because we can't do it in the same way that they do it. Because we as well, we would like to create something, search for something new. But it always stays in the *esprit* of the *tsapiky*. (Interview Rajery, 17.12.2007)

For Rajery, rhythm plays an important role within his compositions. As the example of the "*Tandremo*" song shows, he says that he uses a particular rhythm to underline the message of his song; by choosing this particular rhythm he adapts the song for a particular audience (young people). At the same time, it becomes clear that "rhythm" needs to be understood in a wider sense when he speaks of *tsapiky*. By explaining that his group created their own version of *tsapiky* music, it becomes evident that *tsapiky* for him describes everything from guitar-playing and singing style to tempo and rhythmic structure. However, he puts a particular emphasis on the "rhythmic root" of *tsapiky,* which is the only musical feature they kept from *tsapiky* as it is played in the South. This mirrors many musicians' ideas that there is a common rhythmical structure in Madagascar, one that all Malagasy people share regardless of home region.

In his description of how the composition of the song developed, Rajery points to ideas of both sameness and difference, on a variety of levels. He explains that *tsapiky* and reggae music have something in common, a similarity he uses to evoke certain musical associations. At the same time, he points out the particularity of *tsapiky* music, which lies especially in its tempo; but with regard to *tsapiky* music, he also draws a clear line between *tsapiky* as played in the South—in its region of origin— and his own version of *tsapiky*, which he says retains the "*esprit* of *tsapiky* music." Although he emphasises the similarity of rhythmic root between these two *tsapiky* musics, he explains his group are unable to play *tsapiky* like the people in the South. He points to regional differences within *tsapiky* regarding both singing style (the way of entering the voice, for example) and the manner of playing the guitar.

A kind of counterpart of Rajery's statement can be found in Mallet's book on *tsapiky* music (Mallet 2009). He analyses how *tsapiky* musicians create a very strong regional identity through their music-making, expressing negativity—even a sense of exclusion—towards both the

capital and the land of the *Merina* people (Mallet 2009: 151). In one of the
musicians' statements quoted in Mallet's analysis of the regional identity,
the topic of "rhythm" also comes to the fore. The musician claims that
people from other regions are not capable of playing *tsapiky* music
correctly:

> *À Tana par exemple il y a des gens qui étudient le tsapiky mais ils
> n'arrivent pas. La batterie ils arrivent, mais le rythme non, c'est différent.
> Même à Tamatave ils ont voulu le tsapiky mais non* (Quoted in Mallet
> 2009: 149).[7]

It is striking to see that the musician distinguishes "rhythm" from what
is played on the drum kit in *tsapiky* music, arguing both that their rhythm
is different to that of other regions and also that people from other regions
cannot capture the *tsapiky* rhythm. Once again, this points at the necessity
of understanding "rhythm" in a wider sense, for example analysing
different musical features in their interdependence—a topic I will return to
because it has been part of my own musical experiences and learning
process.

Rajery's description of his song evoking different kinds of musical
journeys while retaining Malagasy, particularly *tsapiky* at its base,
resembles a general trend among musicians I have discovered through
interviews with musicians as well as projects we have worked on together:
many musicians create Malagasy versions of already existing tunes or
"Malagasise" music, as they often refer to it. Every time musicians talk
about these processes of "Malagasising" music, the topic of "rhythm"
seems to play a crucial role. It is particularly within these discussions on
"Malagasising" tunes and on compositions that regional differences are
described or emphasised by the musicians, as Rajery's example above
shows.

One of the main arguments within the musicians' explanations of
"Malagasising" music is that it is about a change of the rhythmic structure,
often adding a ternary rhythmic structure to a binary one or vice versa.
Jazz saxophone player Seta leads the so-called "Tana Gospel Choir." He
says that he realised people like it very much if they "Malagasise"
protestant chants, which are normally in a 4/4 metre. From his experiences
as a jazz musician, including involvement in international and therefore
intercultural music projects, he argues that the Malagasy rhythm can easily

---

[7] "In Tana, for example, there are people who study *tsapiky,* but they don't get it.
The drum kit yes, but the rhythm no, it's different. Even in Tamatave they wanted
the *tsapiky,* but no..." (my translation).

be integrated into jazz standards.[8] In 2010, I was involved in a project by Erick Manana that included "Malagasising" jazz standards, an experience that I will describe in more detail later in this chapter.[9]

Ricky and Jean-Claude told me in our interview that they were planning to record a Malagasy version of a song by Jimmy Hendrix. Jean-Claude immediately introduced the topic of "rhythm," to be here understood in the wider sense; melodies, for example, can be rhythmical as well and can enrich the main "6/8 rhythm," as Jean-Claude explains. This is about mixing and combining the main rhythm with "rhythmical melodies" or "riffs:"

Il y a la guitare, le sax, mais le riff, c'est rythmique. C'est une mélodie qui revient et elle devient rythmique... Les Rolling Stones, quand tu fais [il chante le début de la chanson 'Satisfaction'], ça, c'est rythmique. Donc, lorsque on joue une musique dans le 6/8 et on met en plus une mélodie qui est un riff, la rythmique, elle est beaucoup plus riche. Enfin je sais pas [il rit]... Une mélodie peut être rythmique et ce qui va aussi enrichir la musique 6/8, c'est la mélodie et le riff qu'on va mettre dessus, elle sera en général dans l'esprit 6/8. Donc, le 6/8 devient encore plus chargé et beaucoup plus riche. (Interview Jean-Claude, 18.7.2008)

There is the guitar, the sax, but the riff, it's rhythmical. It's a melody that returns and that becomes rhythmical... The Rolling Stones, when you do [he sings the beginning of the song 'Satisfaction'], that, that's rhythmical. So, when you play music in a 6/8 and you add a melody that is a riff, the rhythm becomes richer. Actually I don't know [he laughs]... A melody can be rhythmical and what will also enrich music in a 6/8 is the melody and the riff you will add, generally it's in the esprit of the 6/8. So, the 6/8 becomes heavier and even richer. (Interview Jean-Claude, 18.7.2008)

According to the musicians' descriptions, rhythmical structure is never the only element to be changed. Melody, for example, is always closely related to rhythm, a relationship that changes dramatically between the

---

[8] Discussion with Seta, 11.12.2007.

[9] It is a common phenomenon that jazz is being taken up by musicians around the world. This has also attracted the interest of researchers. Johnson (2002) develops the notion of a "jazz diaspora" and gives a detailed account of various jazz practices around the world. He argues that jazz "was not 'invented' and then exported. It was invented in the process of being disseminated. As both idea and practice, jazz came into being through negotiation with the vehicles of its dissemination, and with conditions it encountered in any given location" (Johnson 2002: 39). Jazz practices by Malagasy musicians in Madagascar and abroad is yet another research field to be explored.

different regional styles of Malagasy music (as, for example, with regard to where the strong beats are felt). Hence, it is also about changing the accentuation and playing the right tempo as well as the singing and guitar-playing style. Erick Manana, for example, often argues that he mainly creates "High Plateaux" versions of music tunes as this is the region musical style from where he originates, claiming that a Malagasy version of the same music by a musician from the South would be completely different. He argued that if you gave the same song to be "Malagasised" by each of the five musicians in the "Madagascar AllStars"—all from different areas of the island—the result would be five completely different, yet all Malagasy, versions of it.[10]

To sum up, it is in the musicians' narratives on their compositions and on their projects of "Malagasising" music that regional differences and peculiarities within Malagasy music are of most importance to the musicians. At the same time, their references do not only point to the local or regional but also relate their ideas of regional particularities to the global, as when talking about "global music styles" such as jazz or reggae, or in talking about particular musical icons, such as Jimmy Hendrix or the Rolling Stones.

Tapping Feet, Counting and Clapping

The musicians' emphasis on regional particularities does not tally with another topic that persistently reoccurred in narratives of their musical experiences: counting, tapping feet, clapping or any other body movements felt or made while musicking. When discussing these latter topics, musicians would tend to emphasise differences between themselves and non-Malagasy people.[11] Ways of counting while musicking are, at the same time, sometimes described as individualised and personal, as the analysis of the following examples will show.

During one research stay in Antananarivo, I spent an afternoon with violin player Samy listening to music—a collection of tunes from all around the island across a span of decades he had assembled for me. It had been his idea that we should spend some time listening to these tunes together; he wanted to show me that even the way of listening to music

---

[10] Erick Manana during a discussion at the TnMundi conference in Southampton, 15-17th October 2009.

[11] This is also a topic raised by many European people. For example, during and after concerts of Malagasy music, many people say that they are puzzled; they could not understand nor follow the clapping or tapping of the musicians or the Malagasy audience—they were always tapping or clapping differently.

was very different between Malagasy and European people, particularly as regards the rhythm and how one would count or clap to the music. Samy always emphasised the structure of overlapping binaries and ternaries in Malagasy music; this is exactly where he argues these differences come to the fore: Europeans would often hear (and clap to) the binary structure; Malagasy to the ternary structure:

C'est justement ça que je vais te démontrer là maintenant... 1, 2, 3, 4 quand un Européen écoute ça, il dit 1, 2, 3, 4 alors que nous, dans notre tête, c'est 1, 2, 3, 4, 5, 6, 1, 2, 3, 4, 5, 6...[12] (Interview Samy, 7.12.2007)

That's exactly what I will demonstrate to you now... 1, 2, 3, 4 when a European listens to that, he says 1, 2, 3, 4 whereas we, in our head, it's 1, 2, 3, 4, 5, 6, 1, 2, 3, 4, 5, 6...[13] (Interview Samy, 7.12.2007)

Rakotomavo also often brought up the topic of overlapping binaries and ternaries in Malagasy music. As already shown in the previous chapter, he has his own theory distinguishing a "synthetic metre" from an "analytic metre," the latter based on the Malagasy language (see chapter 5). In one interview he gave an example that resembles Samy's idea above, but pointing the opposite way. He argues here that the French waltz "*L'étoile de neige*" in Madagascar was typically played in a binary metre:

Tu connais la chanson là? 'L'étoile des neige'? [Il chante] C'est une valse, mais ici [il chante et clappe à deux temps].[14] *Ça se joue à deux temps, ça c'est typiquement malgache ça.* (Interview Rakotomavo, 1.8.2008)

Do know this song? '*L'étoile des neige*'? [He sings] It is a waltz, but here [he sings and claps in two].[15] We play it in two, that's typical Malagasy. (Interview Rakotomavo 1.8.2008)

Ricky also talks about the coexistence of binaries and ternaries in Malagasy music; he describes it as one of the particularities through which Malagasy music creates difference upon which harmony can be built. He talks about *Mpihira Gasy* violin, trumpet and accordion player Doné (alias Doné Sahondrafinina), who always automatically joins in any 4/4 piece

---

[12] Sound example 8 on DVD.
[13] Sound example 8 on DVD.
[14] Sound example 9 on DVD.
[15] Sound example 9 on DVD.

with a 6/8 rhythm; i.e. he adds the ternary structure to the existing binaries:

> *Mais l'influence aussi, l'ouverture, l'influence, ça va expliquer beaucoup de choses. Par exemple, quand on fait des trucs avec Doné, un truc qui est vraiment en 4/4 comme funk ou je sais pas quoi, mais lui il rentre tout de suite en 6/8 sur le 4/4! Tu vois? Et c'est bien, parce que ça nous a donné vraiment une différence, mais cette différence, ça va créer l'harmonie si c'est bien géré.* (Interview Ricky, 18.7.2008)

> But also the influence, the openness, the influence, that will explain many things. For example, when we play some stuff with Doné, something which is really in 4/4 like funk or I don't know, but he immediately plays a 6/8 on the 4/4! You see? And that's good, because it really has given us a difference, but this difference, it will create harmony if it's well handled. (Interview Ricky, 18.7.2008)

Within the musicians' discussions of different metres or overlapping rhythmic structures, questions of accentuation and the placement of strong beats seem to be key issues. Ricky first argues that the placement of strong beats in Malagasy music was different from that in the music of the "other side of the ocean," referring to the African mainland.[16] During the same interview, Ricky later describes the placement of strong beats as something very personal and individual. He gives the example of singer and fellow musician Dama Mahaleo whose strong beats, Ricky argues, are very different to his own. Here, Ricky describes the placement and feeling of strong beats as something determined by each person's individual education, sensibility for the environment and the music they carry in ourselves:

> *Parce qu'avec Dama, lui, le temps fort de Dama, quand il joue, c'est vraiment différent de nous! Et ça c'est lui. C'est lui et là, tu ne peux pas dire: 'Dama, ça c'est faux, non!' Mais vraiment c'est comme ça. C'est une question de sensibilité par rapport d'environnement, d'éducation, la forme de la musique à l'intérieur de lui-même.* (Interview Ricky, 18.7.2008)

> Because with Dama, Dama's strong beats, when he plays, it's really different to us! And that's him. It's him and here you can't say: 'Dama, that's wrong, no!' But really, it's like that. It's a question of sensibility with regard to the environment, education, one's inner music. (Interview Ricky, 18.7.2008)

---

[16] Interview with Ricky, Antananarivo, 18.7.2008.

Bilo also speaks of the placement of strong beats and the way it creates differences between Malagasy and European people. Although European and Malagasy people both have the "6/8 rhythm," he argues that Malagasy people tend not to play exactly on the beat. For him, Malagasy musicians never follow the beat "correctly," which is the biggest difference:

La différence, c'est le temps. Le temps du 6/8, parce que nous les Malgaches, on ne suit pas les temps correctement, juste au temps, juste dans la mesure. On fait des contretemps, ou mi-temps ou avant-temps ou avec le temps, c'est comme ça qu'on fait le 6/8. Et c'est ça un peu la différence entre les 6/8 européens et les 6/8 malgaches, parce qu'on chante pas direct dans le temps. Le rythme, ça tombe pas directement dans le temps, tac tac tac tac... Mais on peut chanter à mi-temps, le temps avant et on chante après. Ou on fait contretemps. Tu vois, c'est ça la différence. (Interview Bilo, 19.8.2008)

The difference, that's the beat. The beat of the 6/8, because we the Malagasies, we do not follow the beat correctly, exactly on the beat, exactly in the metre. We play *contretemps*, or 'half-beat' or 'before the beat' or with the beat, that's the way we play the 6/8. And that's the difference between the European and the Malagasy 6/8, because we don't sing directly on the beat. The rhythm, it doesn't fall exactly on the beat, tac tac tac tac... but we can sing in 'half-beat,' a bit before or a bit after. Or we play *contretemps*. You see, that's the difference. (Interview Bilo, 19.8.2008)

This resembles what Jaojoby explained to me: *salegy* music is for him something "round," with the accent never on the first beat but instead on the *contretemps*. Jaojoby does not speak of a difference from European people but describes this as a problem that Europeans have with Malagasy music. He says that this is a question of "being bathed" in a music, something that could be learnt with a few years of practice and training:

Quand c'est pas carré, quand c'est rond, souvent on rentre en contretemps, on rentre jamais dans le premier temps. C'est ça le problème des Européens. Mais une fois qu'on est baigné dedans, toi qui t'intéresses au salegy depuis deux, trois ans là, tu peux jouer de ça! (Interview Jaojoby, 21.8.2008)

When it's not 'square,' when it is round, often you enter on the *contretemps*, you never enter on the first beat. That's the problem of the Europeans. But once you get used to it; like you who have been interested in *salegy* for two or three years, you can play it! (Interview Jaojoby, 21.8.2008)

In summary, apart from Ricky's argument that it finally is a very individual question, musicians seem to agree that when it comes to counting to music or tapping or clapping along while musicking, differences between Malagasy and non-Malagasy—usually meaning European—people are striking. Most of these statements are based on experiences as well as observations made by musicians, as the following part will show.

Intercultural Musical Encounters— Examples of Musicians' Experiences

Singer and guitarist Erick Manana told me he was once in a studio recording in France working with a technician who was fascinated by what he was playing rhythmically. The technician decided to play in a 6/8 beat from a metronome, which irritated Erick and made it so he was unable to play.[17]

The technician then recorded what Erick was playing, keen to find the musician's "system" using sound diagrams on his computer. It turned out that the way Erick played was somehow irregular but forming an irregular pattern that repeated itself regularly.[18] Erick said this is because he never

---

[17] Singer Bebey also told me the story that someone had tried to let legendary flute player Rakoto Frah to play with a metronome; this did not work out. Rakoto Frah was horrified, saying "This thing kills me!" Discussion with Bebey, 15.7.2008.

[18] Different scholars have made use of real time measuring. Stobart and Cross (2000), in their study on Bolivian "Easter songs" write that "[w]hen the rhythmic values of individual notes were measured in milliseconds it was discovered that relationships between the durations of individual notes were often asymmetrical and variable, but that the pulse and durations of rhythmic groups (e.g. of two or three notes) were highly regular" (Stobart and Cross 2000: 72). Another approach using real time measuring, also with a particular focus on rhythm, is a method that investigates the role of "entrainment" (Clayton, Sager and Will 2005; Clayton 2008), a concept originally identified by Dutch physicist Christiaan Huygens already in the 17th century. Clayton, Sager and Will (2005) developed a method that correlates musicological description, ethnography and the analysis of movements of both performers and listeners through the analysis of video recordings. They argue that "entrainment" has been proven to be a powerful tool also in research areas of ethnomusicology, for example as it has been inspiring new perspectives on research concerning "metre" (Clayton, Saga, and Will 2005: 20). Therefore, research on Malagasy music following or inspired by a model of "entrainment" could be useful and highly interesting as it offers further ways to tackle the issue of the "6/8 rhythm" and debates on rhythmic perception in Malagasy music-making.

plays exactly on the beat. Instead, it is a very special timing of the *"temps forts,"* the strong beats. His very first tour manager in France was not so much curious as frightened. Erick Manana said that the manager had asked him to stop tapping his feet during the concerts; the manager worried it would confuse Western audiences. He was unable to keep his feet from tapping—getting rid of the tour manager instead—but tends to leave out the "complicated Malagasy rhythms" if playing for a non-Malagasy audience; instead, he plays rhythms with which the people can identify (*"se retrouvent"*). In Madagascar, he does exactly the opposite. For this reason, a primarily European audience containing only a handful of Malagasy people those Malagasy might be disappointed by the music. At the same time, Erick Manana argues that he enjoys playing for people who do not know him because it makes him realise that there is something really special in Malagasy music.[19]

The examples of Erick Manana's experiences in France resemble other intercultural encounters experienced by many of the other musicians. As all the musicians I worked with are to some extent involved in the so-called "world music" business (see chapter 1), almost all of them have played with musicians from outside Madagascar or attended musical events, such as festivals, concerts and recording sessions abroad. Here, I will focus on how musicians describe their experience of working with non-Malagasy musicians and their observations on intercultural musical encounters.

Ricky told me about a situation he had seen at a festival in La Réunion where Malagasy accordionist Régis Gizavo (based in Paris; member of the Madagascar AllStars) was accompanied by a percussionist who had problems capturing the right rhythm. Ricky laughed as he explained that he immediately understood what was going on. The percussionist had played a ternary rhythm, like a waltz, which did not fit to the rhythm that Régis Gizavo had been playing. Ricky, confirming his point of view that rhythmical feeling is something very individual, says that it is not a question of being Malagasy, French or any other nationality, but rather the question of whether you get the rhythm:

J'ai vu un percussionniste qui joue avec Régis à la Réunion au «Kabardock», eux, ils ont des problèmes. Et moi, j'étais dans le public et moi je sais c'est quoi le problème [il rit]. Parce que Régis il donne des trucs comme [il montre][20], et le gars il rentre dans le 3/4 [il montre][21] et

---

[19] Discussion with Erick Manana, 27.2.2008.
[20] Sound example 10 on DVD.
[21] Sound example 10 on DVD.

c'est comme la valse ou je sais pas. Mais j'ai bien compris la situation. Donc, ça c'est pas l'histoire d'être Malgache ou Français ou Comorien ou..., mais c'est vraiment... tu captes ou tu captes pas. (Interview Ricky, 18.7.2008)

I have seen a percussionist who plays with Régis in La Réunion at the "Kabardock," they had problems. And I was in the audience and I knew what the problem was [he laughs]. Because Régis, he plays things like [he demonstrates],[22] and then the guy he starts playing in a 3/4 [he demonstrates][23] and that's like a waltz or I don't know. But I have understood the situation. So, it's not a question of being Malagasy, or French, or Comorian or... but it's really... you get it or you don't. (Interview Ricky, 18.7.2008)

However, for the majority of musicians the fact of being Malagasy or not seems to be the most essential one. As already seen, some musicians speak of a Malagasy "soul" necessary to play this music correctly. Bebey, for example, argues that the music never sounds properly Malagasy when foreign people play it: the "Malagasy soul" is missing.[24] Similarly, Ratovo says that it is not too difficult for foreigners to capture the "6/8 rhythm," but the "soul" would always be missing in their playing:

C'est très facile, surtout le 6/8... Mais c'est l'âme qui manque! (Interview Ratovo, 26.7.2008)

That's very easy, especially the 6/8... But it's the soul that is missing! (Interview Ratovo, 26.7.2008)

Echoing the examples analysed above, strong beats and accentuation are key issues that come up in the musicians' discourses on their intercultural musical experiences. This is also the case for choreographer and dancer Ariry. In an interview he talks about a French dancer who had lived in Madagascar for nine years. Despite these nine years of collaboration, there had always been what Ariry calls a "*contretemps* of placement of the strong beats." The problem lay in where to place the first

---

[22] Sound example 10 on DVD.
[23] Sound example 10 on DVD.
[24] Discussion with Bebey, 15.7.2008. Bebey further explained that this "soul" was something that Malagasy people could easily lose as well. Young people, for example, who mainly listen to foreign music would lose the Malagasy soul, the Malagasy rhythm and the Malagasy polyphonic singing.

beat (*"l'attaque"*)—this matched what he had experienced when he went to Europe and the United States to give dancing classes:

> Ariry: *Un Français, il était ici pendant neuf ans. Mais même neuf ans de pratique de ce qu'on avait fait, il y avait toujours... ce que moi je vais dire, un contretemps de temps fort que moi, je voudrais suivre. Et des fois, j'ai donné des cours en Europe ou aux Etats-Unis et il y a toujours ce problème-là.*
> Jenny: *Mais tu peux expliquer ce qu'ils font? Si tu expliques la différence...*
> Ariry: *La différence, la différence c'est toujours l'attaque...*
> Jenny: *L'attaque?*
> Ariry: *L'attaque du rythme. Le premier temps du rythme... Ah j'arrive pas vraiment à expliquer, mais je sais pas pourquoi, je sais pas comment, mais il y a toujours l'attaque du premier temps [il clappe] de ce que moi je pense le premier temps que moi j'aimerais bien suivre. Mais les autres personnes, ils ont une autre... leur propre premier temps.* (Interview Ariry, 26.7.2008)

> Ariry: A French, he was here for nine years. But even nine years of practice of what we did, there was always…what I would call a *contretemps* of the strong beats that I would follow. And sometimes, I have given classes in Europe and in the Unites States and there was always this problem.
> Jenny: But can you explain what they do? If you explain the difference…
> Ariry: The difference, the difference is always the attack…
> Jenny: The attack?
> Ariry: The rhythm attack. The first beat of the rhythm… oh I don't really manage to explain, but I don't know why, I don't know how, but there is always the attack of the first beat [he claps] of what I think is the first beat and that I would like to follow. But the other persons, they have another… their own first beat. (Interview Ariry, 26.7.2008)

Hajazz is equally convinced that accentuation and the placement of strong beats differ and can create problems for foreigners trying to play Malagasy music. However, he distinguishes between different kinds of foreigner; African people, he argues, have fewer difficulties than European people:

> Hajazz: *Entre par exemple Africains, ça marche plus vite, avec des Européens c'est un peu difficile pour eux. Mais si, par exemple, on sait lire les notes comme ça, on peut déchiffrer quelques notes. Mais le problème de temps en temps, on peut pas, chacun a sa façon de jouer après... Le problème c'est l'accentuation, les accents, il y a des accents, il y a du temps fort et temps faible. C'est pour cela par exemple que les gens*

étrangers n'arrivent pas à jouer comme les Malgaches. Parce qu'il y a l'accent [il tape le pied]...
Jenny: *C'est quoi...*
Hajazz: *Le placement des temps forts et temps faibles et des soupirs et tout ça... Des nuances comme ça.* (Interview Hajazz,12.8.2008)

Hajazz: For example between Africans, it works quicker, with the Europeans it's a bit difficult for them. But, for example, if you know how to read sheet music like this, you can decipher some notes. But from time to time the problem is, you cannot, finally everyone has his own way of playing... The problem is the accentuation, the accents, there are accents, there are strong beats and weak beats. That's for example why foreign people do not manage to play like the Malagasies. Because there is the accent [he taps his foot]
Jenny: What is it...
Hajazz: The placement of the strong and weak beats and crotchets rests and all this... Nuances like that. (Interview Hajazz, 12.8.2008)

Rajery sees the difficulties for *vazahas* as lying in the structure of overlapping binaries and ternaries. In a discussion similar to that we have already seen in the section on musicians' discourses about "Malagasising" music, Rajery argues that Malagasy people are capable of adding a ternary rhythm to a binary or vice versa:

Là, le problème de la musique malgache aussi avec les vazaha, c'est l'existence de binaire et ternaire en même temps dans une chanson, c'est... Tu vois [il rit]... Des fois si on fait des rencontres avec des musiciens étrangers, ils ont eu du mal. Parce que nous, on est capable aussi d'introduire des rythmes ternaires dans les rythmes binaires ou l'envers. (Interview Rajery, 17.12.2007)

The problem with Malagasy music and the *vazaha* is the existence of binaries and ternaries at the same time in one song, it's... you see [he laughs]... Sometimes when we meet foreign musicians, they have difficulties. Because we are capable of adding ternary rhythms to binaries and vice versa. (Interview Rajery, 17.12.2007)

Justin Vali also points to the structure of overlapping binaries and ternaries, arguing it is the "6/8 rhythm" that foreigners have difficulties in following. The reason for this is that the rhythm is always *"en l'air,"* referring to the coincidence of the strong beat with the moment when the musicians' tapping foot is up (see also chapter 5). Here, Justin also uses *salegy* as a synonym for "6/8 rhythm," a phenomenon discussed in the previous chapter:

Parce que les musiciens, quand ils jouent le 6/8, le rythme était en l'air. Donc, c'est pour cela que souvent les musiciens à l'extérieur, ils ont toujours du mal à suivre le rythme. Et quand on fait le salegy, c'est toujours quand on donne des concerts à l'extérieur, les étrangers, c'est difficile pour eux de suivre le rythme salegy. (Interview Justin, 23.11.2007)

Because the musicians, when they play the 6/8, the rhythm is in the air. So, that's why often foreign musicians, they have difficulties in following the rhythm. And when we play the *salegy*, every time we give concerts abroad, foreigners, it's difficult for them to follow the *salegy* rhythm. (Interview Justin, 23.11.2007)

To sum up, apart from Ricky's opinion on every musician's individuality, all musicians stress differences to non-Malagasy people and without exception talk about disappointments and situations that did not work out with regard to intercultural musical encounters.

Participating Musically Myself

So, how do I fit my own musical experiences into narratives about the failed musical adventures of non-Malagasy people venturing into Malagasy music-making?

First of all, many of the musicians have argued that one needs to play Malagasy music in order to properly understand it. They have also expressed a certain degree of discontent about the prevalence of non-musicians writing about music and musicians' inability to write about music and explain properly what they are doing.[25] In various interview situations and even more so during informal conversation at rehearsals, concerts and recording sessions, I have been encouraged not only by the musicians but also by people involved in the organisation or from the audience. So far, I have not had any sceptical or generally negative responses towards my participation in Malagasy music making. Rather to the contrary, Malagasy people very often express hope about as well as interest and curiosity in my work, saying that this kind of research and work—but especially event of a *vazaha*, performing live Malagasy music—was necessary. During our concert tour in June 2011 and also before and after our concert in May 2012 at the "Palais des Sports" in Antananarivo, there was significant media interest in me, emphasising that I am a German musician and researcher focusing much energy and time on

---

[25] An argument that also appears in musicological scholarly debates; see for example Cook (1999).

Malagasy music.[26] It often happens that people from the audience come to speak to me after a concert, to ask when my academic work would be available to the public and how I was planning to make it accessible, especially to the Malagasy communities.

I have also drawn confidence in practicing Malagasy music (and using these practices and experiences for my research and analysis) from Agawu's notion of a "presumption of sameness" (Agawu 2003: 171). Intercultural musical encounters are at base all about interaction, communication and musical exchange. Even though it was the case that I was learning "their music," I can recall many situations in which I have become the one being "researched" and "observed" (see chapter 1 for a detailed discussion). I argue that every musician has their own musical "baggage,"[27] created by their musical education, training, experiences, listening habits, access to musical events, recordings etc. Whatever the form of our "baggage," we can draw on it for exchange and interaction. We can use this to create a shared musical experience when musicking and thereby widen and enrich our shared experiential horizon. The following examples will show that my practical engagement in Malagasy music did not aim at "becoming Malagasy" in any way. Instead, my approach has been self-reflexive and sensitive, taking into account my own musical "baggage," my double role as researcher and as a musician and the particular research context (the research language, the role of Antananarivo, the musicians' aim at the international music market etc.).

Examples

The Importance of *Lova-tsofina*

Engaging in discussions with musicians alongside listening to and analysing their discourses about music has given me much inspiration and help for learning and playing Malagasy music. I have become aware of topics, ideas and methods that otherwise I would have never thought about, never used or never felt and experienced.

I would like to start by giving what might be the most obvious example, as it has been the starting point for many others. If the musicians had not talked so much about their ways of learning music using nothing

---

[26] For examples of newspaper articles, see Rado (2011), Ratsara (2011), Solhar (2011) and Heimer (2011).

[27] A term also often used by the Malagasy musicians when talking about their own musical background, knowledge or training.

but their ears, emphasising the *lova-tsofina,* as the base of Malagasy music-making, I would not have tried to understand and use the concept myself. Many musicians encouraged me to learn using only my ears, such as Doné Andriambaliha in my very first *valiha* lesson in Antananarivo or Erick Manana who keeps teaching me new songs and compositions by singing to me; but musicians also indirectly encouraged me to discover and use the *lova-tsofina,* by emphasising the significance of the Malagasy language or Malagasy everyday life, as I will discuss in more detail below.

The counterpart to this first example is that only through experiencing and performing the music and therefore sharing experiences with musicians was I able to understand the essential idea of the *lova-tsofina* as the base for Malagasy music-making. Following the musicians' ideas and their own experiences of learning and playing by ear has helped me to understand the music without searching for any kind of authoritative text or indeed any kind of written source behind it. Through engaging in these musical practices, I have found other musical references (e.g. for tempi, accentuation etc.) and playing techniques that have in turn helped me to better understand the musicians' discourses. Engaging musically has made me realise that it is not about searching for any kind of exact musical "instructions" within the musicians' discourses on music but—as the examples below will show—listening to their individual concepts, ideas, and experiences.

"6/8 rhythm" and the Opportunity of Binaries and Ternaries

These first examples concerning the *lova-tsofina* return me to the crux of my research, the issue of the "6/8 rhythm." My own experiences of learning and playing Malagasy music by following the *lova-tsofina* have led to one particularly striking fact: any attempt to count to the music or imagine a particular metre—with a fixed accentuation—would confuse or even disturb rather than help me. However, I have discovered another way—for me, at least—to keep the tempo, play around with accentuations and "keep the dialogue" with other musicians. It is something I could describe as a kind of "inner dance," a way of moving and using my body movements as a reference. I am speaking of an "inner" dance only because I am not properly dancing, merely moving in subtle ways, such as swaying my head or the upper part of my body just a little bit.[28] It is also through

---

[28] Examples of these subtle body movements can be seen in video example 4 ("*Fofompofony ihany sisa*"), video example 5 ("*Bitika*") and video example 6 ("*Tsofy Rano*").

using this reference that I have come to understand one element related to the "6/8 rhythm" in a new way: the structure of overlapping binaries and ternaries.

As seen in chapter 2, this structure is crucial for Malagasy music, as other scholars also have pointed out. Malagasy musicologist Rakotomalala (2003), for example, argues that the Malagasy rhythm is either in two, but thought in three, or it is in three, but thought in two (Rakotomalala 2003: 43-44). The topic of a structure of binaries and ternaries also persistently appears in the musicians' discourses. As a result of my analysis of both discourses and musical experiences, I argue that this structure could best be described as a constant opportunity, meaning that no accentuation is fixed through a particular metre (as defined in Western music theory; see chapter 2) but that there is instead a constant opportunity for musicians to play with accents on both binary and ternary patterns. This implies that the two patterns are not both always audibly present, or that they are consistently felt and experienced equally by all musicians and music-listeners involved.

Using my body as a reference to follow this constant opportunity helps me to avoid falling into any particular metre (with its determined accentuation) and helps me follow other references for accentuation, such as the language, as I will explain below. The use of body movements as a reference and source for musicking is a well-known phenomenon. Rice (1994) for example speaks of physical behaviour that becomes part of the conceptual source of new musical ideas, referring to his personal discovery of how to make use of hand motions when playing the Bulgarian bagpipe (Rice 1994: 83). As seen in the last chapter, the musicians also point to the relation between music and dance, for example, or see rhythm as inherent to everyday movements like walking. The topic of body movements also reappears in other examples that I will give below, such as with regard to playing techniques of particular instruments or to the topic of individuality in music.

I remember how confused and irritated I was when during one of my first research stays in Antananarivo I happened to be at a Christmas party where the song "Silent Night" was sung; people were tapping their feet differently: some in two (focusing on the binary structure), some in three (focusing on the ternary structure). Since then, I have come across many other examples of this kind; Rakotomavo, for example, argues that a French waltz would be played in a binary rhythm in Madagascar, whilst Rajery explains that the coexistence of both binaries and ternaries is often the major obstacle within Malagasy music for Europeans (see interview quotations above).

Another example in which this structure of overlapping binary and ternary patterns becomes obvious is the accompaniment of singing with hand-clapping. A typical moment when hand-clapping comes into play is when a singer starts improvising, e.g. in musical styles like *saova* and *jijy* (see also chapter 2). Whereas the hand clapping varies with regard to the patterns or tempo in the different regional musical styles, there are always both clapping patterns emphasising a binary structure and ones emphasising a ternary structure.[29]

Engaging in "Malagasising" Music

As I highlighted at the beginning of this chapter, the structure of binaries and ternaries appears particularly prominently in the musicians' discourses about their way of composing, or when they talk about how they "Malagasise" other music.

Throughout the last years, Erick Manana has "Malagasised" many different musics, including Brazilian *bossa* songs, jazz standards, French chansons or German folk songs. In 2010, we prepared a performance at the "Festival Nuits Atypiques" in Langon, France. With the "Erick Manana Quintet"[30] we performed standard jazz and *manouche* tunes which Erick Manana had transformed into his own Malagasy versions, including lyrics in Malagasy.[31] Erick Manana says that in all his "Malagasised" version of songs he mainly draws on regional musical styles of the High Plateaux music, particularly the style of the *hira gasy*.[32] In the course of this music project, I have observed that people hear, experience and perceive the rhythmic structure of these "Malagasised" tunes differently. For example, sometimes people tend to concentrate more on the ternary rhythmical structure, whereas others tap their feet to a binary pattern.

---

[29] See video example 2: In May 2013 we prepared an intercultural music workshop for the "Stiftung Berliner Philharmoniker" (education programme) in Berlin. In this workshop we also demonstrated the accompaniment of singing with hand-clapping. In the video, we rehearse a typical hand clapping rhythm from Northern Madagascar.

[30] Erick Manana: guitar and voice, Rija Randrianianivosoa: guitar and voice, Modeste Ratsimandresy: saxophone and voice, Dina Rakotomanga: bass and voice, Jenny Fuhr: violin.

[31] Examples of "Malagasised" tunes by Erick Manana are on the DVD: two pieces by Django Reinhard (sound example 11: "*Nuages*"; sound example 12: "Tears"), two Brazilian *bossa* songs (sound example 13: "*Você Abusou*" by Antonio Carlos; sound example 14: "*Sampa*" by Caetano Veloso); and an extract from Erick Manana's version of Edith Piaf's "*La vie en rose*" (sound example 15).

[32] Various conversations with Erick Manana during rehearsals.

This project confirmed me in my feeling and understanding of a constant opportunity of binaries and ternaries in Malagasy music-making as described above. Playing this "Malagasised" music has also made me realise that counting to the music or thinking of a particular metre would not help when musicking. I am generally familiar with the original tunes, such as "*La vie en rose*" (Edith Piaf), "What a Wonderful World" (Louis Armstrong), or "*Nuages*" or "Tears" by Django Reinhardt, all of which we played in Erick Manana's Malagasy version. This has been helpful and challenging at the same time; knowing the original tunes has given me a detailed view of what exactly changes in the process of "Malagasising" them. At the same time, being familiar with the original tune has sometimes made it difficult to "loosen" myself from the rhythmical and melodic structures or arrangements of the original. Again, I have realised that using my subtle body movements as a rhythmical reference works well and avoids any attempt to try and count to the music while playing.

So what happens if music becomes "Malagasised"? I do agree with many musicians who say "Malagasising" is definitely always about changing the rhythmical structure of the music; I think that it could best be described as giving this constant opportunity of binaries and ternaries to any music. Sometimes it is about adding a ternary structure to a binary, sometimes vice versa. This does not imply that both are necessarily always audibly present; rhythmical perception can differ between different people. According to what I have experienced for myself, I could also describe it as a change of listening habit; I even realised that I start to hear a rhythmical structure of binaries and ternaries in non-Malagasy music I would have previously heard as either in two or in three. This experience mirrors some of the musicians' arguments—e.g. about hearing or dancing a waltz in a binary rhythm—as well as an aspect of Justin London's understanding of "metre," which he regards as a kind of "entrained behaviour" (London 2004: 4-6; see discussion on theories on "rhythm" and "metre" in chapter 2). I would therefore argue that what I describe as an opportunity is often misleadingly referred to as "6/8 rhythm." It is misleading in the sense that the particular metre of a "6/8 rhythm" as understood in its original context would determine a fixed accentuation (as argued in chapter 2).

The idea of a "constant opportunity" of binaries and ternaries raises the following questions: if there is no fixed indication in the music, such as a "metre," what determines accentuation or the rhythmical structure more generally? And how are regional particularities in Malagasy music related to rhythmical structure, given the claim by Erick Manana that he mainly creates High Plateaux versions of songs?

My focus on the connection between our shared musical experiences and discourses about Malagasy music-making have made me question my own understanding of the concept of "rhythm." Most importantly, it has made me understand that "rhythm" cannot be understood separately from other musical elements. Rather, the importance lies in seeing the interdependencies of different elements in music, such as between language and musical accentuation.

The Importance of Language and Lyrics

In the last chapter I identified language as one of the *topoi* that the musicians refer to in their ideas about the origin and meaning of "rhythm" in Madagascar. As I have argued that all *topoi* are closely related, aspects of language can also be found in other *topoi*, such as in everyday life—speaking is of course a daily activity. Musicians emphasise that Madagascar (unlike other African countries) has the same language, Malagasy, across its whole territory; some point to the close relation of language to both tempo and accentuation in music. For many musicians, language is an important factor to reflect upon when composing new songs (see beginning of this chapter).

If the topic of the Malagasy language had not appeared so persistently in the musicians' discourses, I probably would have not tried to use my knowledge of it in my experiences of musicking.

When I first started to play Malagasy music on my violin and recorder, I tried to learn the lyrics or at least keep the sound of them in my mind when learning a new song. This helped me to capture the story, emotion, or idea told within the song. On a more concrete level, mirroring Rakotomavo's idea about language determining accentuation in music, it has helped me find the right tempo and in placing accentuations. I often play an introduction to a song, mirroring the melody that will be sung afterwards. Here, I actually imagine the singing while playing the instrument. Similarly, when I play the counter-melody while the song is sung, I listen carefully to the lyrics and therefore the accentuation and tempo; it feels as though I am responding to or engaging in a dialogue.[33]

In the project of "Malagasising" tunes, mentioned above, I use lyrics and language as a reference, imagining the lyrics or singing while

---

[33] Examples of songs in which I play an introduction imagining the lyrics: video example 4 (*"Fofompofony ihany sisa"*), video example 7 (*"O Rakoto"*) and sound example 16 (*"Taralila an-dRasaraka"*). For an example of a counter-melody that I play as an introduction, see video example 6 (*"Tsofy Rano"*).

musicking. This has been especially useful, as it helps me not to fall back into the original non-Malagasised tune.

In turn, it is also true that it is through using aspects of the language while musicking and experimenting with language and tempo or accentuation that I have come to better understand the musicians' statement and ideas. I remember, for example, that I had difficulties at the very beginning when Erick Manana started singing to me in order to teach me new songs or new parts or accompaniments to a song. At first, I only listened to the actual notes and was surprised that he was not satisfied when I replayed the same notes he had just sung to me. Only a gradual process of learning through both listening to discourses and experimenting musically solved this. Through them, I realised I need to listen carefully to more than just the pitch of the notes, paying heed to the exact length of each note, the exact accentuation and tempo; finally, I realised it is not at all arbitrary which lyrics and words he chose to teach me.

The more I engage in singing, the more I understand the direct link between the Malagasy language and the rhythmical structure of the music. As much as I imagine singing the lyrics when playing my instruments, I also use imagination while singing, on a different level; the singing style that has fascinated me most since I began researching Malagasy music, the style to which my own singing has often been compared is that of the *mpihira gasy* (see also chapter 1). So far, there has not been any research focusing primarily on the musical aspect of the *hira gasy*; ethnographic studies include only a few very brief musical descriptions (Edkvist 1997:76-79; 118-119 and Mauro 2001: 205-206). *Hira gasy* singers need not only a loud voice, performing outside for a large number of people. They also need to pronounce every word carefully as the lyrics are of crucial importance. Further, *hira gasy* is not only about telling stories through songs. It is also about giving advice, discussing moral issues, debating politics and asking critical questions—it is about engaging the audience, entering into a dialogue. When I sing myself, I often automatically think about and imagine *hira gasy* singers. I have not had any singing lessons. Instead, I started to sing by getting to know Malagasy musicians, who encouraged me to sing along with them. To me, learning to sing involves watching singers and listening to their voices and their singing as well as getting to know them personally and understanding their everyday lives. An example where this aspect becomes obvious is the song "2CV an-dRandria," composed by Erick Manana in 2010, the first song that I publicly performed as a singer.[34] It is a song dedicated to the witty

---

[34] See video example 1 ("*Ny 2CV an-dRandria*").

and resourceful Antananarivo taxi drivers, praising their expertise and knowledge of the old 2CV cars and demanding more esteem for the profession. More generally, the song is also a tribute to the creative and optimistic Malagasy attitude to life. When Erick Manana first composed the song, it was based on a Brazilian *bossa* melody that he had "Malagasised."[35] However, he then decided that the story and lyrics of the song would be easier to perform in the *hira gasy* style; people would better understand the message of the song. Interestingly, he also told me that my voice and singing style would automatically make him compose in that style. When we perform "*2CV an-dRandria*" I am not only imagining *hira gasy* singers. I also think of all the taxi drivers I know and whose stories I have heard during my research stays in Antananarivo.

The Importance of the Instrument and its Playing Technique

The idea of using imagination while musicking has also come to me through yet another example of how the musicians' discourses influenced my musical experiences, an example which again is closely related to the *lova-tsofina*.

Many of the musicians are not only autodidacts, but have also built their own instruments. This might be one of the reasons why they often talk about particular playing techniques and the material and shape of an instrument as influences on the music. Many claim the playing technique is an important factor, including the percussion caused through the blowing technique of the *sodina* flute, the fall of the fingers on the (bamboo, wooden or plastic) tube of the flute, or the rattling sound of the strings of the bamboo zither *valiha*.

This is the reason why Rakotomavo was very critical about Justin Vali's "Ny Malagasy orkestra," mentioned in chapter 4. Rakotomavo at the time saw difficulties for that project because instruments were often very individual and personal in Madagascar:

> *C'est un projet très difficile, parce que réunir des gens qui n'ont jamais quitté leur coin, avec des instruments très personnels qu'ils ont fabriqué eux-mêmes, donc... Quand je fabrique un instrument, c'est pour moi. C'est moi qui va le jouer, c'est pas les autres. Et comme je vous ai dit tout à l'heure, entre deux valiha, ça ne passe pas. Il faut qu'il joue son instrument. Et cet instrument-là n'a pas été conçu d'être dans un*

---

orchestre. C'est pour jouer seul. Donc, c'est ça le problème pour ce genre de projets. (Interview Rakotomavo, 1.8.2008)

It's a difficult project, because bringing together people who have never left their area, with very personal instruments that they have built themselves, well... When I build an instrument, it's for me. It's me who will be playing it, it's not the others. And as I just told you, between two *valiha*, it doesn't work. He must play his instrument. And this instrument was not designed to be in an orchestra. It is for playing alone. So, that's the problem for this kind of project. (Interview Rakotomavo, 1.8.2008)

My first attempts to learn to play the bamboo zither *valiha* and my amateurish *valiha* playing ever since has helped me because Malagasy music, especially in the High Plateaux region, has its origin in *valiha* music. The instrument is mostly tuned in a diatonic scale; it is played with both hands, the notes alternating left and right.[36]

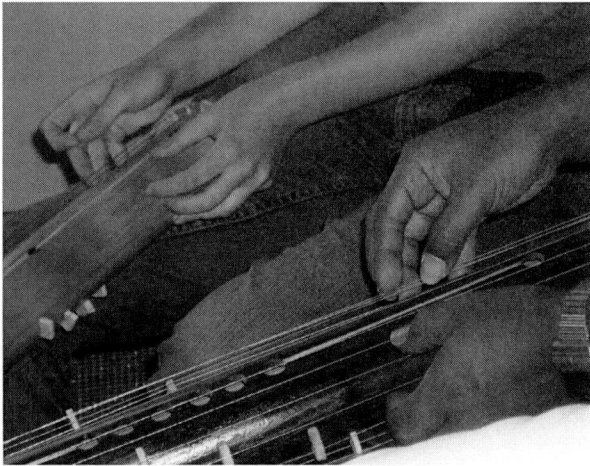

Fig. 6-1: *Valiha* playing technique. Picture taken during my *valiha* lesson with Doné Andriambaliha, Antananarivo, April 2005.

The instrument's tuning, with the notes alternating left and right, combines with its playing technique to shape the sound and style of *valiha* music, for example with regard to tempo and accentuation. If I now play a typical *valiha* phrasing on my violin or my recorder, it will help note

---

[36] See video example 8 for a demonstration of the *valiha* playing technique.

placement, accentuation and tempo if I imagine playing it on the *valiha*, i.e. by imagining the playing technique, shape and sound of the *valiha* itself.

I would like to explain this further with a concrete example. In Erick Manana's song *"Bitika,"*[37] which we played at the Olympia concert in Paris, I played a chorus that Erick Manana developed beforehand and taught me through singing it to me. The way Erick Manana arranged *"Bitika"* for that concert was mainly in the *hira gasy* style of the High Plateaux region. However, a few parts range through Madagascar as it plays with other regional styles. One element during the chorus is a musical reference to the musician Rakotozafy, a famous *marovany* player from the Northeast of the island I mentioned in chapter 2. Rakotozafy is known and admired for his virtuosic playing and special phrasings—such as a typical run downwards which Malagasy people immediately associate with him—, his playing style and the sound of his self-built *marovany*. When I play these runs on my violin or recorder,[38] imagining playing them on the *valiha* helps enormously; the playing technique (picking the strings, using both hands) and tuning of the instrument (with notes alternating left and right) create a very particular sound to this phrasing.

If the musicians had not talked so much about the interdependence between the instrument, its playing style and the sound and style of the music, I would probably not have tried to use my knowledge of *valiha* playing for my violin and recorder playing. At the same time, my practical experiences of having learnt *valiha* from scratch and learning and playing Malagasy music using my own violin (played in Western classical style) and my own Renaissance recorder (not a Malagasy *sodina*) has made me understand the musicians' discourses on these musical interdependencies; it has made me focus more on how a particular instrument or playing technique can shape and become part of music-making.

The Malagasy *sodina* in the High Plateaux region is made of bamboo, wood or plastic and is played slightly to the side because there is no mouth piece like that of the Western treble recorder. The blowing technique instead resembles that of the transverse flute. It is played with lots of air; watching *sodina* players, it almost looks as though the flute were "dancing" or "jumping" in front of the mouth. Various musicians explained to me that the sound created through this playing technique, the percussive sound of the blowing air and the sound of the fall of fingers onto the flute mentioned earlier, form part of the music. One typical

---

[37] See video example 5 (*"Bitika"*).
[38] See video example 5: 02:14-02:30 and 03:57-04:09

element of Malagasy *sodina* playing is to "close" every last note of a phrase by descending a few notes and thereby let the fingers fall onto the flute. Often, two or more flutes play together, with the second flute playing around the principal melody and thus engaging in a "dialogue."[39]

When I play Malagasy music on my Renaissance recorder, I take the instrument slightly to the side, not in imitation of the look of a Malagasy player but for reasons concerning particular elements in the music that I have described in the examples above: holding the recorder to the side and blowing with more air approaches the sound of the *sodina* flute and also allows me to play more easily with and differentiate more in terms of accentuation. It further helps in imagining the lyrics, i.e. imagining the vocal element of the performance while actually playing my instrument.[40]

I have had comparable experiences with my violin playing. I have mainly played music from the High Plateaux region or music in the style of this region in which the sound of the violin is mainly associated with the *hira gasy*. *Hira gasy* violin players often hold their instrument against their upper part of the body but often also in the "Western way" with the violin resting on the shoulder. They often tighten the bow's hair with the same hand they are holding the bow, gripping it towards the middle rather than at the bow frog as in the Western classical way. I have not changed the way I hold my violin and bow. However, as for the recorder, I have discovered certain interdependencies between the playing technique of the instrument and the music.

Erick Manana, who grew up surrounded by *hira gasy* musicians and who says that many of his own compositions are inspired by this particular style of Malagasy music, told me a few times during our rehearsals that the most typical element of *hira gasy* violin playing for him was a rather rhythmical playing style with the bow hardly ever resting. He often asks me to "put in more little notes" ("*mettre plus des petites notes*"), especially if I play a counter-melody with my violin (or recorder); this is often about adding particular rhythmical runs specific to *hira gasy* music.[41] In order to play these runs correctly in terms of accentuation and tempo, it helps

---

[39] For examples of the typical "closing down" of last notes and for "flute dialogues", see video example 3 ("*Ilay tany niaviako*"), video example 4 ("*Fofompofony ihany sisa*"), video example 5 ("*O Rakoto*") and sound example 16 ("*Taralila an-dRasaraka*").

[40] See for example video example 4 ("*Fofompofony ihany sisa*") and video example 7 ("*O Rakoto*").

[41] Examples of these runs can be seen in video example 5 ("*Bitika*"): 0:27-0:31 (violin) or 3:33-3:36 (flute), video example 6 ("*Tsofy Rano*"): 0:52-0:59 and 2:40-2:43.

enormously to use what I have described as my subtle body movements as a rhythmical reference. Imagining the lyrics or the singing is another way of getting these runs "right," just as I imagine the lyrics when I play the instrumental introduction to a song.

It is often when I play these runs (a reference to *hira gasy* music; similar to the example above of the reference to the playing style of Rakotozafy) that the Malagasy audience reacts during the songs.[42] Similarly, the audience also often reacts through clapping or shouting comments when I first start singing in a song.

In chapters 1 and 3, I have reflected upon my double role as musician and researcher. Within my research, the boundary between "researcher" and "researched" has become more and more blurred the more I perform Malagasy music, especially in Madagascar; this relates to another topic that draws on the connection between the analyses of discourses and shared musical practices, namely the emphasis put on personality and individuality in Malagasy music-making.

The Emphasis on Personality and Individuality in Malagasy Music

My focus on identity issues throughout the book has shown that identities often shift and, depending on the topic, theme and context, references are drawn to various places of belonging. Fitting myself and my own role, experiences and feelings into these layers of shifting identities is challenging. And yet, it is exactly my participatory approach and the lived experience of accepting my double role as both researcher and researched (as both researcher and musician) that has brought another significant aspect of Malagasy music-making to the fore.

With regard to the significance of the *lova-tsofina* for the musicians, I have mentioned the importance that places of learning (such as the streets of the musicians' home towns and villages or the neighbouring courtyard), or learning sources (such as the radio or a grandfather's singing) play for the musicians; they often express this in songs dedicated to these places and persons.[43]

---

[42] This can also be observed in video example 5 ("*Bitika*"): 0:27-0:31 and video example 6 ("*Tsofy Rano*"): 2:40-2:43.

[43] For example: Erick Manana composed the song "*O Rakoto*" as a tribute to the flutist Rakoto Frah with whom he played and learned over a long period of time (see video example 7). He also made his own Malagasy version of "Crying in the rain" called "*Revirevinay Tamboho*"—a song dedicated to a small wall in

As explained above, the *marovany* player Rakotozafy is not only a well-known musical personality but certain musical features are associated with him and with his particular playing style and sound. According to my own experience, Malagasy people tend to stress the importance of personality within music and the influence of a musician's personality on the shape of music. In Western classical music, for example, it is more often the musical piece or oeuvre as such that becomes the centre of attention, although nowadays there is definitely a tendency to focus on the interpreters (as the marketing of certain "classical superstars" shows).[44] Within Malagasy music, however, I have sensed the attention that people give to the interplay of musician—i.e. their personality—and the music they create and perform. Musicians argue that the *lova-tsofina* itself is always already personal and individual—it is with your very own ears that you learn, play and create music. This also shines through in the musicians' explanations about the self-built and therefore personal instruments. I will try to explain this aspect with more detailed examples that also concern my own experiences of musicking.

Playing a *sodina* (a Malagasy flute) is in Madagascar inevitably associated with one particular person: Philibert Rabazoza, alias Rakoto Frah, who I mentioned before. This legendary flute player performed over many years, forming the sound of Malagasy flute music, particularly in the High Plateaux region, before he died in Antananarivo in 2001. I have not experienced one occasion, be it in Madagascar or abroad, where *sodina* music was played, heard or spoken of without Rakoto Frah being mentioned and becoming the source of numerous stories, memories, and anecdotes. It would exceed the framework of this book to recall all of these moments and retell the vivid memories people have of this musical folk hero.[45]

However, I will give a brief sample of them because they are of great importance to many of the musicians I worked with. They not only give an idea of Rakoto Frah's personality and character but also provide an insight into his playing techniques and styles, showing that these two aspects are highly interdependent.

Antananarivo where he used to sit with his fellow musician-friends and where they composed their first songs in the 1970s.

[44] I am thinking for example of pianist Lang Lang, or violinist Anne-Sophie Mutter.

[45] The idea of collecting these memories, stories, and anecdotes remains a project that I would like to undertake, not least because these memories are immensely important and a treasure within Malagasy culture. They could also function as a kind of window into Malagasy flute-playing.

Despite his great popularity as a musical folk hero, Rakoto Frah never became a wealthy man; until his death, he lived in his home neighbourhood in Isotry, one of the poorest quarters of Antananarivo. People often mention with regret and anger that Rakoto Frah was never properly supported and his popularity never officially recognised or rewarded, a topic raised in songs composed for and dedicated to him.[46] A picture of his face was printed on the 1000 FMG banknote, the former currency of the country.[47] Rakoto Frah is known for always carrying at least one of his flutes in his pockets, ready to take it out at any moment, making it part of his everyday life. It is his everyday activities, movements, and attitudes that people relate to his flute-playing. If you watched Rakoto Frah eating his daily rice with his own special technique of dividing the rice in small portions on his spoon and chewing the rice in his own peculiar way, you would see him playing the flute. If you listened to Rakoto Frah speaking to his friends, flirting with girls, or arguing during a discussion, you would hear the sound of his flute. People would even applaud when he spoke as his way of speaking and telling stories was like he was playing the flute. Rakoto was known for speaking in the same manner to every person, not making any difference between a politician, a foreigner, a child, or a beggar; always speaking in his mother tongue, Malagasy, or more specifically the language of his quarter Isotry. When abroad, Rakoto Frah would be crying from homesickness, longing to go home. As soon as he saw musicians, no matter in which occasion and at which place, he could not be stopped from taking out his flute to join in. I cannot go into more detail here, but the essence of these memories and stories is that Rakoto Frah was (and still remains) a folk hero for many Malagasy people. They regard Rakoto and his flutes as inseparable and within those memories emphasise the interplay between Rakoto's personality and his music. The flute-playing was part of his everyday experiences, even as far as his way of speaking, his everyday movements were related to his playing styles and the sound produced on his flutes.

Unfortunately, I did not get to know Rakoto Frah personally. I have also never properly played a Malagasy flute. So far, I have always performed on my Renaissance recorder, having tried to develop my own way of adapting my playing technique to Malagasy music. And yet, after the concert at the "Olympia" in Paris and especially since the concerts in Madagascar in 2011 and 2012, Malagasy people have come to me asking

---

[46] See "*Lasa i Rakoto*," and "*O Rakoto*" composed by Erick Manana.
[47] In 2003 the Malagasy currency changed from FMG to Ariary. 1000 FMG was worth between € 0.14 and € 0.30. For further information on the currency change, Péguy (2003).

whether and how I have learned with Rakoto Frah, telling me that everything (including my way of moving on stage, for example the way of taking out my recorder) reminded them of Rakoto Frah. I have even been given nicknames, often shouted during the performances or written in comments on videos online or in newspaper articles that all create a kind of European or even German version of Rakoto Frah, such as "Rakoto Françoise," "Rakoto Fräulein," "Rakoto Frau" or "Jenny Rakoto." I have never tried to properly imitate Rakoto Frah's playing, but—as for everyone—Malagasy flute music for me has always been the sound and style of Rakoto Frah's flute-playing; that is the sound and playing style that I have tried to approach using my Renaissance recorder. Further, Erick Manana, with whom I do the bulk of my learning and performing, was one of the closest companions of Rakoto Frah, founded the group "Feo Gasy" with him and obviously is more than familiar with Rakto Frah's playing style.

Ben Mandelson and Roger Armstrong produced in 1988 a recording with Rakoto Frah, entitled *Rakoto Frah. Flute Master of Madagascar.*[48] Mandelson writes in the sleeve notes to the album that there were many other flute players in the same tradition who were equally good, or some younger ones who one day would even be better, but who were holding themselves back to honour and respect Rakoto Frah because in Madagascar the elders are always the elders.[49]

As stated earlier, Rakoto Frah is still the most obvious presence when it comes to *sodina* music in Madagascar. I was told by different musicians that Rakoto Frah always had many students around him in Isotry, almost like a kind of "school," which did not continue after his death, as no one would take over his role. The only *sodina* player I met in Antananarivo is Rageorge (alias George Ranaivoson),[50] himself former student of Rakoto Frah. The German producer Birger Gesthuisen released an album in 2010 of Sammy's group "Samy Izy."[51] Interestingly, on this recording, Sammy

---

[48] The recording was released on CD in 1999 with an updated version of the sleeve notes by Ben Mandelson, see: Rakoto Frah (1999).

[49] Mandelson (1999).

[50] In sound example 1 Regeorge, together with Sammy, gives an example of the *jijy*.

[51] Samy Izy (2010). It is remarkable that this CD and also the CD by Erick Manana mentioned earlier in this chapter (Erick Manana Orchestra 2008) contain the name of the country in the title. I mentioned in chapter 2 that the marketability of the name "Madagascar" is a topic frequently raised by the musicians. Particularly interesting here is that both cases use of name in Malagasy language: "Madagasikara." It would be interesting to conduct some further research on these

invited Rageorge to join in two songs with his *sodina*. As written in the sleeve notes by Gesthuisen (2010), it was to honour and show respect to this "old master," who until now has never recorded on his own. However, just before Rageorge is mentioned in the sleeve notes, Rakoto Frah also appears in the text, as Gesthuisen describes how Rakoto Frah, like *valiha* master Randafison or *hira gasy* director Ramilison, made their mark solely through their personalities, their expertise, and artistic skills. These stories and this admiration for Rakoto Frah could have easily scared me away from getting involved in Malagasy flute music just as much as the musicians' discourses of *vazahas* having difficulties within intercultural musical encounters.

However, understanding the significance of the *lova-tsofina*, and thus accepting and following the idea of it, I have quickly realised that it is not about becoming Malagasy or getting myself a "Malagasy soul"—and even less about trying to become Rakoto Frah.

As described above, I perform on my own Renaissance recorder and do not try when playing violin to look like a *hira gasy* violin player. In fact, I have embraced new musical challenges whilst accepting, keeping and making use of my own "musical baggage." Following the *lova-tsofina* while learning and playing with musicians from Madagascar allows me to engage in Malagasy music-making whilst expressing my own (musical) personality. From what I have experienced in discussions with musicians and Malagasy audiences (as well as through musicking) is that it seems to be essential for Malagasy people that they can identify with the music they play and listen to ("*se retrouvent dans la musique*" is the French expression people use). When and how people are able to do so is difficult to define. According to my own experiences, accepting the *lova-tsofina* as the base for Malagasy music making, and learning and performing Malagasy music with Malagasy musicians using nothing but your ears— for the actual musicking as much as for listening to and engaging in discussions with musicians—has proven to be a fruitful way to learn about Malagasy music-making.

I have argued that the music the musicians I work with play and create could best be understood as "Contemporary Malagasy music" as the term is used by Randrianary (2001). One important element in this definition is that he describes it as an attitude rather than a particular musical style. The idea of a certain "openness" and "creation" (Randrianary 2001: 128) is therefore of great significance. The musicians' projects of "Malagasising"

---

albums (and similar cases) in order to find out the process that led to this marketing decision. Is the use of the word "Madagasikara" linked to notions within discourses on "world music," such as "authenticity"?

music for example fit very well into this idea. Based on my continuous collaboration with musicians from Madagascar, I therefore tend to think of Malagasy music-making more as a particular way of musicking than as one particular music.

Having said this, my aim here has not been to give a clear definition of Malagasy music or to give instructions of how to learn and play it. My aim was to show how my analysis of discourses inform my musical experience, and how in turn, my analysis of experiences gained through musicking inform discourses. Instead of seeing both as separate worlds or treating musical experiences as "untranslatable," I have tried to show that the analysis in both directions and the focus on their connection is necessary for ethnomusicological research.

Conclusion

This chapter has focused on my participatory approach, showing with concrete examples how I analysed the interdependencies of musical experiences and discourses about music and music-making. Thereby I have challenged boundaries, such as that between "researcher" and "researched" or between those who make and play music and those who write about it; I have also tried to go beyond the study of the seemingly contradictory discourses that exist on Malagasy music. By analysing discourses and musical experiences interdependently, I have tackled the seeming contradiction between the *lova-tsofina* and the 6/8 rhythm, arguing that the latter should not be understood as a Western concept which has travelled or "migrated" to Madagascar. Rather, its appearance, individual usages and understandings in the Malagasy context suggest a close interdependency with the *lova-tsofina*; I have argued that with regard to the shared rhythmical structure that all musicians point to there exists a constant opportunity of binaries and ternaries in Malagasy music, even if both are not always audibly present for everyone. The differences in rhythmical perception emphasise the general importance of individuality in Malagasy music that the *lova-tsofina* suggests. Further, accentuation and the perception of where the strong beats seem to be are closely related to other elements, such as language, dance, body movements and the instruments and their playing techniques, as I have tried to demonstrate with the examples I have given. This is also where regional differences come into play. My aim was not to depict and explain different regional rhythmical particularities. Concentrating on the musicians' argument that there is a shared rhythmical base in Malagasy music, I have tried to guard against the misunderstandings, misinterpretations and contradictions caused by the usage of the Western term of "6/8 rhythm." To do so, I searched for individual understandings of and experience with "rhythm" in order to find relevant criteria. "Rhythm" in the context of "Contemporary Malagasy music" cannot be understood separately as something like a particular "rhythm" (or metre) notated in a musical score in Western style. It is the different interdependencies within Malagasy music-making that my research has brought to the fore that hold the key for a better understanding of both the shared rhythmical base—which I have described as a constant opportunity of binaries and ternaries—as well as the differences between regional musical particularities.

CHAPTER SEVEN

CONCLUSION

In this book, I have presented my research on experiences of "rhythm" in "Contemporary Malagasy music" (Randrianary 2001). Throughout the last seven years, I have had the privilege of conducting thorough ethnographic fieldwork in Madagascar and Europe made up of numerous interviews, encounters, observations and discussions; I have also been learning, playing and regularly performing with musicians from Madagascar the very music I am researching. Thus, my work is based on my own and *shared* experiences of "musicking" as a practising violinist, flutist and singer.

Many ethnomusicologists over the past decades have emphasised the need to follow the discipline's long-standing claim (Hood 1960) of the need for a more performance-based approach in research, arguing that crucial knowledge can be gained through making musical participation a part of research. However, only very few scholars have applied this aim on a practical level (e.g. Baily 2008). How can we translate our musical experiences into words and fully integrate them into our academic works? Many scholars and many musicians have reflected on this challenge and often conclude that talking about music and experiencing music through playing and performing are two different worlds, with translation between them difficult or even impossible. I have argued throughout this book that we should not accept this methodological challenge as an insurmountable obstacle. Things are rather to the contrary; we need to explore more and new ways to further the use of performative research within ethnomusicological studies.

While we tend to give too much attention to the problematic issue of expressing in words what we feel or experience musically, we do not give enough value to the actual *connection* between our musical experiences and our discourses on music and music-making. I have argued that it is not a one-directional phenomenon, but that both musical experiences and discourses on music need to be analysed in a constant interrelation—both constantly inform one another. By following this approach, we will also be able to address scholarly debates on the very nature of ethnographic fieldwork.

Most recent research confirms that music remains a powerful tool that offers us paths of understanding topical issues such as globalisation and migration (Kiwan & Meinhof 2011) and identity debates (e.g. Connell and Gibson 2003, Biddle and Knights 2007). Musics associated with or identified as so-called "world music" have not only attracted attention from diverse disciplines but have actually made scholars reflect upon, challenge and debate the very nature of their own research, especially their research methodologies. Scholars emphasise the need for highly self-reflexive research and point to the importance of reflecting upon our relationships during field research and our impact as researchers, to name but two very prominent examples (see for example Barz & Cooley 2008). However, despite these on-going methodological debates, criticism remains of the tendency of researchers to apply a merely Western analytical perspective on music, often one based on musical notation, that favours prevailing Western discourses (Agawu 2003) and which also carries the risk of "essentialising music" (Bohlman 1993), particularly with regard to music based on an oral culture.

This becomes especially relevant with regard to the context of "Contemporary Malagasy music" (Randrianary 2001), where "rhythm" plays a crucial role as the starting point for the musicians' search for a collective musical identity (see chapter 1). Within the musicians' discourses on "rhythm," two discourses come to the fore that at first glance contradict each other: the musicians' constant use of the term "6/8 rhythm," a concept based in Western music theory and grounded in the idea of musical notation (Arom 1991, Dudley 1996; see chapter 2); musicians also repeatedly state that they see the base of Malagasy music in the Malagasy concept of oral tradition, the *lova-tsofina* (*lova* = heritage; *sofina* = ear). However, instead of understanding these two discourses as either opposing tendencies or as mutually isolated, I have decided to go beyond the statement of difference and contradiction and investigate the phenomenon further by bringing in our shared musical experiences as a means to explore new ways of understanding.

While musicians constantly use the term "6/8 rhythm," many different understandings and meanings are attached to it (see chapter 4). Thus, instead of analysing it as a Western concept that has "migrated" to Madagascar, I have carefully focused on the analyses of individual experiences with this term, linking them with the musicians' usage and understanding of the *lova-tsofina* (see chapter 5) and with our shared experiences of playing and performing the music (see chapter 6). Thereby,

I have shown how discourses on the music and on musical experiences constantly inform our actual music making and vice versa.

I have deliberately decided against the use of Western notation or transcriptions within this book. Following my own argument about the danger of imposing a merely Western analytical perspective and the importance of integrating the voices, perspectives and understandings of the musicians I have worked with and our shared musical experiences (see chapter 3), I have presented representative interview material and have included sound and video examples to highlight the most important aspects of my analyses.

At present, so-called "world music" is leaving its niche existence to become an everyday experience (e.g. Aubert 2007). Furthermore, it becomes more and more difficult to define cultures or music cultures as fixed entities. The diversity of musical styles, genres, instruments and music projects that I have presented throughout this book gives a vivid example. As cultural boundaries become increasingly blurred it becomes much more useful to concentrate on *individual* trajectories, perspectives and experiences (e.g. Rice 2003; Kiwan & Meinhof 2011). While scholarly discussions are already moving towards more self-reflexive research, including a bottom-up approach that focuses on individuals (including the researcher), we still need to give more attention to answering the many methodological challenges in practice. With this book, I argue that musical practices and ethnomusicological research form an excellent partnership that we need to use and explore more; musicking researchers and researching musicians together hold the key to finding new ways of understanding today's musical phenomena and intercultural musical encounters.

BIBLIOGRAPHY

Acosta, Leonardo. 2005. "On Generic Complexes and Other Topics in Cuban Popular Music." *Journal of Popular Music Studies* Vol. 17: 227-254.

Agawu, Kofi. 2003. *Representing African Music: Postcolonial Notes, Queries, Positions*. London: Routledge.

Anderson, Benedict. 1991. *Imagined Communities. Reflections on the Origin and Spread of Nationalism*. London and New York: Verso. Revised edition.

Anderson, Ian. 1994. "Mad about Madagascar: Indian Ocean Music from Southeast Africa." In *World Music: The Rough Guide*, edited by Simon Broughton et al., 363-370. London: Rough Guides Ltd.

Appadurai, Arjun. 1996. *Modernity at Large*. Minneapolis: Minnesota University Press.

Armbruster, Heidi 2008. "Researching a Beleaguered Community." In *Taking Sides: Ethics, Politics, and Fieldwork in Anthropology*, edited by Heidi Armbruster and Anna Laerke, 119-142. New York and Oxford: Berghahn Books.

Arnaud, Gérald. 2003. "Madagascar: Nouvelles Frontière de la World Music." *Africultures* No. 55: 161-168.

Arom, Simha. 1984. "Structuration du Temps dans les Musiques d'Afrique Centrale: Periodicite, Metre, Rythmique et Polyrythmie." *Revue de Musicologie* T. 70e, No.1: 5-36.

—. 1991. *African polyphony and polyrhythm. Musical Structure and Methodology*. Cambridge, New York, Melbourne and Sidney: Cambridge University Press and Editions de la Maison des Sciences de l'Homme.

Aubert, Laurent. 2007. *The Music of the Other: New Challenges for Ethnomusicology in a Global Age*. Aldershot: Ashgate.

Baily, John. 2001. "Learning to Perform as a Research Technique in Ethnomusicology." *British Journal of Ethnomusiocology* Vol. 10, No.2: 85-98.

—. 2008. "Ethnomusicology, Intermusability, and Performance Practice." In *The New (Ethno)musicologies*, edited by Henry Stobart, 117-134. Lanham, ML: Scarecrow Press.

Bakhtin, Mikhail M. et al. 1990. [1919]. *Art and Answerability: Early Philosophical Essays*. Austin: University of Texas Press.

Barz, Gregory, and Timothy Cooley, eds. 1997. *Shadows in the Field: New Perspectives for Fieldwork in Ethnomusicology*. Oxford: Oxford University Press.

Barz, Gregory. 1997. "Chasing Shadows in the Field: An Epilogue." In *Shadows in the Field: New Perspectives for fieldwork in ethnomusicology* edited by Gregory F. Barz and Timothy J. Cooley, 205-209. New York: Oxford University Press.

Biddle, Ian and Vanessa Knights, eds. 2007. *Music, National Identity and the Politics of Location: between the Global and the Local*. Aldershot: Ashgate.

Blacking, John. 1973. *How Musical is Man?*. Seattle and London: University of Washington Press.

Blanchy, Sophie and Francoise Raison-Jourde and Malanjaona Rakotomalala 2001. *Les Ancêtres au Quotidien: Usages Sociaux du Religieux sur les Hautes-Terre Malgache*. Paris: L'Harmattan.

Bloch, Maurice. 1968. "Tombs and Conservatism among the Merina of Madagascar." *The Journal of the Royal Anthropological Institute* Vol. 3, No.1: 94-104.

—. 1971. *Placing the Dead: Tombs, Ancestral Villages, and Kinship Organization in Madagascar*. New York: Seminar Press.

—. 1986. *From Blessing to Violence: History and Ideology in the Circumcision Ritual of the Merina of Madagascar*. New York: Cambridge University Press.

—. 1999. "'Eating' young men among the Zafimaniry." In *Ancestors, Power and History in Madagascar*, edited by Karen Middleton, 175-190. Leiden et al.: Brill.

—. 2006. "Teknonymy and the Evocation of the 'Social' among the Zafimaniry of Madagascar." In *Anthropology of Names and Naming*, edited by Gabriele Bruck and Barbara Bodenhorn, 97-114. Cambridge: Cambridge University Press.

Blum, Stephen. 1991. "European Musical Terminology and the Music of Africa." In *Comparative Musicology and Anthropology of Music: Essays on the History of Ethnomusicology*, edited by Bruno Nettl and Philip V. Bohlman, 1-36. Chicago and London: University of Chicago Press.

Boas, Franz. 1936. "History and Science in Anthropology, a reply." *American Anthropologist* Vol. 38: 137-151.

Bohlman, Philip. 1993. "Musicology as a Political Act." *The Journal of Musicology* Vol. 11, No. 4: 411-436.

—. 2002. "World Music at the 'End of History.'" *Ethnomusicology* Vol. 46, No. 1: 1-32.

Bolton, T.L. 1894. "Rhythm." *American Journal of Psychology* Vol. 6: 145-238.

Brandel, Rose. 1959. "The African Hemiola Style." *Ethnomusicology* Vol. 3, No. 3: 106-117.

Brettell, Caroline, B., ed. 1993. *When they Read What We Write: the Politics of Ethnography*. London: Bergin and Garvey.

Brown, Mervyn. 1979. *Madagascar Rediscovered*. Hamden, Conn.: Archon Books.

Bruner, Jerome. 1986. *Actual Minds, Possible Worlds*. Cambridge, MA: Harvard University Press.

Chailley, Jaques. 1951. *La Musique Médiévale*. Paris: Ed. du Coudrier.

Chang, Heewon. 2008. *Autoethnography as Method*. Walnut Creek: Left Coast Press.

Chernoff, John Miller. 1979. *African Rhythm and African Sensibility: Aesthetics and Social Action in African Musical Idioms*. Chicago and London: The University of Chicago Press.

Cheshire, Jenny and Sue Ziebland. 2005. "Narrative as a Resource in Accounts of the Experience of Illness." In *The Sociolinguistics of Narrative*, 17-40. Amsterdam and Philadelphia: John Benjamins Publishing Company.

Clayton, Martin R. L. 1996. "Free Rhythm: Ethnomusicology and the Study of Music without Metre." *Bulletin of the School of Oriental and African Studies, University of London* Vol. 59, No.2: 323-332.

Clayton, Martin and Rebecca Sager and Udo Will. 2005. "In Time with the Music: the Concept of Entrainment and its Significance for Ethnomusicology." *European Meetings in Ethnomusicology 11, ESEM Counterpoint* 1: 3-75.

Clayton, Martin. 2008. "Toward an Ethnomusicology of Sound Experience." In *The New (Ethno)musicologies*, edited by Henry Stobart, 135-169. Lanham, ML: Scarecrow Press.

Clifford, James and George E. Marcus, eds. 1986. *Writing Culture: The Poetics and Politics of Ethnography*. Berkeley: University of California Press.

Clifford, James. 1997. *Routes: Travel and Translation in the Late Twentieth Century*. Cambridge, Massachusetts and London: Harvard University Press.

Cole, Jennifer. 2001. *Forget Colonialism?: Sacrifice and the Art of Memory in Madagascar*. Berkeley: University of California Press.

Connell, J. and C. Gibson. 2003. *Sound Tracks: Popular Music, Identity and Place*. London: Routledge.

Conquergood, D. 1985. "Performing as a Moral Act: Ethical Dimensions of the Ethnography of Performance." *Literature in Performance* 2(5): 1-13.

Cook, Nicholas. 1999. "Analysing Performance and Performing Analysis." In *Rethinking Music*, edited by Nicolas Cook and Mark Everist, 239-261. Oxford and New York: Oxford University Press.

Cooley, Timothy. 2003. "Theorizing Fieldwork Impact: Malinowski, Peasant-love and Friendship." *Ethnomusicology* Vol. 12/i: 1-17.

Cooper, Grosvenor and Leonard B. Meyer. 1960. *The Rhythmic Structure of Music*. Chicago: University of Chicago Press.

Deleris, Ferdinand. 1986. *Ratsiraka: Socialisme et Misère à Madagascar*. Paris: L'Harmattan.

Denzin, Norman K. 2003. *Performance Ethnography: Critical Pedagogy and the Politics of Culture*. London, Thousand Oaks, and New Dehli: Sage Publications.

Deschamps, Hubert. 1972. *Histoire du Madagascar*. Paris: Berger-Levrault. 4th edition.

Dregni, Michael. 2006. *Django Reinhardt and the Illustrated History of Gypsy Jazz*. Denver: Speck Press.

Dubois, Robert. 2002. *L'identité Malgache: la Tradition des Ancêtres*. Paris: Édition Karthala.

Dudley, Shannon. 1996. "Judging 'By the Beat'. Calypso versus Soca." *Ethnomusicology* Vol. 40, No.2: 269-298.

Edkvist, Ingela. 1997. *The Performance of Tradition: An Ethnography of Hira Gasy Popular Theatre in Madagascar*. Uppsala, Acta Universitatis Upsaliensis: Uppsala Studies in Cultural Anthropology 23.

Ellis, Carolyn. 2004. *The Ethnographic I: A Methodological Novel about Autoethnography*. Walnut Creek: Mira Press.

Ellis, Stephen D.K. 1985. *The Rising of the Red Shawls: a Revolt in Madagascar, 1895-1899*. Cambridge: Cambridge University Press.

Emoff, Ron. 2002. *Recollecting from the Past: Musial Practice and Spirit Possession on the East Coast of Madagascar*. Middletown: Wesleyan University Press.

Erlmann, Veit. 1993. "The Politics and Aesthetics of Transnational Musics." *The World of Music* Vol. 35(2): 3-15.

Fabian, Johannes. 1983. *Time and the Other: how Anthropology makes its Object*. New York: Columbia University Press.

—. 1991. [1983]. *Time and the Work of Anthropology: Critical Essays 1971-1991.* Chur: Harwood Academic Publishers.

Feld, Steven. 1981. "'Flow like a Waterfall': The Metaphors of Kaluli Musical Theory." *Yearbook for Traditional Music* Vol. 13: 22-47.

Frith, Simon. 1996. "Music and Identity." In *Questions of Cultural Identity*, edited by Stuart Hall and Paul du Gay, 108-127. London: Sage Publications.

—. 2000. "The Discourses of World Music." In *Western Music and its Others: Difference, Representation and Appropriation in Music*, edited by Georgina Born and David Hesmondhalgh, 305-322. Berkely: University of California Press.

Fuhr, Jenny. 2006. "Malagasy Roots Musicians in Contemporary Antananarivo." Master's dissertation, SOAS, University of London.

—. 2011. "'6/8 rhythm' meets '*Lova-tsofina*'–Experiencing Malagasy Music." *Music and Arts in Action*, Vol. 3, No. 3: 56-76.

Gellner, Ernest. 1998. *Language and Solitude: Wittgenstein, Malinowski and the Habsburg Dilemma.* Cambridge: Cambridge University Press.

Gelly, David and Rod Fogg. 2005. *Django Reinhardt: Know the Man, Play the Music.* San Francisco: Backbeat Books.

Giddens, Anthony. 1991. *Modernity at Large: Self and Society in the Late Modern Age.* Stanford: Stanford University Press.

Gjerdingen, Robert O. 1989. "Meter as a Mode of Attending: A Network Simulation of Attentional Rhythmicity in Music." *Integral* No. 3: 67-91.

Gow, Bonar A. 1980. *Madagascar and the Protestant Impact.* New York: Holmes and Meier.

Guilbault, Jocelyne. 1997. "Interpreting World Music: A Challenge in Theory and Practice." *Popular Music* Vol. 16, No.1: 31-44.

Hall, E.T. 1983. *The Dance of Life–The Other Dimension of Time.* New York: Anchor Press.

Harison, Marie Aimé Joël. 2005. *Musikgeschichte Madagaskars: Unter besonderer Berücksichtigung der europäischen Einflüsse.* Hamburg: Verlag Dr. Kovač.

Heims, Ernst. 1976. "Letter to Ethnomusicology regarding Judith Becker's Review of Music in Java." *Ethnomusicology* XX(1): 97-101.

Hellier-Tinoco, Ruth. 2003. "Experiencing People: Relationships, Responsibility and Reciprocity." *Ethnomusicology* Vol. 12, No.1: 19-34.

Herzfeld, Friedrich. 1974. *Ullstein Lexikon der Musik.* Frankfurt, Berlin, and Vienna: Ullstein Verlag.

Hood, Mantle. 1960. "The Challenge of 'Bi-musicality'." *Ethnomusicology* 4/2: 55-59.

Huntington, Richard. 1987. *Gender and Social Structure in Madagascar.* Bloomington: Indiana University Press.

Johnson, Bruce. 2002. "The Jazz Diaspora." In *The Cambridge Companion to Jazz*, edited by Mervyn Cooke and David Horn, 33-54. Cambridge: Cambridge University Press.

Kauffmann, Robert. 1980. "African Rhythm: A Reassessment." *Ethnomusicology* Vol. 24, No.3: 393-415.

Khosravi, Shahram. 2010. *'Illegal' Traveller: an Auto-ethnography of Borders.* Basingstoke and New York: Palgrave Macmillan.

Kisliuk, Michelle. 1997. "(Un)doing Fieldwork: Sharing Songs, Sharing Lives." *Shadows in the Field: New Perspectives for Fieldwork in Ethnomusicology*, edited by Gregory F. Barz and Timothy J. Cooley, 34-44. New York: Oxford University Press.

Kiwan, Nadia and Ulrike H. Meinhof. 2011. *Cultural Globalization and Music: African Artists in Transnational Networks.* Basingstoke and New York: Palgrave MacMillan.

Kolinksi, Mieczyslaw. 1973. "A Cross-Cultural Approach to Metro-Rhythmic Patterns." *Ethnomusicology* Vol. 17, No.3: 494-506.

Kubik, Gerhard. 1969. "Transmission et Transcription des Éléments de Musique Instrumentale Africaine." *Bulletin of the International Committee on Urgent Anthropological and Ethnological Research* XI: 47-61.

—. 1974, contributor to "African Peoples, Arts of III, African Music." London: Encyclopaedia Britannica.

—. 2010. *Theory of African Music.* Chicago: University of Chicago Press. Vol. I & II.

London, Justin. 2004. *Hearing in Time.* New York: Oxford University Press.

Malinowski, Bronislaw. 1962. [1922]. *Argonauts of the Western Pacific: an Account of Native Enterprise and Adventure in the Archipelagoes of Melanesian New Guinea.* New York: E.P. Dutton & Co. Reprint.

Mallet, Julien. 2000. "Histoire de Vies, Histoire d'une Vie. Damily, Musicien de Tsapiky, Troubadour des Temps Modernes." *Cahier de Musiques Traditionelles* 15: 113-132.

—. 2004. "Liens Sociaux et Rapports Ville/Campagne: Analyse d'une Pratique Musicale du Sud de Madagascar." Kabaro II, 2-3: *Diversité et Spécificités des Musiques Traditionnelles de l'Océan Indièn*: 155-168.

—. 2007. "Industrie du Disque, Musique Africaines et Naissance du Tsapiky: 'Jeune musique' de Tuléar (Sud-Ouest de Madagascar)." In

Madagascar et l'Afrique: Entre Identité Insulaire et Appartenance Historique, edited by Didier Nativel and Faranirina V. Rajaonah, 469-481. Paris: Karthala.

—. 2008. "'Asio Elany'" Le Tsapiky, une 'Jeune Musique' qui Fait Danser les Ancêtres." *Cahiers d'Ethnomusicologie* 21: 155-174.

—. 2009. *Le Tsapiky, une Jeune Musique de Madagascar: Ancêtres, Cassettes et Bals-poussière*. Paris: Édition Karthala.

Marcus, George E. and Michael M. J. Fischer. 1986. *Anthropology as Cultural Critique: An Experimental Moment in the Human Sciences.* Chicago: University of Chicago Press.

Mauro, Didier. 2001. *Madagascar, l'opéra du People: Anthropologie d'un Fait Social Total: l'art Hira Gasy entre Tradition et Rébellion.* Paris: Édition Karthala.

McLeod, Norma. 1964. "The Status of Musical Specialists in Madagascar." *Ethnomusicology* 8: 278-289.

—. 1977. "Musical Instruments and History in Madagascar." In *Essays for a Humanist: An Offering to Klaus Wachsmann*, 189-215. New York, The Town House Press.

Meinhof, Ulrike H and Dariusz Galasinski. 2005. *The Language of Belonging.* Basingstoke: Palgrave Macmillan.

Meinhof, Ulrike Hanna. 2005a. "Initiating a Public: Malagasy Music and Live Audiences in Differentiated Cultural Contexts." In *Audiences and Publics: When Cultural Engagement Matters for the public Sphere*, edited by Sonia Livingstone, 115-138. Bristol: Intellect books.

Meinhof, Ulrike Hanna and Zafimahaleo Rasolofondraosolo. 2005b. "Malagasy Song-Writer Musicians in Transnational Settings." *Moving Worlds. A Journal of Transcultural Writings*, 144-158. University of Leeds.

Meinhof, Ulrike Hanna and Anna Triandafyllidou. 2006. "'Beyond the Diaspora: Transnational practices as transcultural capital.'" In *Transcultural Europe: Cultural Policy in a changing Europe*, edited by Ulrike H. Meinhof and Anna Triandafyllidou, 200-222. London: Palgrave.

Merriam, Alan. 1964. *The Anthropology of Music.* Evanston, Ill.: Northwestern University Press.

Meumann, Ernst. 1894. "Untersuchungen zur Psychologie und Aesthetik des Rhythmus." *Philosophische Studien* Vol. 10: 249-322; 393-430.

Middleton, Karen, ed. 1999. *Ancestors, Power and History in Madagascar.* Leiden et al.: Brill.

Middleton, Karen. 1999. Introduction to *Ancestors, Power and History in Madagascar*, edited by Karen Middleton, 1-36. Leiden et al.: Brill.

Monson, Ingrid. 1999. "Riffs, Repetition, and Globalization." *Ethnomusicology* Vol. 43, No. 1: 31-65.

Mumford, L. 1934. *Technics and Civilisation*. New York and Harcourt: Brace.

Neustadt, Robert. 2002. "Buena Vista Social Club versus La Charanga Habanera: The Politics of Cuban Rhythm." *Journal of Popular Music Studies* Vol. 14: 139-162.

Nketia, J.H. Kwabena.1963. *Folk Songs of Ghana*. Legon: University of Ghana.

Nketia, J.H. Kwabena. 1974. *The Music of Africa*. New York: Norton.

Pacaud, Pierre-Loïc. 2003. *Un Culte d'Exhumation des Morts à Madagascar, le Famadihana: Anthropologie Psychanalytique*. Paris: L'Harmattan.

Rabemananjara, Raymond-William. 2001. *Le Monde Malgache: Sociabilité et Culte des Ancêtres*. Paris: L'Harmattan.

Rabetafika, Roger. 1990. *Réforme Fiscale et Révolution Socialiste à Madagascar*. Paris: L'Harmattan.

Rakotomalala, Mireille Mialy. 1986. *Bibliographie Critique d'Intérêt Ethnomusicologique sur la Musique Malagasy*. Antananarivo: Musée d'Art et d'Archéologie de l'Université de Madagascar: Travaux et Documents XXIII.

—. 2003. *Madagascar: La Musique dans l'Histoire*. Fontenay sous Bois: Editions Anako.

Randafison, Silvestre. 1980. *Etude sur la Fabrication des Instruments de Musique*. Antananarivo: CENAM.

Randrianary, Victor. 2001. *Madagascar: Les Chants d'une île*. Paris: Cité de la Musique/Actes Sud.

Randrianja, Solofo. 2012. *Madagascar: Le Coup d'Etat de Mars 2009*. Paris: Édition Karthala.

Randrianja, Solofo and Stephen Ellis. 2009. *Madagascar: a Short History*. London: Hurst&Co.

Rasolofondraosolo, Zafimahaleo and Ulrike H. Meinhof. 2003. "Popular Malagasy Music and the Construction of Cultural Identities." *Africa and Applied Linguistics. AILA Review* Vol. 16: 127-148.

Reed-Danahay, Deborah, ed. 1997. *Auto/Ethnography: Rewriting the Self and the Social*. Oxford and New York: Berg Publishers.

Reed-Danahay, Deborah. 2001. "Autobiography, Intimacy, and Ethnography." In *Handbook of Ethnography*, edited by Paul Atkinson et al., 407-425. London: Sage Publications.

Rice, Timothy. 1994. *May it Fill your Soul: Experiencing Bulgarian music*. Chicago and London: University of Chicago Press.

—. 1997. "Toward a Mediation of Field Methods and Field Experience in Ethnomusicology." In *Shadows in the Field: New Perspectives for Fieldwork in Ethnomusicology*, edited by Gregory F. Barz and Timothy J. Cooley, 101-120. New York: Oxford University Press.

—. 2003. "Time, Place, and Metaphor in Musical Experience and Ethnography." *Ethnomusicology* Vol. 47, No. 2: 151-179.

Rouget, Gilbert. 1946. "La Musique à Madagascar." In *L'Ethnographie de Madagascar* by Jacques Faublée, 85-92. Paris: Les Editions de France et d'Outre-Mer.

Sachs, Curt. 1938. *Les Instruments de Madagascar*. Paris: Institut d'Ethnologie, Travaux et Mémoires de l'Institut d'Ethnologie 28.

Schechner, Richard. 2006. *Performance Studies: an Introduction*. New York and London: Routledge.

Schiffrin, Deborah. 1996. "Narrative as Self-portrait: Sociolinguistic Constructions of Identity". *Language in Society* 25: 167-203.

Schmidhofer, August. 1995. *Das Xylophonspiel der Mädchen: Zum afrikanischen Erbe in der Musik Madagaskars*. Frankfurt am Main: Peter Lang Europäischer Verlag der Wissenschaften.

—. 2013. "Musikheilung im Kulturellen Kontext: Bilo und Tromba in Madagaskar" In *Heilung in den Religionen. Religiöse, Spirituelle und Leibliche Dimensionen*, edited by Veronica Futterknecht, Michaela Noseck-Licul and Manfred Kremser, 313-322. Wien: Lit Verlag.

Seeger, Charles. 1977. *Studies in Musicology 1935-1975*. Berkeley, Los Angeles and London: University of California Press.

Sharp, Lesely A. 1993. *The Possessed and the Dispossessed: Spirits, Identity, and Power in a Madagascar Migrant Town*. Berkeley: University of California Press.

Slobin, Mark. 1993. *Subcultural Sounds: Micromusics of the West*. Hanover and London: Wesleyan University Press.

Small, Christopher. 1998. *Musicking: The Meanings of Performing and Listening*. Middletown: Wesleyan University Press.

Stobart Henry and Ian Cross. 2000. "The Andean Anacrusis? Rhythmic Structure and Perception in Easter Songs of Northern Potosí, Bolivia." *British Journal of Ethnomusicology* Vol. 9/ii: 63-94.

Stobart, Henry, ed. 2008. *The New (Ethno)musicologies*. Lanham, ML: Scarecrow Press.

Stocking, George. 2001. *Delimiting Anthropology: Occasional Reflections*. Madison, Wisconsin: University of Wisconsin Press.

Stokes, Martin. 1994. *Ethnicity, Identity and Music: The Musical Construction of Place*. Oxford: Berg.

—. 2004. "Music and the Global Order." *Annual Review of Anthropology* Vol. 33: 47-72.

Taylor, Timothy. 1997. *Global Pop: World Music, World Markets.* New York and London: Routledge.

Temperly, David. 2000. "Meter and Grouping in African Music: A View from Music Theory." *Ethnomusicology* Vol. 44, No.1: 65-96.

Terramorsi, Bernard and Elie Rajaonarison. 2004. "Jaojoby et Samoela: Les deux Grandes Figures de la Chanson Malgache Moderne." Kabaro, II, 2-3: *Diversité et Spécificités des Musiques Traditionnelles de l'Océan Indien*: 170-205.

Théberge, Paul. 2003. "'Ethnic Sounds.' The Economy and Discourses of World Music Sampling." In *Music and Technoculture*, edited by René Lysloff and Leslie Gay, 93-108. Middletown: Wesleyan University Press.

Thornborrow, Joanna and Jennifer Coates. 2005. Introduction to *The Sociolonguistics of Narratives*, 1-16. Amsterdam and Philadelphia: John Benjamins Publishing Company.

Titon, Jeff Todd. 1997. "Knowing Fieldwork." In *Shadows in the Field: New Perspectives for Fieldwork in Ethnomusicology*, edited by Gregory F. Barz and Timothy J. Cooley, 87-100. New York, Oxford University Press.

Turnbull, Collin. 1965. *Wayward Servants: The Two Worlds of the African Pigmies*. London: Eyre and Spottiswoode.

Turner, Victor. 1986. *The Anthropology of Performance.* New York: PAJ Publications.

Van Leeuwen, Theo. 1999. *Speech, Music, Sound.* London: Macmillan Press Ltd.

Vatan, Géraldine. 2004. *Hira Gasy, l'Opéra du Peuple à Madagagscar.* Paris: L'Harmattan.

Verma, Ritu. 2009. *Culture, Power and Development Disconnect in the Central Highlands of Madagascar.* PhD thesis. SOAS, University of London.

Vivier, Jean-Loup. 2007. *Madagascar sous Ravalomanana: la Vie Politique Malgache Depuis 2001.* Paris: L'Harmattan.

Waterman, Richard Alan. 1952. *African Influence on the Music of the Americas. Acculturation in the Americas.* Proceedings and Selected papers of the XXIXth International Congress of Americanists, 207-218. Chicago: University of Chicago press.

Waterman, Christopher A. 1990. "'Our Tradition Is a Very Modern Tradition': Popular Music and the Construction of Pan-Yoruba Identity." *Ethnomusicology* Vol. 34, No.3: 367-379.

Watson, C.W., ed. 1999. *Being There: Fieldwork in Anthropology.* London: Pluto Press.

Woolley, Oliver. 2002. *The Earth Shakers of Madagascar: an Anthropological Study of Authority, Fertility, and Creation.* London and New York: Continuum.

Zemp, Hugo. 1978. "'Are'are Classifications of Musical Types and Instruments." *Ethnomusicology* Vol. 22, No.1: 37-67.

—. 1979. "Aspects of 'Are'are Musical Theory." *Ethnomusicology* Vol 23, No.1: 5-48.

Newspaper/Magazine Articles

Eyre, Banning. 2002. "Salegy Central, Salegy is north Madagascar's hot dance export: Banning Eyre gets to meet the King, Jaojoby, and new star Lego." *froots* 223/224:40-41.

Heimer, Klaus. 2012. "Menschen im Gespräch: Auf Madaskar schon ein Star." *Kölner Stadt-Anzeiger,* May 4. Accessed 26.06.2013. http://www.ksta.de/region/menschen-im-gespraech-auf-madagaskar-schon-ein-star,15189102,16205442.html.

Péguy, Olivier. 2003. "Madagascar. L'Ariary Remplace le Franc Malgache." *RFI, July 31.* Accessed 10.06.2013. http://www.rfi.fr/actufr/articles/043/article_23988.asp

Rado, Maminirina. 2011. "CCESCA Antanimena: Bà gasy Classique avec Erick et Jenny." *L'Express de Madagascar,* June 20. Accessed 14.06.2013. http://www.lexpressmada.com/4947/cc-esca-antanimena-madagascar/24573-ba-gasy-classique-avec-erick-et-jenny.html.

Ratsara, Domoina. 2011a. "Erick Manana – Jenny, duo Unique." *L'Express de Madagascar,* May 20. Accessed 14.06.2013. http://www.lexpressmada.com/4923/spectacle-madagascar/23684-erick-manana-jenny-tuhr-duo-unique.html.

—. 2011b. "Erick Manana et Jenny en Apothéose." *L'Express de Madagascar,* September 8. Accessed 10.06.2013. http://www.lexpressmada.com/concert-madagascar/27169-erick-manana-et-jenny-en-%20apotheose.html.

Solhar. 2011. "Spectacle Eric Manana et Jenny au CCESCA: Deux fois à guichet fermé." *Madagascar Tribune,* June 21. Accessed 14.06.2013. http://www.madagascar-tribune.com/Deux-fois-a-guichet-ferme,16058.html.

Turfan, Barbara. 2013. *The Hardyman Madagascar Collection at SOAS Library.* Accessed 23.05.2013. http://www.iias.nl/iiasn/iiasn4/iswasia/hardyman.txt.

Websites and Online Resources

Angaredona. 2008. *Angaredona Festival 2008. 5ème édition.* Accessed 08.06.2013. http://www.angaredona.mg.

AVMM. 2013. *Archives Virtuelles de la Musique Malgache.* Accessed 23.05.2013. http://www.avmm.org/home_english.htm.

Berliner Philharmoniker. 2013. *Unterwegs: Ein kultureller Dialog.* Accessed 10.06.2013. http://www.berliner-philharmoniker.de/konzerte/unterwegs/

Hiley, David. 2007-2012. "Bar." In *Grove Music Online. Oxford Music Online.* Accessed 20.02.2012. http://www.oxfordmusiconline.com/subscriber/article/grove/music/01972.

Latham, Alison. 2007-2012. "Metre." In *The Oxford Companion to Music.* Accessed 20.02.2012. http://www.oxfordmusiconline.com.

Oxford Music Online. 2007-2012. *The Oxford Companion to Music.* Accessed 20.02.2012. http://www.oxfordmusiconline.com.

The World Bank. 2013. *Madagascar Overview.* Accessed 26.06.2013. http://www.worldbank.org/en/country/madagascar/overview.

WDR3 Musikkulturen. 2010. *Klanglandschaft Madagaskar. Hira Gasy-Das Theater der Reisbauern aus dem Hochland,* March. Accessed 10.06.2013. http://www.wdr3.de/musik/musikkulturenbeiwdr3/videos116.html.

WWF. 2013. *Facts about Madagascar.* Acccssed 23.05.2013. http://www.wwf.mg/ourwork/cssp/species_report/factsmada/.

Youtube Madatsara. 2013. *Playlist Jenny Fuhr.* Accessed 10.06.2013. http://www.youtube.com/playlist?list=PL5AC4293CDB79398E&feature=view_all

Films

Gray, Ian and Mary Summerill, producer. 2011. *Madagascar: The land where evolution ran wild.* Burbank, CA: BBC/Warner Home Video.

Raymond Rajaonarivelo, César Paes and Marie-Clémence Paes, producer. 2005. *Mahaleo,* Laterit Production, Cobra Films, ARTE France Cinéma and RTBF.

Cécila Lowenstein, producer. 1998. *Like a God when He Plays,* featuring Paddy Bush. First broadcasted on 30th August 1998 by Channel 4.

CDs and DVDs

Erick Manana Orchestra. 2008. *Made in Madagasikara,* Audio-CD. France: artist's own production.

Erick Manana and Jenny. 2012. *Ny 2CV an-dRandria: LIVE,* DVD 1-2. Antananarivo, Madagascar: MiRitsoka Production.

Erick Manana and Jenny. 2013. *Ny 2CV an-dRandria,* Audio-CD. France: artists' own production.

Feo Gasy. 2000. *Ramano,* Audio-CD. France: Daqui 332008.

Rajery. 2007. *Sofera,* Audio-CD. France: Marabi Productions, MARABI 46820.2.

Rakoto Frah. 2009. *Flute Master of Madagascar,* produced by Roger Armstrong and Ben Mandelson, Audio-CD. UK: Ace Records Ltd. and Globe Style Records, CDORBD027.

Samy Izy. 2010. *Tsara Madagasikara,* Audio-CD. Germany: Network Medien GmbH, 495132.

World Network 18. 1993. *Madagaskar,* edited by WDR (Westdeutscher Rundfunk), Audio-CD. Germany, Network Medien Gmbh, 55.835.

INDEX